SECRET AVENGERS

CRET AVENGERS BY RICK REMENDER VOL. 1. Contains material originally published in magazine form as SECRET AVENGERS #21.1 and #22-25. First printing 2012. Hardcover ISBN# 978-0-7851-18-9. Softcover ISBN# 978-0-7851-6119-6. Published by MARVEL WORLDWIDE, INC., a subsidiary of MARVEL ENTERTAINMENT, LLC. OFFICE OF PUBLICATION: 135 West 50th Street, New York, NY 020. Copyright © 2012 and 2013 Marvel Characters, Inc. All rights reserved. Hardcover: $24.99 per copy in the U.S. and $27.99 in Canada (GST #R127032852). Softcover: $19.99 per copy in the U.S. d $21.99 in Canada (GST #R127032852). Canadian Agreement #40668537. All characters featured in this issue and the distinctive names and likenesses thereof, and all related indicia are trademarks Marvel Characters, Inc. No similarity between any of the names, characters, persons, and/or institutions in this magazine with those of any living or dead person or institution is intended, and any such milarity which may exist is purely coincidental. Printed in the U.S.A. ALAN FINE, EVP - Office of the President, Marvel Worldwide, Inc. and EVP & CMO Marvel Characters B.V.; DAN BUCKLEY, Publisher & esident - Print, Animation & Digital Divisions; JOE QUESADA, Chief Creative Officer; TOM BREVOORT, SVP of Publishing; DAVID BOGART, SVP of Operations & Procurement, Publishing; RUWAN JAYATILLEKE, P & Associate Publisher, Publishing; C.B. CEBULSKI, SVP of Creator & Content Development; DAVID GABRIEL, SVP of Publishing Sales & Circulation; MICHAEL PASCIULLO, SVP of Brand Planning & mmunications; JIM O'KEEFE, VP of Operations & Logistics; DAN CARR, Executive Director of Publishing Technology; SUSAN CRESPI, Editorial Operations Manager; ALEX MORALES, Publishing Operations anager; STAN LEE, Chairman Emeritus. For information regarding advertising in Marvel Comics or on Marvel.com, please contact Niza Disla, Director of Marvel Partnerships, at ndisla@marvel.com. For Marvel bscription inquiries, please call 800-217-9158. Manufactured between 5/28/2012 and 7/9/2012 (hardcover), and 5/28/2012 and 1/7/2013 (softcover), by R.R. DONNELLEY, INC., SALEM, VA, USA.

9 8 7 6 5 4 3 2 1

SECRET AVENGERS

WRITER
RICK REMENDER

ISSUE #21.1
ARTIST:
PATCH ZIRCHER
COLOR ARTIST:
ANDY TROY
LETTERER:
DAVE LANPHEAR
COVER ART:
PATCH ZIRCHER & DEAN WHITE

ISSUES #22-25
ARTIST:
GABRIEL HARDMAN
COLOR ARTIST:
BETTIE BREITWEISER
LETTERER:
CHRIS ELIOPOULOS
COVER ART:
ARTHUR ADAMS
WITH **LAURA MARTIN** (#22 & #24)
& PETER STEIGERWALD (#23 & #25)

ASSISTANT EDITOR
JOHN DENNING
ASSOCIATE EDITOR
LAUREN SANKOVITCH
EDITOR
TOM BREVOORT

Collection Editor: JENNIFER GRÜNWALD • Assistant Editors: ALEX STARBUCK & NELSON RIBEIRO • Editor, Special Projects: MARK D. BEAZLEY
Senior Editor, Special Projects: JEFF YOUNGQUIST • Senior Vice President of Sales: DAVID GABRIEL
SVP of Brand Planning & Communications: MICHAEL PASCIULLO

Editor in Chief: AXEL ALONSO • Chief Creative Officer: JOE QUESADA • Publisher: DAN BUCKLEY • Executive Producer: ALAN FINE

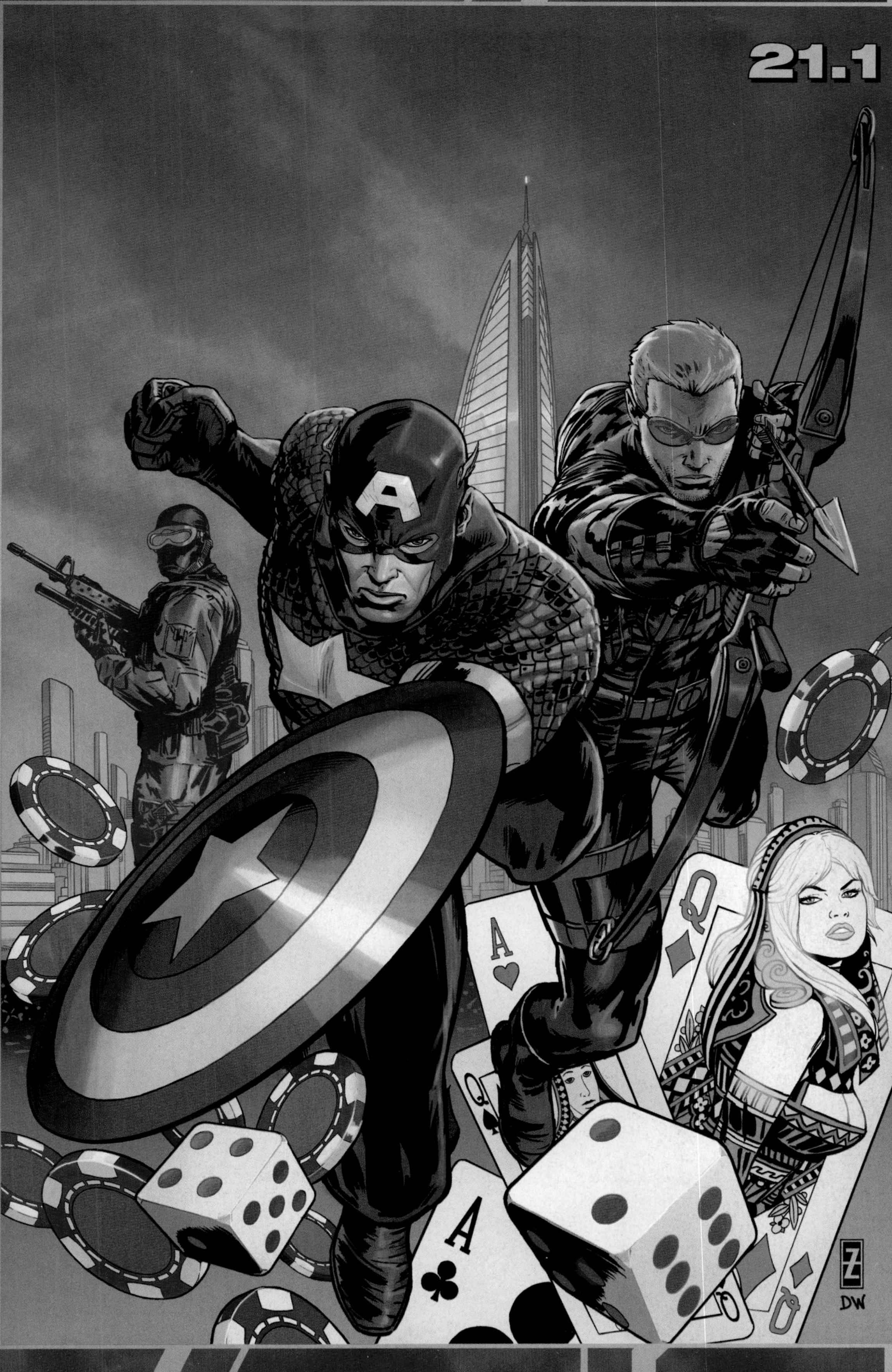
21.1
DW

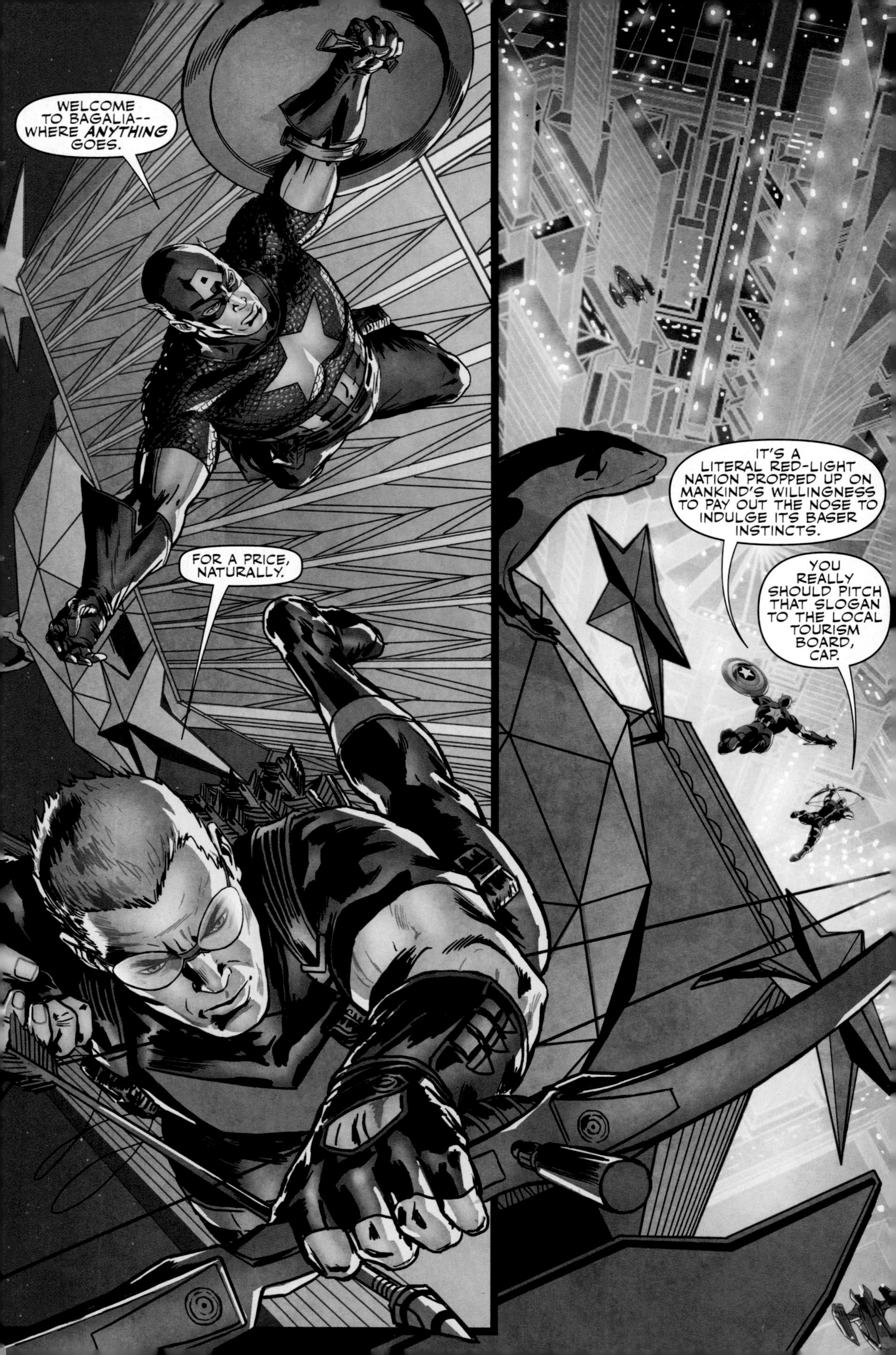
WELCOME TO BAGALIA-- WHERE *ANYTHING* GOES.
FOR A PRICE, NATURALLY.
IT'S A LITERAL RED-LIGHT NATION PROPPED UP ON MANKIND'S WILLINGNESS TO PAY OUT THE NOSE TO INDULGE ITS BASER INSTINCTS.
YOU REALLY SHOULD PITCH THAT SLOGAN TO THE LOCAL TOURISM BOARD, CAP.

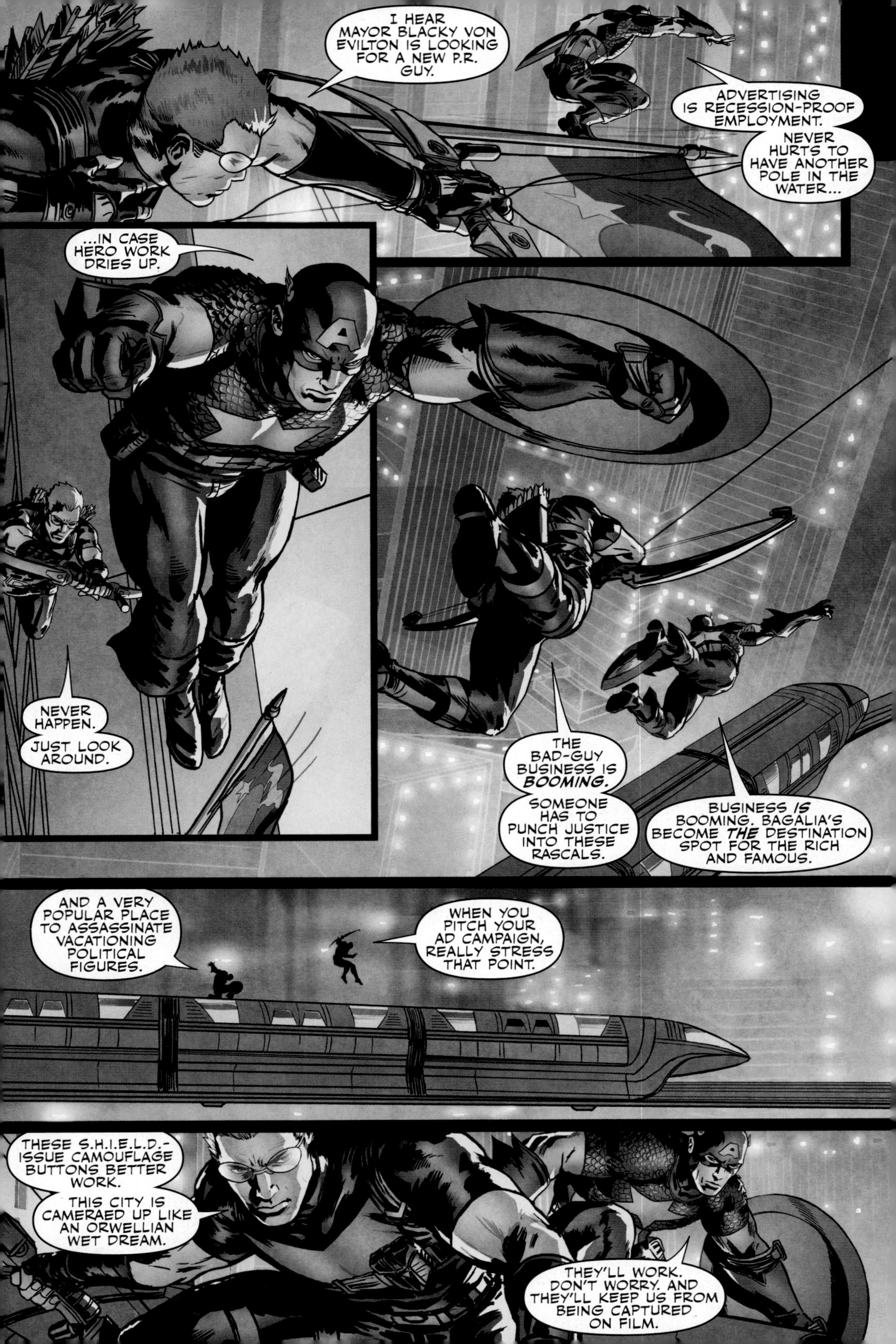
I HEAR MAYOR BLACKY VON EVILTON IS LOOKING FOR A NEW P.R. GUY.
ADVERTISING IS RECESSION-PROOF EMPLOYMENT.
NEVER HURTS TO HAVE ANOTHER POLE IN THE WATER...
...IN CASE HERO WORK DRIES UP.
NEVER HAPPEN.
JUST LOOK AROUND.
THE BAD-GUY BUSINESS IS BOOMING.
SOMEONE HAS TO PUNCH JUSTICE INTO THESE RASCALS.
BUSINESS IS BOOMING. BAGALIA'S BECOME THE DESTINATION SPOT FOR THE RICH AND FAMOUS.
AND A VERY POPULAR PLACE TO ASSASSINATE VACATIONING POLITICAL FIGURES.
WHEN YOU PITCH YOUR AD CAMPAIGN, REALLY STRESS THAT POINT.
THESE S.H.I.E.L.D.-ISSUE CAMOUFLAGE BUTTONS BETTER WORK.
THIS CITY IS CAMERAED UP LIKE AN ORWELLIAN WET DREAM.
THEY'LL WORK. DON'T WORRY. AND THEY'LL KEEP US FROM BEING CAPTURED ON FILM.

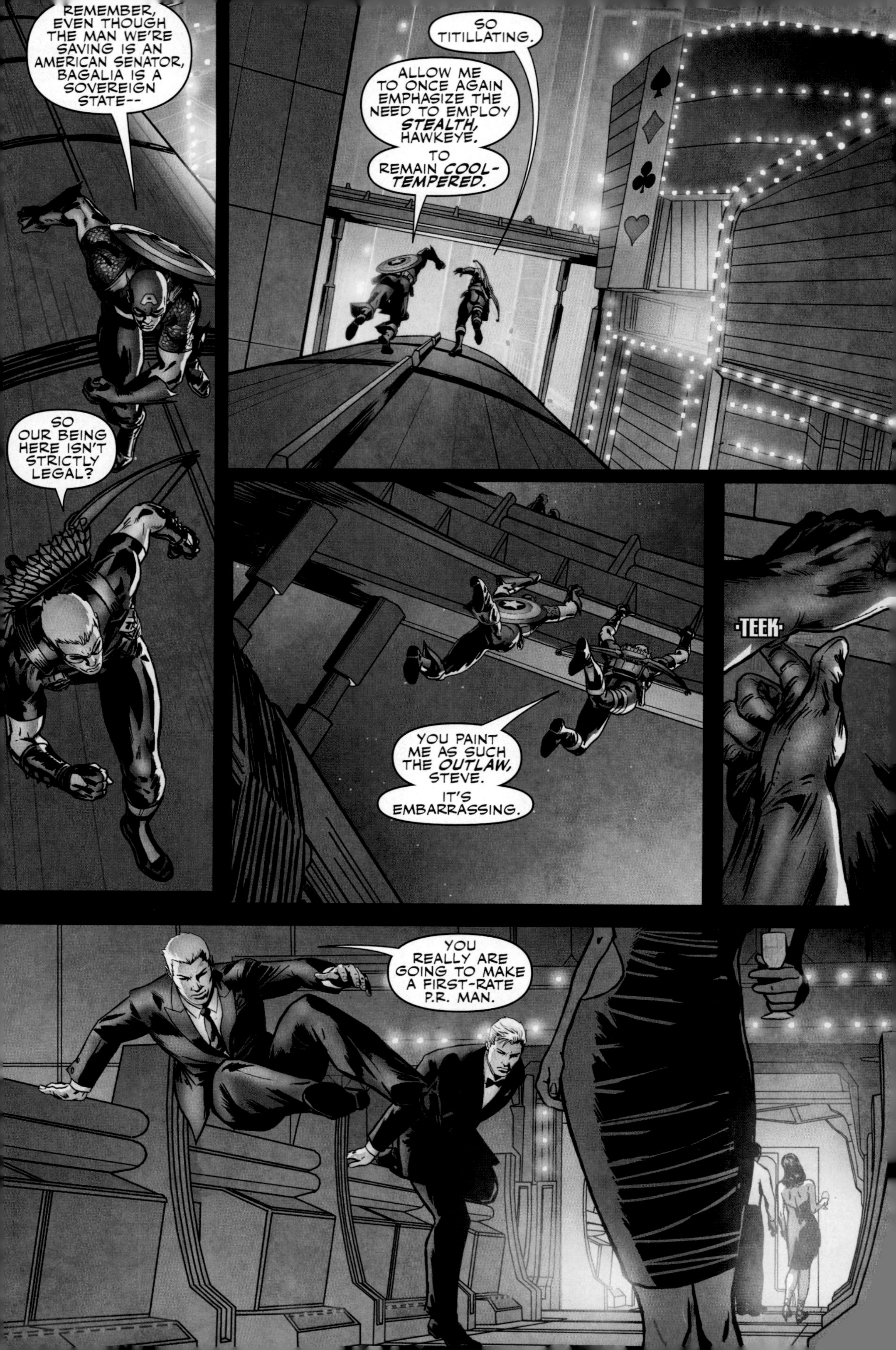

REMEMBER, EVEN THOUGH THE MAN WE'RE SAVING IS AN AMERICAN SENATOR, BAGALIA IS A SOVEREIGN STATE--
SO OUR BEING HERE ISN'T STRICTLY LEGAL?
SO TITILLATING.
ALLOW ME TO ONCE AGAIN EMPHASIZE THE NEED TO EMPLOY STEALTH, HAWKEYE.
TO REMAIN COOL-TEMPERED.
YOU PAINT ME AS SUCH THE OUTLAW, STEVE.
IT'S EMBARRASSING.
·TEEK·
YOU REALLY ARE GOING TO MAKE A FIRST-RATE P.R. MAN.

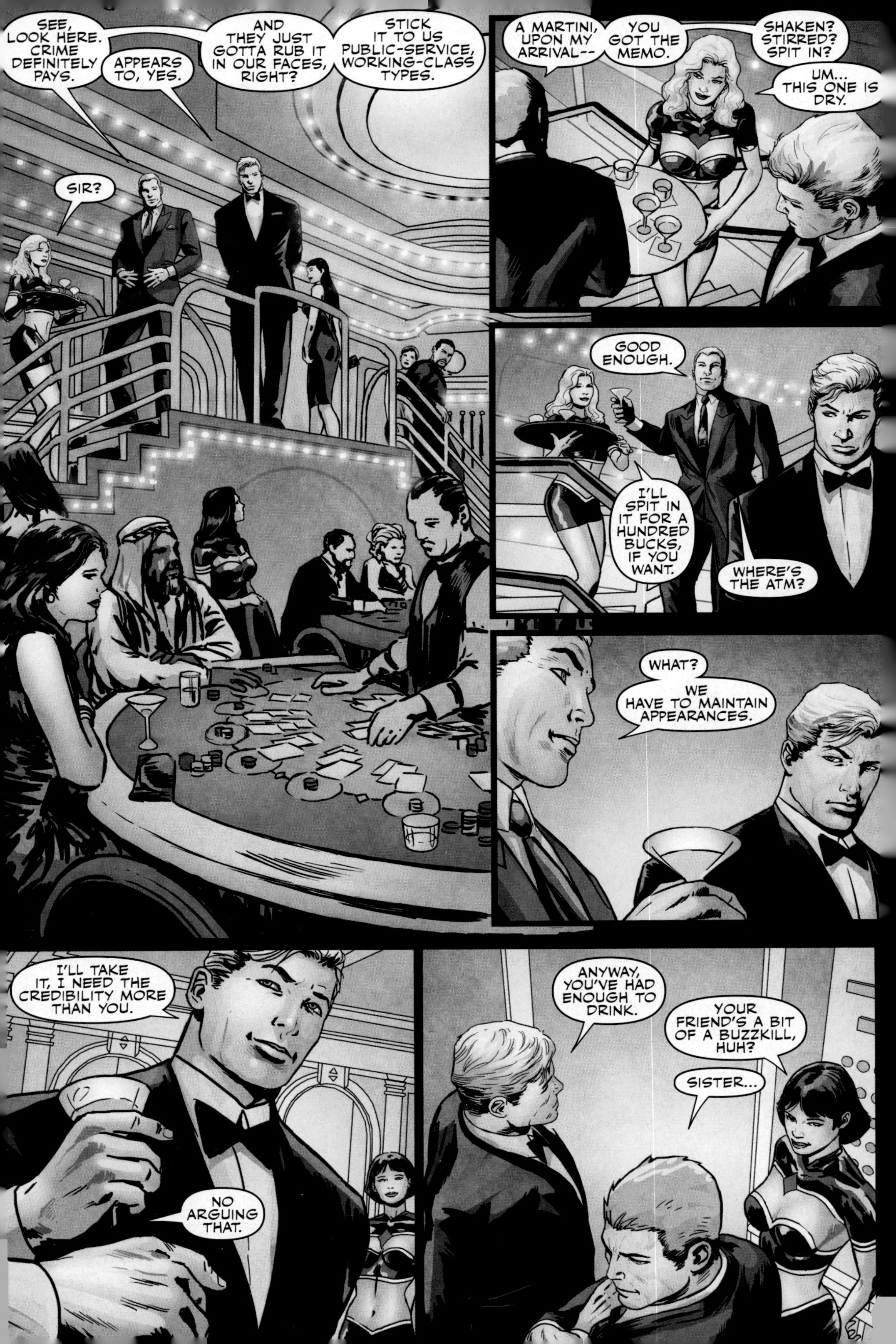
SEE, LOOK HERE. CRIME DEFINITELY PAYS.
APPEARS TO, YES.
AND THEY JUST GOTTA RUB IT IN OUR FACES, RIGHT?
STICK IT TO US PUBLIC-SERVICE, WORKING-CLASS TYPES.
SIR?
A MARTINI, UPON MY ARRIVAL--
YOU GOT THE MEMO.
SHAKEN? STIRRED? SPIT IN?
UM... THIS ONE IS DRY.
GOOD ENOUGH.
I'LL SPIT IN IT FOR A HUNDRED BUCKS, IF YOU WANT.
WHERE'S THE ATM?
WHAT?
WE HAVE TO MAINTAIN APPEARANCES.
I'LL TAKE IT, I NEED THE CREDIBILITY MORE THAN YOU.
NO ARGUING THAT.
ANYWAY, YOU'VE HAD ENOUGH TO DRINK.
YOUR FRIEND'S A BIT OF A BUZZKILL, HUH?
SISTER...

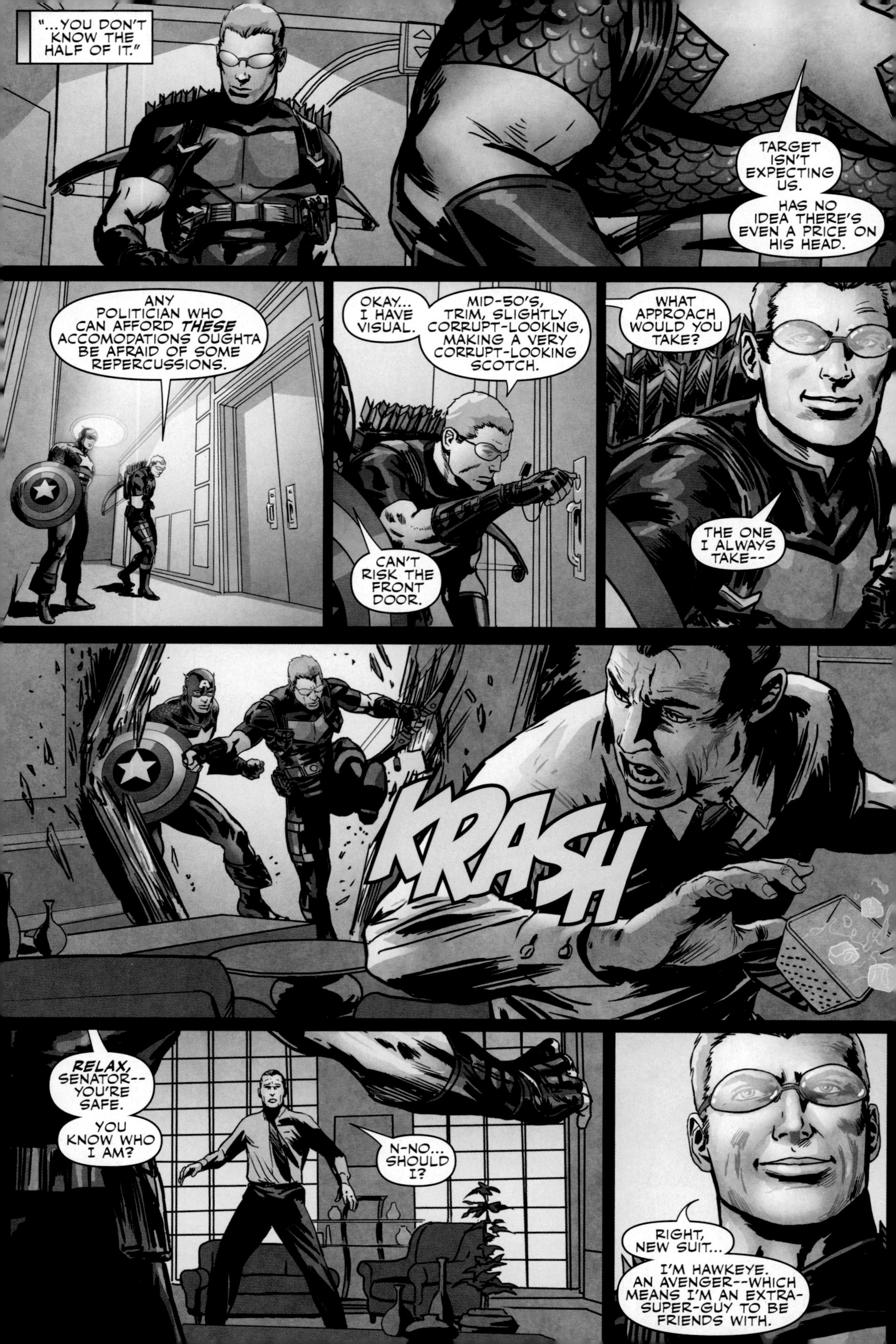
"...YOU DON'T KNOW THE HALF OF IT."
TARGET ISN'T EXPECTING US.
HAS NO IDEA THERE'S EVEN A PRICE ON HIS HEAD.
ANY POLITICIAN WHO CAN AFFORD *THESE* ACCOMODATIONS OUGHTA BE AFRAID OF SOME REPERCUSSIONS.
OKAY... I HAVE VISUAL.
MID-50'S, TRIM, SLIGHTLY CORRUPT-LOOKING, MAKING A VERY CORRUPT-LOOKING SCOTCH.
CAN'T RISK THE FRONT DOOR.
WHAT APPROACH WOULD YOU TAKE?
THE ONE I ALWAYS TAKE--
KRASH
RELAX, SENATOR-- YOU'RE SAFE.
YOU KNOW WHO I AM?
N-NO... SHOULD I?
RIGHT, NEW SUIT...
I'M HAWKEYE. AN AVENGER--WHICH MEANS I'M AN EXTRA-SUPER-GUY TO BE FRIENDS WITH.

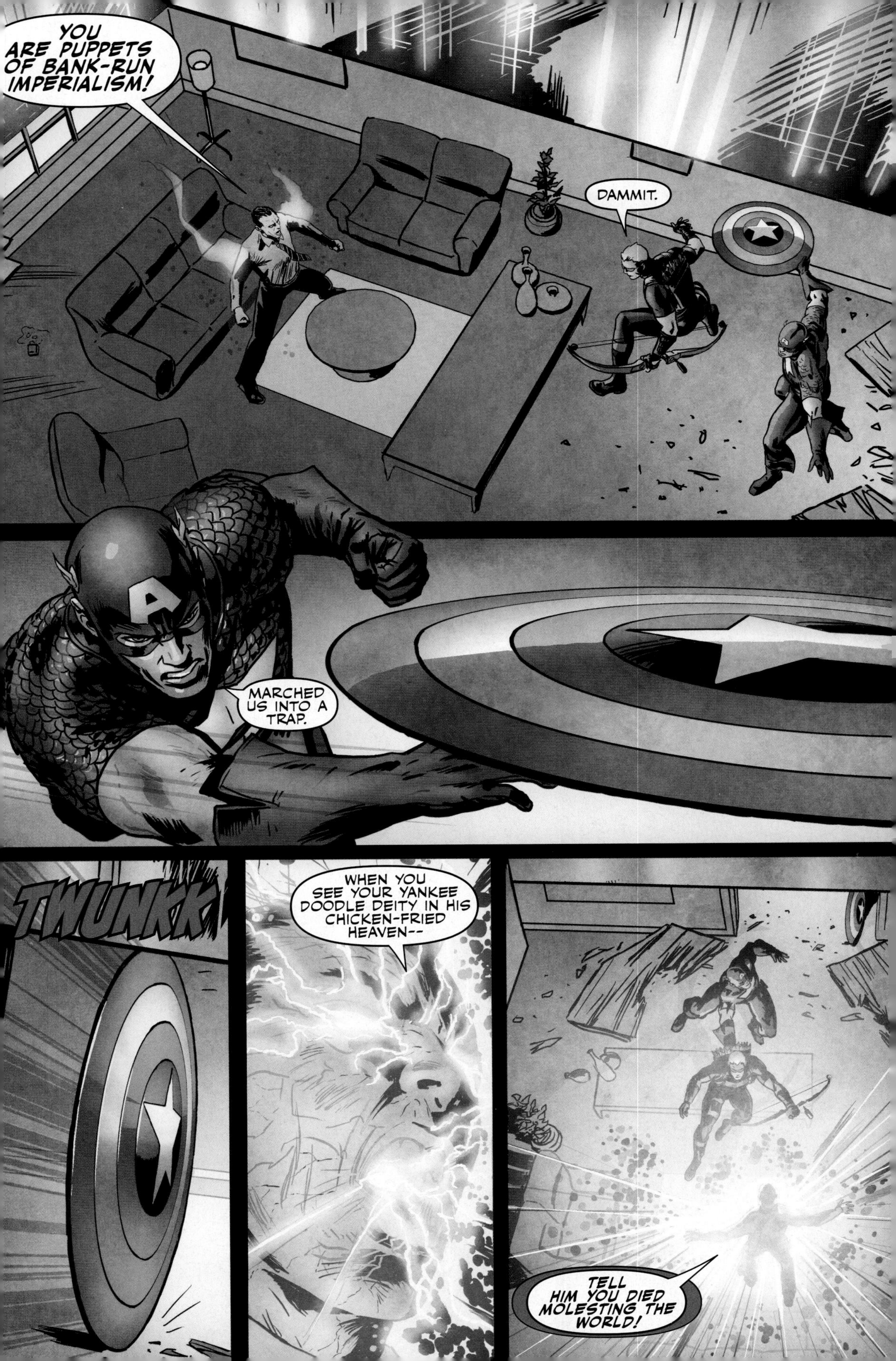
YOU ARE PUPPETS OF BANK-RUN IMPERIALISM!
DAMMIT.
MARCHED US INTO A TRAP.
TWUNKK
WHEN YOU SEE YOUR YANKEE DOODLE DEITY IN HIS CHICKEN-FRIED HEAVEN--
TELL HIM YOU DIED MOLESTING THE WORLD!

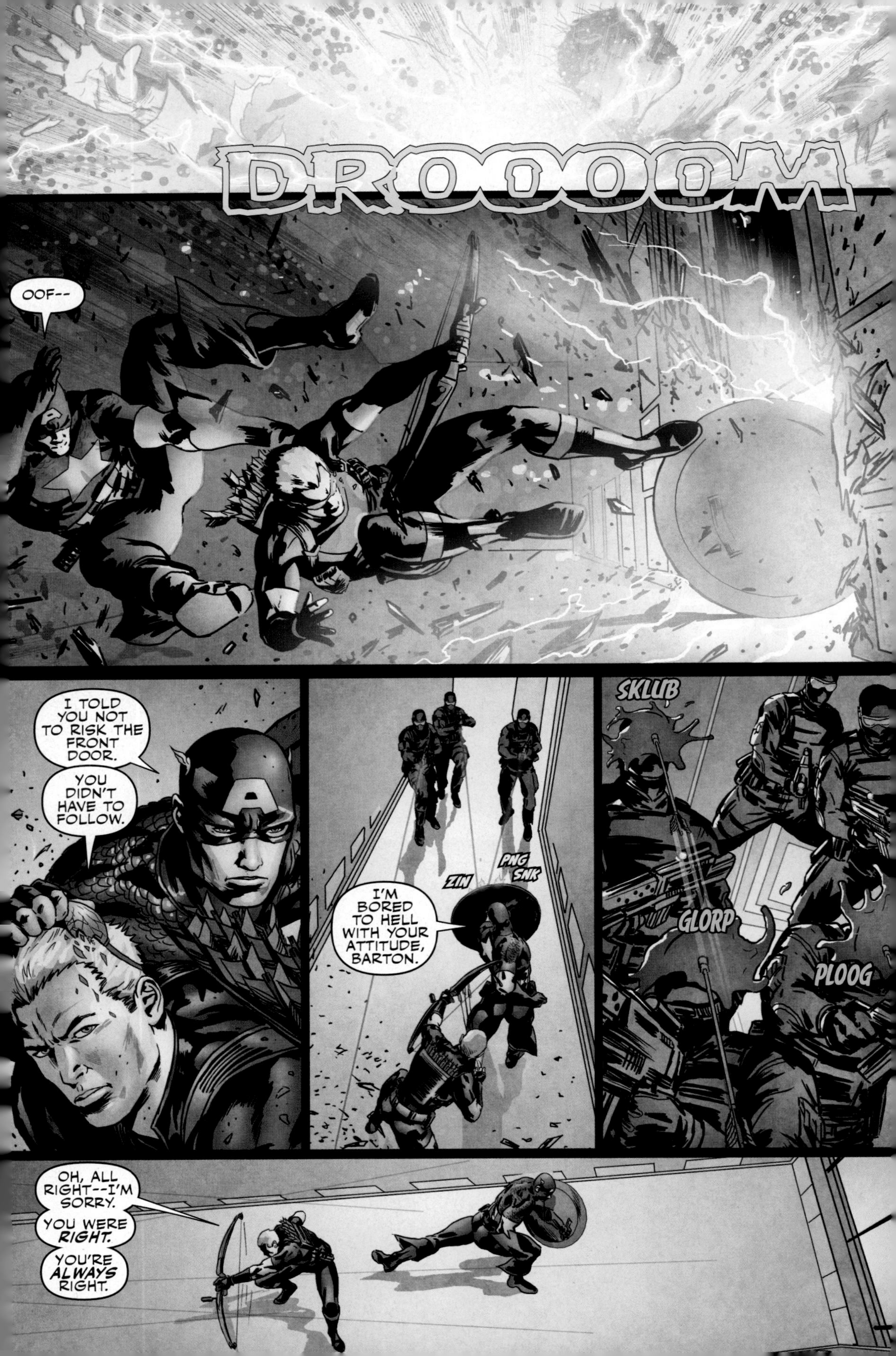
DROOOOM
OOF--
I TOLD YOU NOT TO RISK THE FRONT DOOR.
YOU DIDN'T HAVE TO FOLLOW.
ZIN
PNG
SNK
I'M BORED TO HELL WITH YOUR ATTITUDE, BARTON.
SKLUB
GLORP
PLOOG
OH, ALL RIGHT--I'M SORRY.
YOU WERE *RIGHT.*
YOU'RE *ALWAYS* RIGHT.

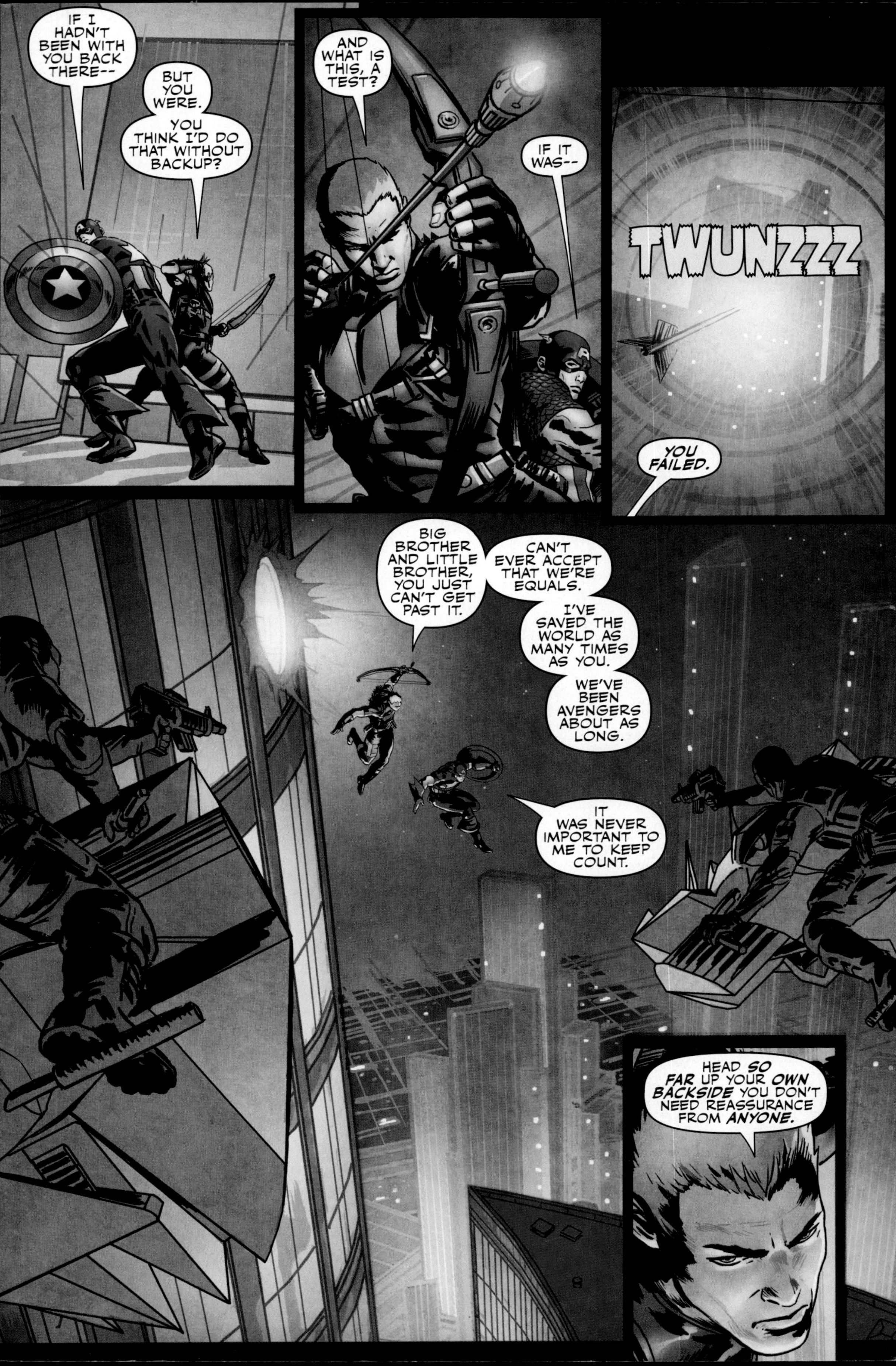
IF I HADN'T BEEN WITH YOU BACK THERE--
BUT YOU WERE.
YOU THINK I'D DO THAT WITHOUT BACKUP?
AND WHAT IS THIS, A TEST?
IF IT WAS--
TWUNZZZ
YOU FAILED.
BIG BROTHER AND LITTLE BROTHER, YOU JUST CAN'T GET PAST IT.
CAN'T EVER ACCEPT THAT WE'RE EQUALS.
I'VE SAVED THE WORLD AS MANY TIMES AS YOU.
WE'VE BEEN AVENGERS ABOUT AS LONG.
IT WAS NEVER IMPORTANT TO ME TO KEEP COUNT.
HEAD SO FAR UP YOUR OWN BACKSIDE YOU DON'T NEED REASSURANCE FROM ANYONE.

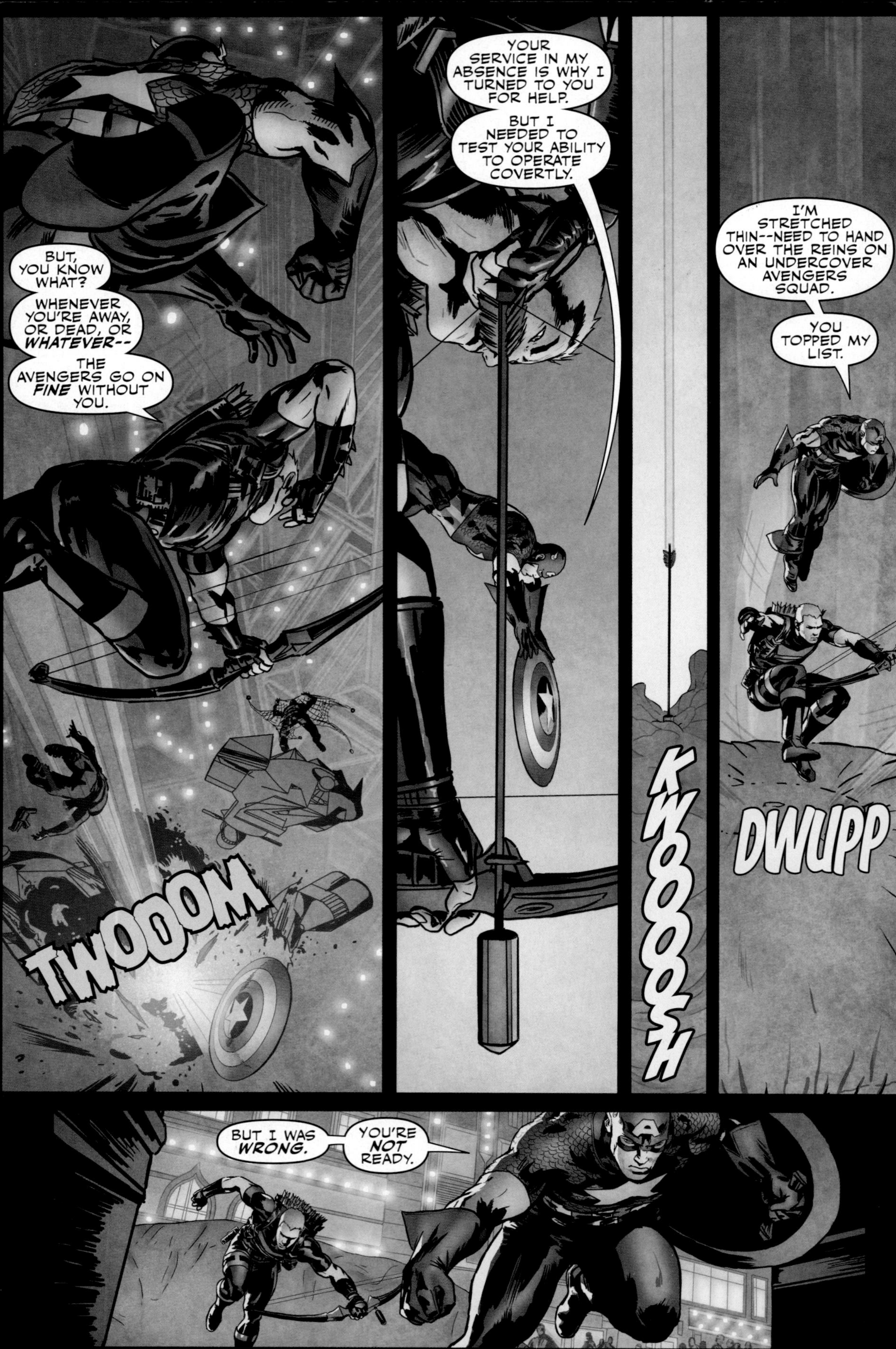

BUT, YOU KNOW WHAT?
WHENEVER YOU'RE AWAY, OR DEAD, OR *WHATEVER*--
THE AVENGERS GO ON *FINE* WITHOUT YOU.
TWOOOM
YOUR SERVICE IN MY ABSENCE IS WHY I TURNED TO YOU FOR HELP.
BUT I NEEDED TO TEST YOUR ABILITY TO OPERATE COVERTLY.
KWOOOOOSH
I'M STRETCHED THIN--NEED TO HAND OVER THE REINS ON AN UNDERCOVER AVENGERS SQUAD.
YOU TOPPED MY LIST.
DWUPP
BUT I WAS *WRONG*.
YOU'RE *NOT* READY.

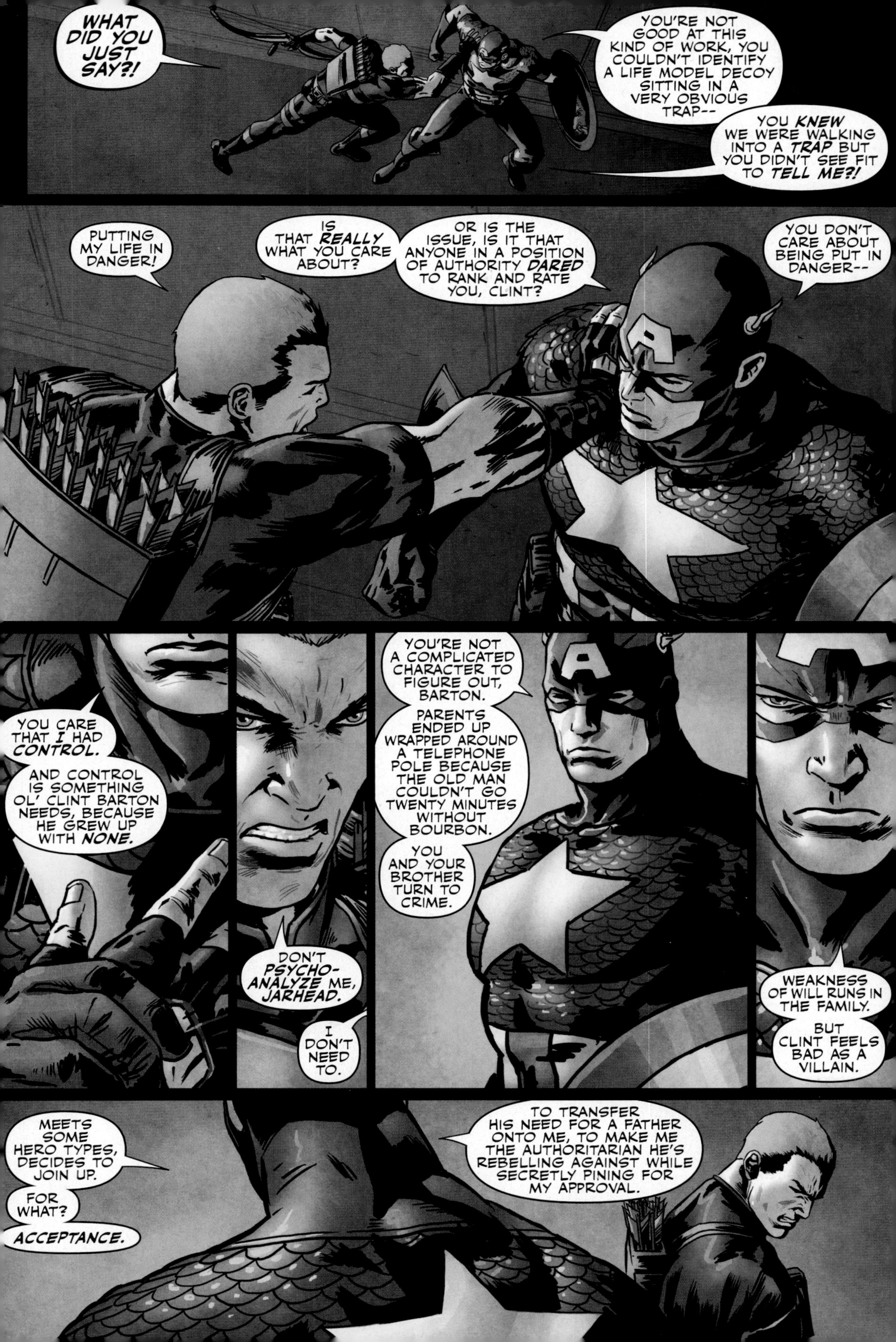
WHAT DID YOU JUST SAY?!
YOU'RE NOT GOOD AT THIS KIND OF WORK, YOU COULDN'T IDENTIFY A LIFE MODEL DECOY SITTING IN A VERY OBVIOUS TRAP--
YOU KNEW WE WERE WALKING INTO A TRAP BUT YOU DIDN'T SEE FIT TO TELL ME?!
PUTTING MY LIFE IN DANGER!
IS THAT REALLY WHAT YOU CARE ABOUT?
OR IS THE ISSUE, IS IT THAT ANYONE IN A POSITION OF AUTHORITY DARED TO RANK AND RATE YOU, CLINT?
YOU DON'T CARE ABOUT BEING PUT IN DANGER--
YOU CARE THAT I HAD CONTROL.
AND CONTROL IS SOMETHING OL' CLINT BARTON NEEDS, BECAUSE HE GREW UP WITH NONE.
DON'T PSYCHO-ANALYZE ME, JARHEAD.
I DON'T NEED TO.
YOU'RE NOT A COMPLICATED CHARACTER TO FIGURE OUT, BARTON.
PARENTS ENDED UP WRAPPED AROUND A TELEPHONE POLE BECAUSE THE OLD MAN COULDN'T GO TWENTY MINUTES WITHOUT BOURBON.
YOU AND YOUR BROTHER TURN TO CRIME.
WEAKNESS OF WILL RUNS IN THE FAMILY.
BUT CLINT FEELS BAD AS A VILLAIN.
MEETS SOME HERO TYPES, DECIDES TO JOIN UP.
FOR WHAT?
ACCEPTANCE.
TO TRANSFER HIS NEED FOR A FATHER ONTO ME, TO MAKE ME THE AUTHORITARIAN HE'S REBELLING AGAINST WHILE SECRETLY PINING FOR MY APPROVAL.

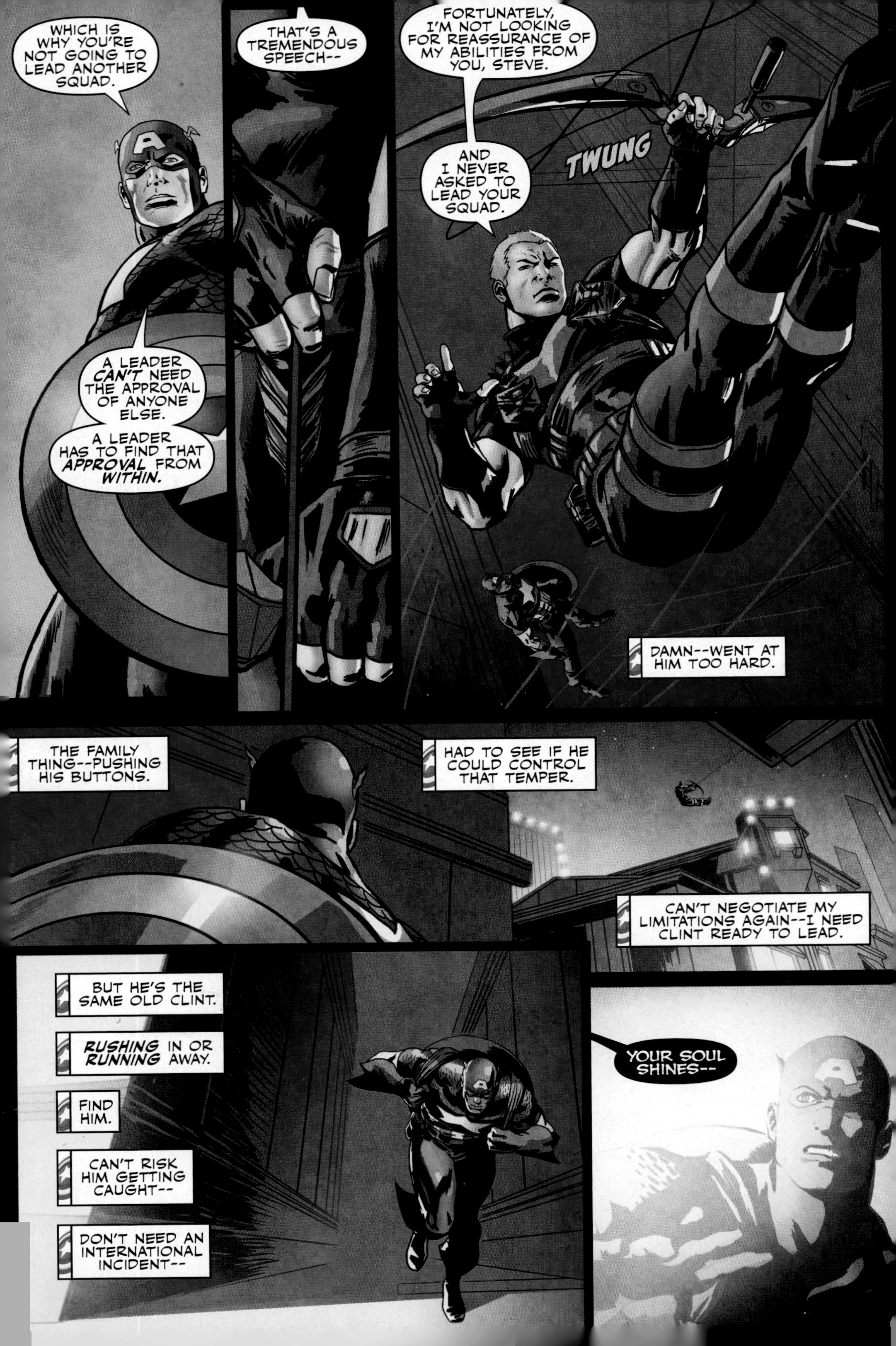

WHICH IS WHY YOU'RE NOT GOING TO LEAD ANOTHER SQUAD.
A LEADER *CAN'T* NEED THE APPROVAL OF ANYONE ELSE.
A LEADER HAS TO FIND THAT *APPROVAL* FROM *WITHIN.*
THAT'S A TREMENDOUS SPEECH--
FORTUNATELY, I'M NOT LOOKING FOR REASSURANCE OF MY ABILITIES FROM YOU, STEVE.
AND I NEVER ASKED TO LEAD YOUR SQUAD.
TWUNG
DAMN--WENT AT HIM TOO HARD.
THE FAMILY THING--PUSHING HIS BUTTONS.
HAD TO SEE IF HE COULD CONTROL THAT TEMPER.
CAN'T NEGOTIATE MY LIMITATIONS AGAIN--I NEED CLINT READY TO LEAD.
BUT HE'S THE SAME OLD CLINT.
RUSHING IN OR *RUNNING* AWAY.
FIND HIM.
CAN'T RISK HIM GETTING CAUGHT--
DON'T NEED AN INTERNATIONAL INCIDENT--
YOUR SOUL SHINES--

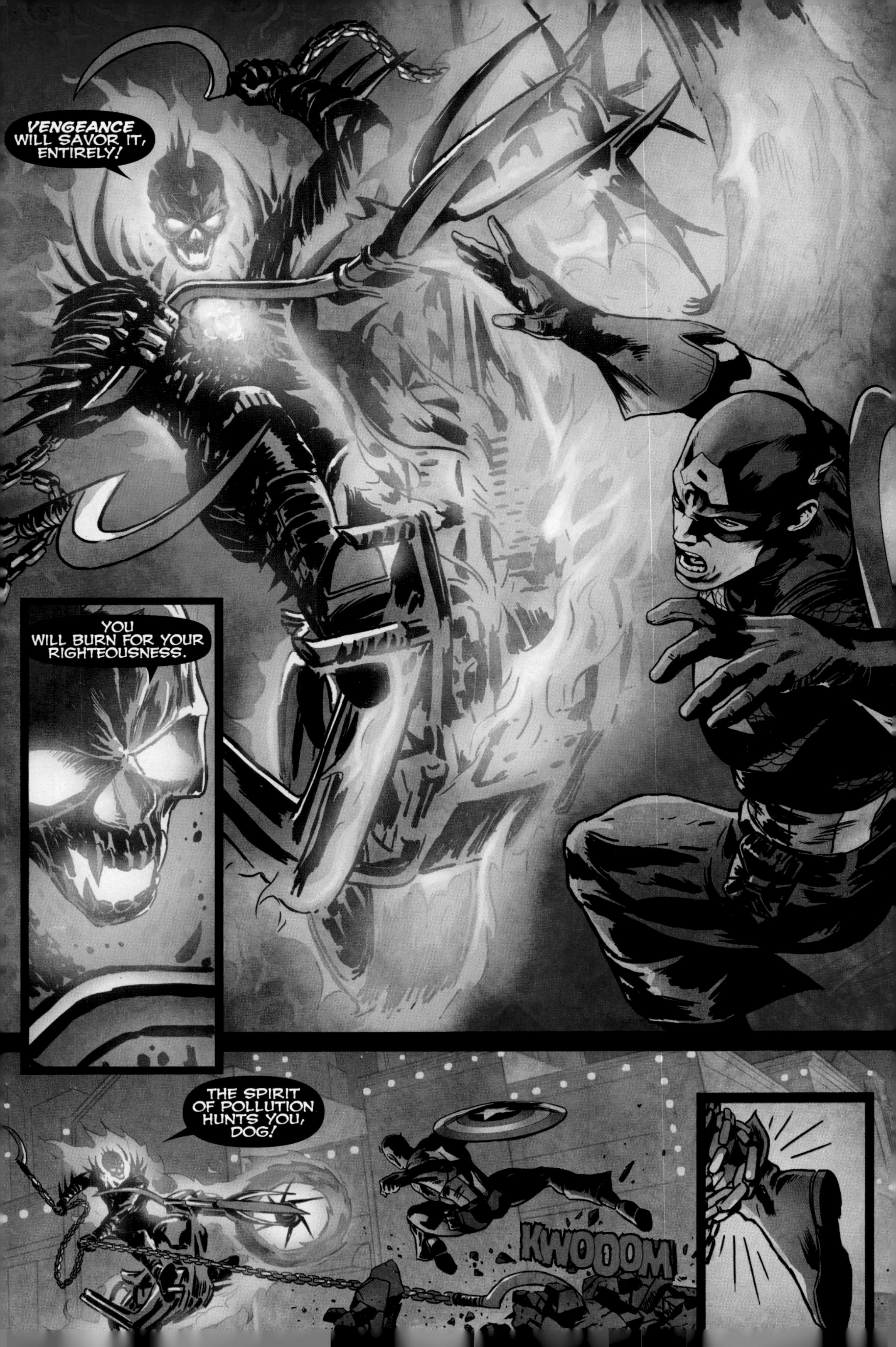
VENGEANCE WILL SAVOR IT, ENTIRELY!
YOU WILL BURN FOR YOUR RIGHTEOUSNESS.
THE SPIRIT OF POLLUTION HUNTS YOU, DOG!
KWOOOM

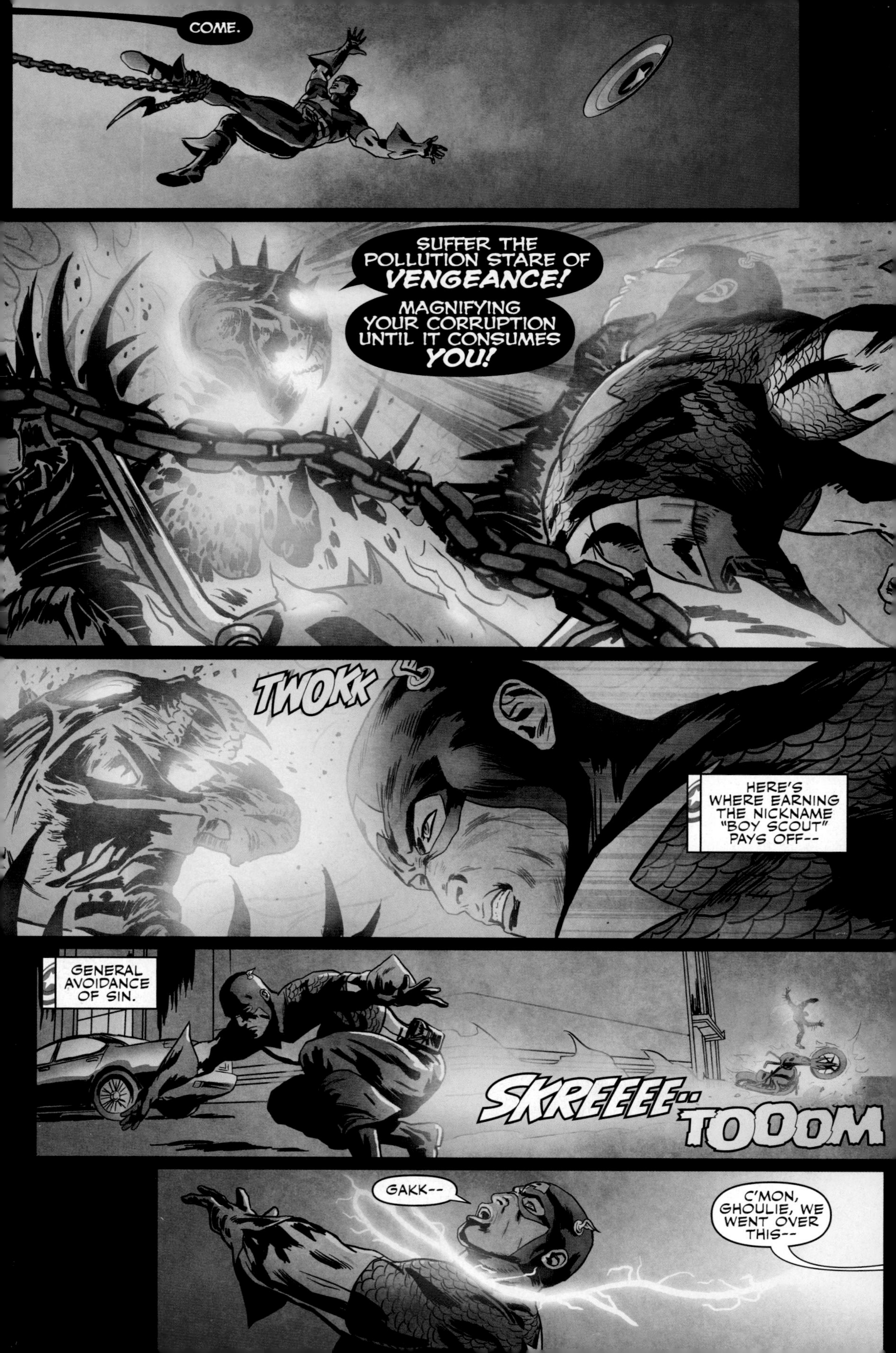
COME.
SUFFER THE POLLUTION STARE OF VENGEANCE!
MAGNIFYING YOUR CORRUPTION UNTIL IT CONSUMES YOU!
TWOKK
HERE'S WHERE EARNING THE NICKNAME "BOY SCOUT" PAYS OFF--
GENERAL AVOIDANCE OF SIN.
SKREEEE.. TOOOOM
GAKK--
C'MON, GHOULIE, WE WENT OVER THIS--

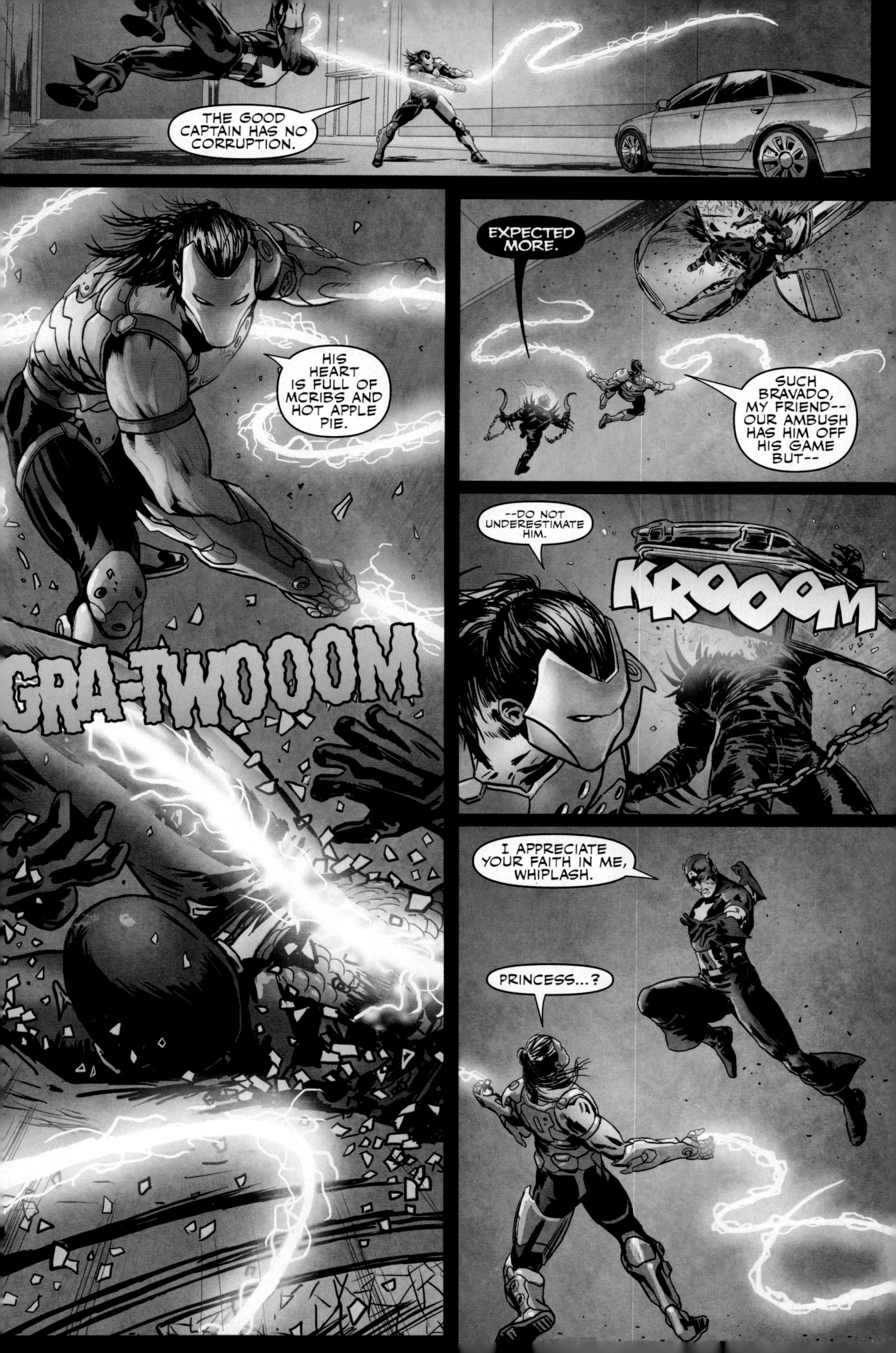
THE GOOD CAPTAIN HAS NO CORRUPTION.
HIS HEART IS FULL OF MCRIBS AND HOT APPLE PIE.
GRA-TWOOOM
EXPECTED MORE.
SUCH BRAVADO, MY FRIEND--OUR AMBUSH HAS HIM OFF HIS GAME BUT--
--DO NOT UNDERESTIMATE HIM.
KROOOM
I APPRECIATE YOUR FAITH IN ME, WHIPLASH.
PRINCESS...?

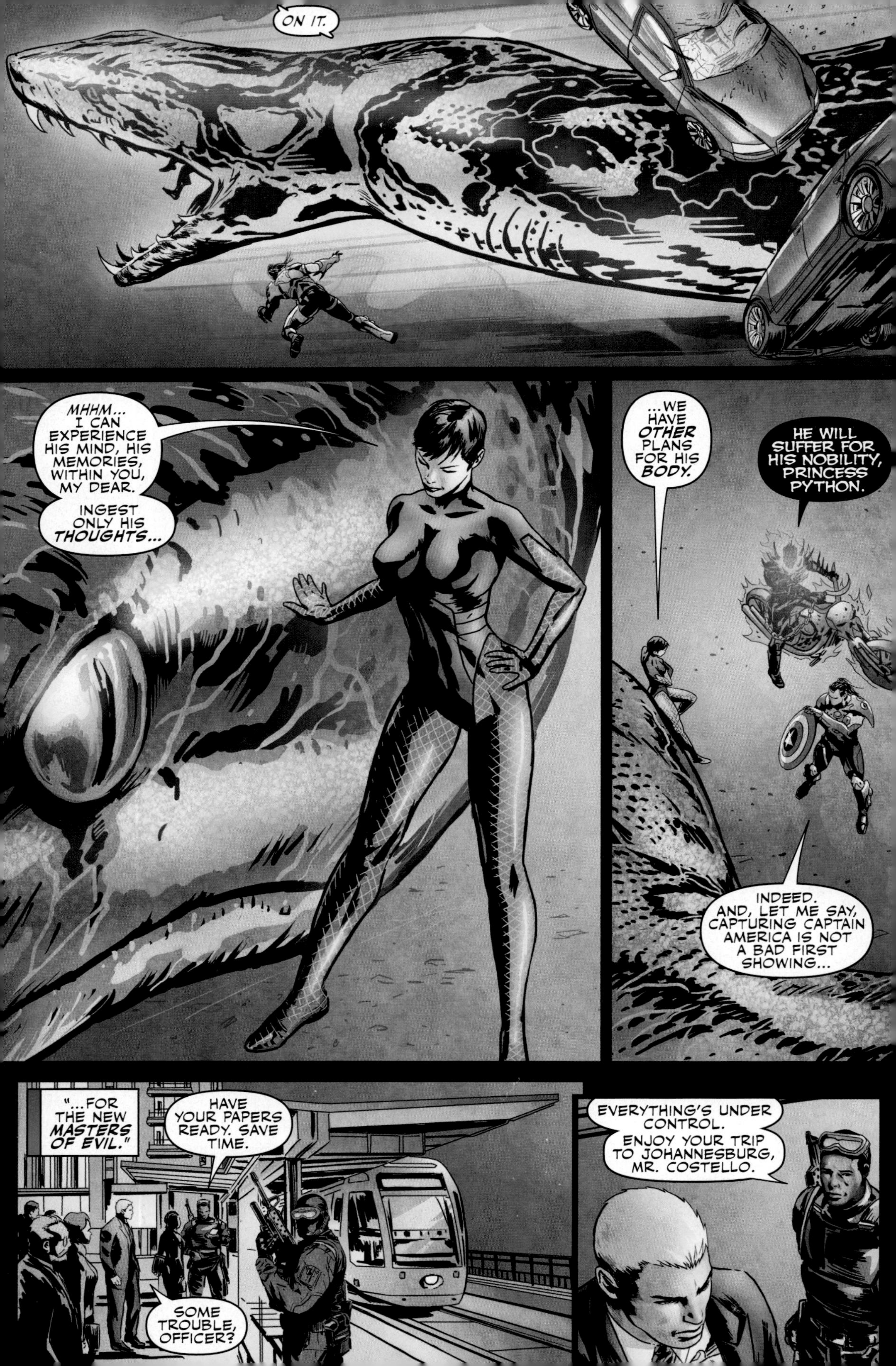

ON IT.
MHHM... I CAN EXPERIENCE HIS MIND, HIS MEMORIES, WITHIN YOU, MY DEAR.
INGEST ONLY HIS *THOUGHTS*...
...WE HAVE *OTHER* PLANS FOR HIS *BODY*.
HE WILL SUFFER FOR HIS NOBILITY, PRINCESS PYTHON.
INDEED. AND, LET ME SAY, CAPTURING CAPTAIN AMERICA IS NOT A BAD FIRST SHOWING...
"...FOR THE NEW *MASTERS OF EVIL*."
HAVE YOUR PAPERS READY. SAVE TIME.
SOME TROUBLE, OFFICER?
EVERYTHING'S UNDER CONTROL.
ENJOY YOUR TRIP TO JOHANNESBURG, MR. COSTELLO.

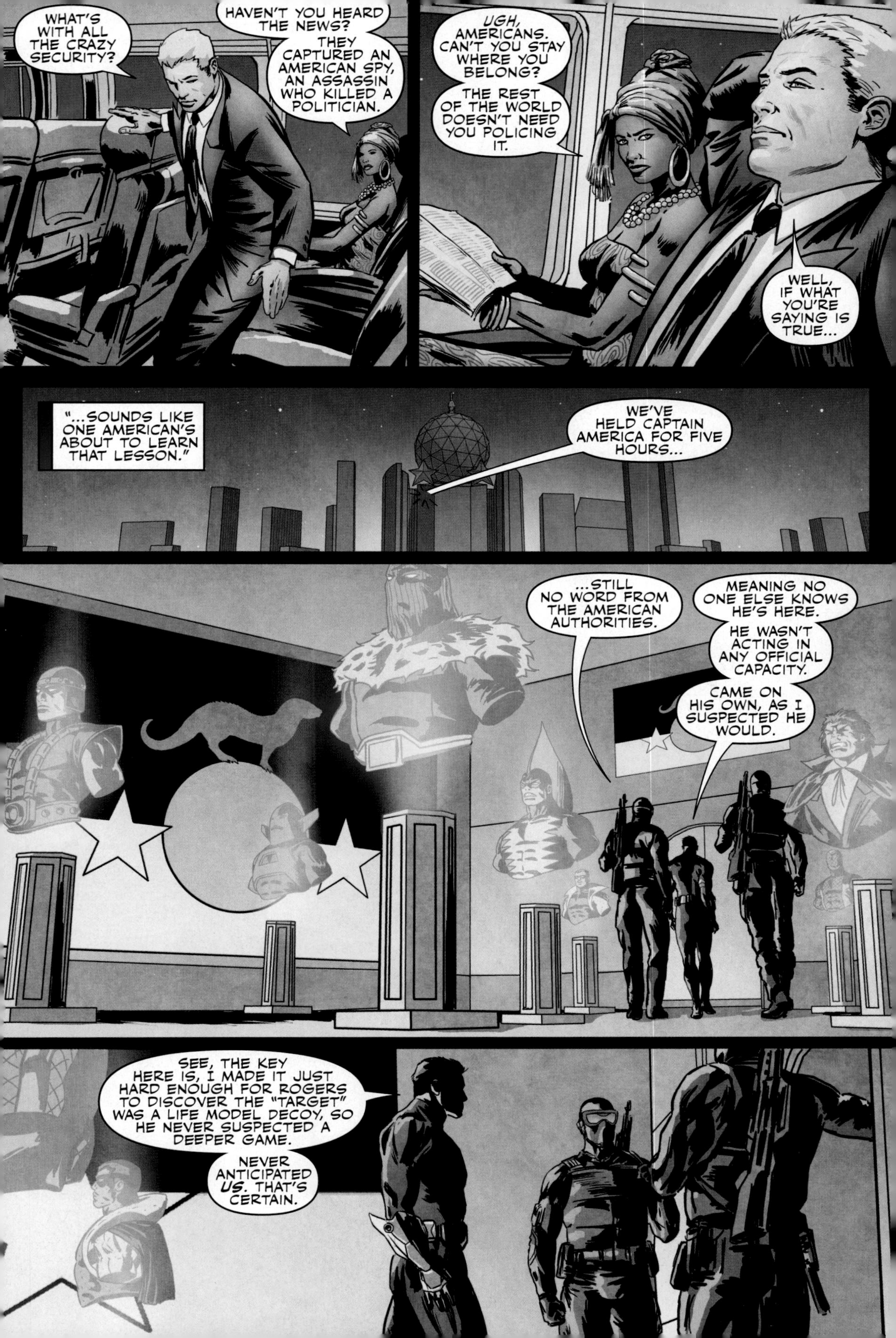
WHAT'S WITH ALL THE CRAZY SECURITY?
HAVEN'T YOU HEARD THE NEWS?
THEY CAPTURED AN AMERICAN SPY, AN ASSASSIN WHO KILLED A POLITICIAN.
UGH, AMERICANS. CAN'T YOU STAY WHERE YOU BELONG?
THE REST OF THE WORLD DOESN'T NEED YOU POLICING IT.
WELL, IF WHAT YOU'RE SAYING IS TRUE...
"...SOUNDS LIKE ONE AMERICAN'S ABOUT TO LEARN THAT LESSON."
WE'VE HELD CAPTAIN AMERICA FOR FIVE HOURS...
...STILL NO WORD FROM THE AMERICAN AUTHORITIES.
MEANING NO ONE ELSE KNOWS HE'S HERE.
HE WASN'T ACTING IN ANY OFFICIAL CAPACITY.
CAME ON HIS OWN, AS I SUSPECTED HE WOULD.
SEE, THE KEY HERE IS, I MADE IT JUST HARD ENOUGH FOR ROGERS TO DISCOVER THE "TARGET" WAS A LIFE MODEL DECOY, SO HE NEVER SUSPECTED A DEEPER GAME.
NEVER ANTICIPATED *US*. THAT'S CERTAIN.

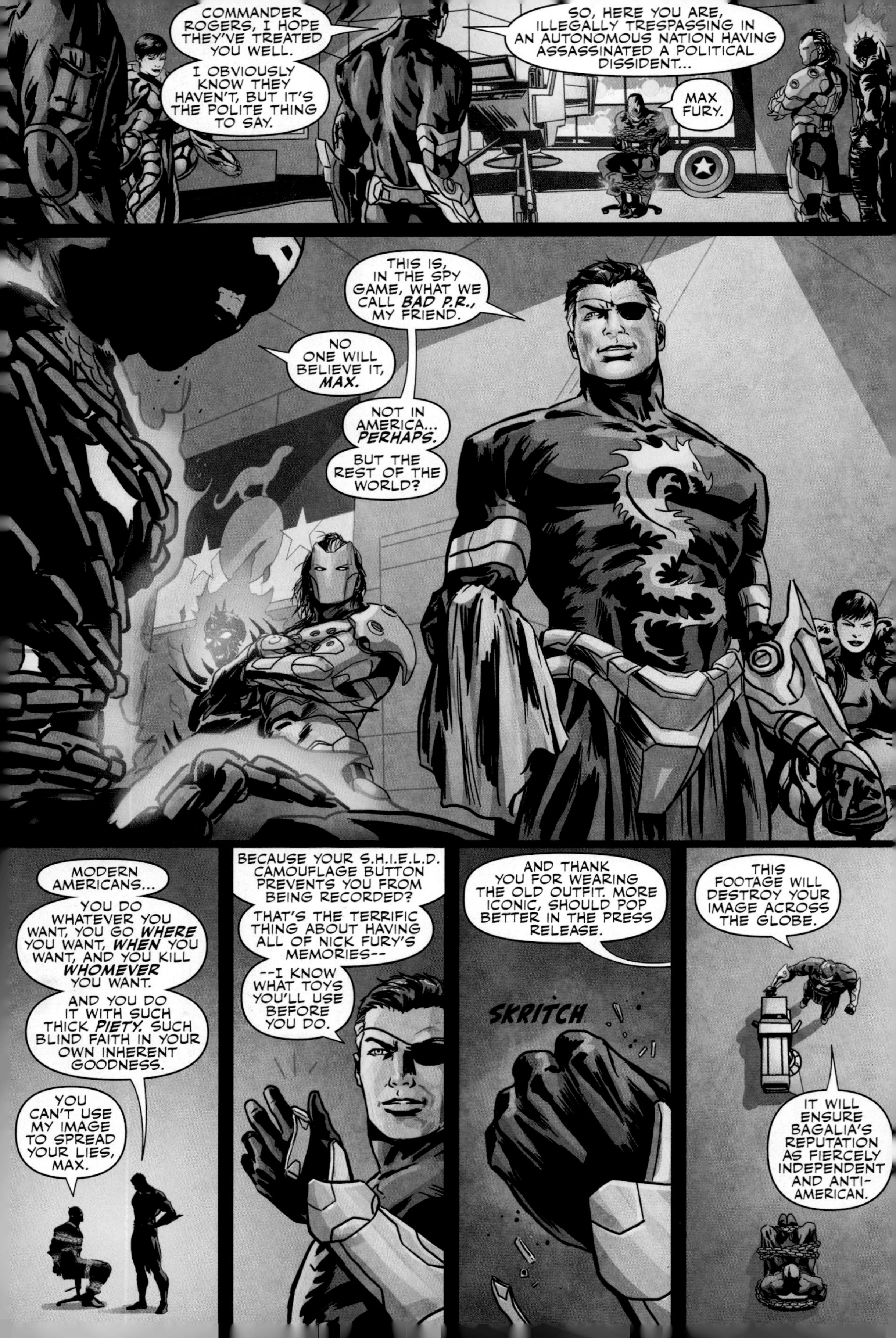
COMMANDER ROGERS, I HOPE THEY'VE TREATED YOU WELL.
I OBVIOUSLY KNOW THEY HAVEN'T, BUT IT'S THE POLITE THING TO SAY.
SO, HERE YOU ARE, ILLEGALLY TRESPASSING IN AN AUTONOMOUS NATION HAVING ASSASSINATED A POLITICAL DISSIDENT...
MAX FURY.
THIS IS, IN THE SPY GAME, WHAT WE CALL BAD P.R., MY FRIEND.
NO ONE WILL BELIEVE IT, MAX.
NOT IN AMERICA... PERHAPS.
BUT THE REST OF THE WORLD?
MODERN AMERICANS...
YOU DO WHATEVER YOU WANT, YOU GO WHERE YOU WANT, WHEN YOU WANT, AND YOU KILL WHOMEVER YOU WANT.
AND YOU DO IT WITH SUCH THICK PIETY. SUCH BLIND FAITH IN YOUR OWN INHERENT GOODNESS.
YOU CAN'T USE MY IMAGE TO SPREAD YOUR LIES, MAX.
BECAUSE YOUR S.H.I.E.L.D. CAMOUFLAGE BUTTON PREVENTS YOU FROM BEING RECORDED?
THAT'S THE TERRIFIC THING ABOUT HAVING ALL OF NICK FURY'S MEMORIES--
--I KNOW WHAT TOYS YOU'LL USE BEFORE YOU DO.
AND THANK YOU FOR WEARING THE OLD OUTFIT. MORE ICONIC, SHOULD POP BETTER IN THE PRESS RELEASE.
SKRITCH
THIS FOOTAGE WILL DESTROY YOUR IMAGE ACROSS THE GLOBE.
IT WILL ENSURE BAGALIA'S REPUTATION AS FIERCELY INDEPENDENT AND ANTI-AMERICAN.

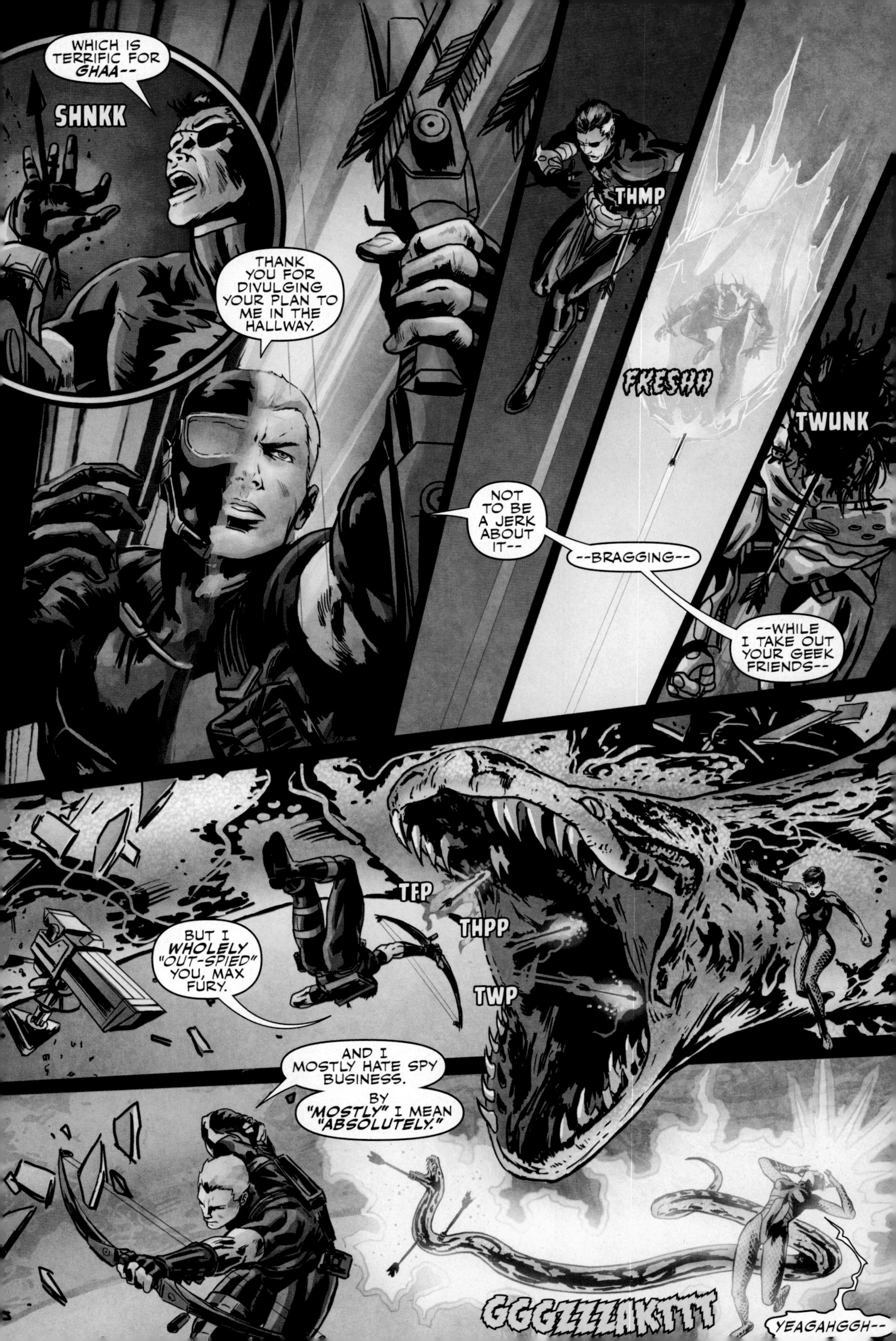
WHICH IS TERRIFIC FOR GHAA--
SHNKK
THANK YOU FOR DIVULGING YOUR PLAN TO ME IN THE HALLWAY.
THMP
FKESHH
TWUNK
NOT TO BE A JERK ABOUT IT--
--BRAGGING--
--WHILE I TAKE OUT YOUR GEEK FRIENDS--
TFP
THPP
TWP
BUT I WHOLELY "OUT-SPIED" YOU, MAX FURY.
AND I MOSTLY HATE SPY BUSINESS.
BY "MOSTLY" I MEAN "ABSOLUTELY."
GGGZZZAKTTT
YEAGAHGGH--

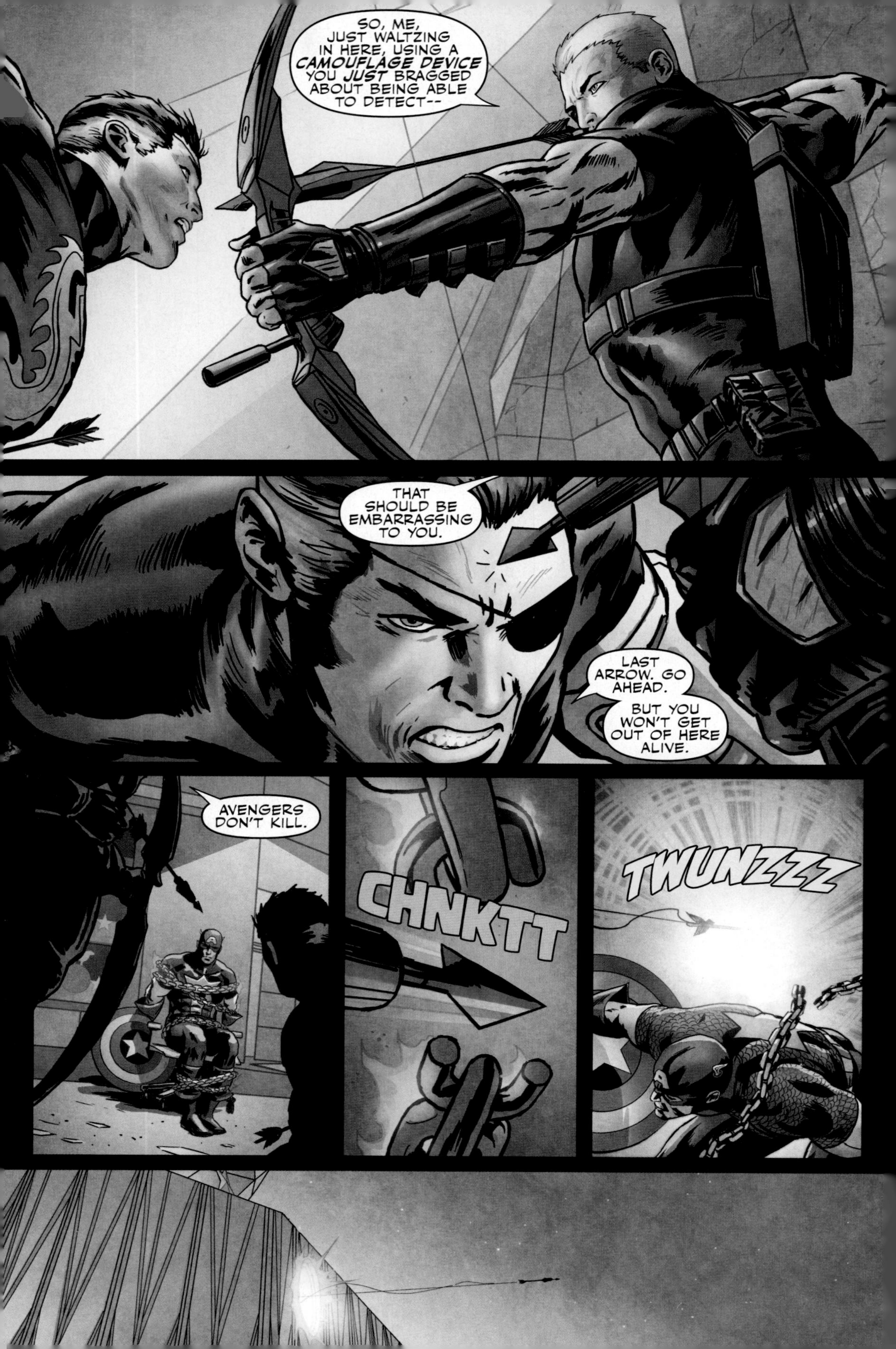
SO, ME, JUST WALTZING IN HERE, USING A CAMOUFLAGE DEVICE YOU JUST BRAGGED ABOUT BEING ABLE TO DETECT--
THAT SHOULD BE EMBARRASSING TO YOU.
LAST ARROW. GO AHEAD.
BUT YOU WON'T GET OUT OF HERE ALIVE.
AVENGERS DON'T KILL.
CHNKTT
TWUNZZZ

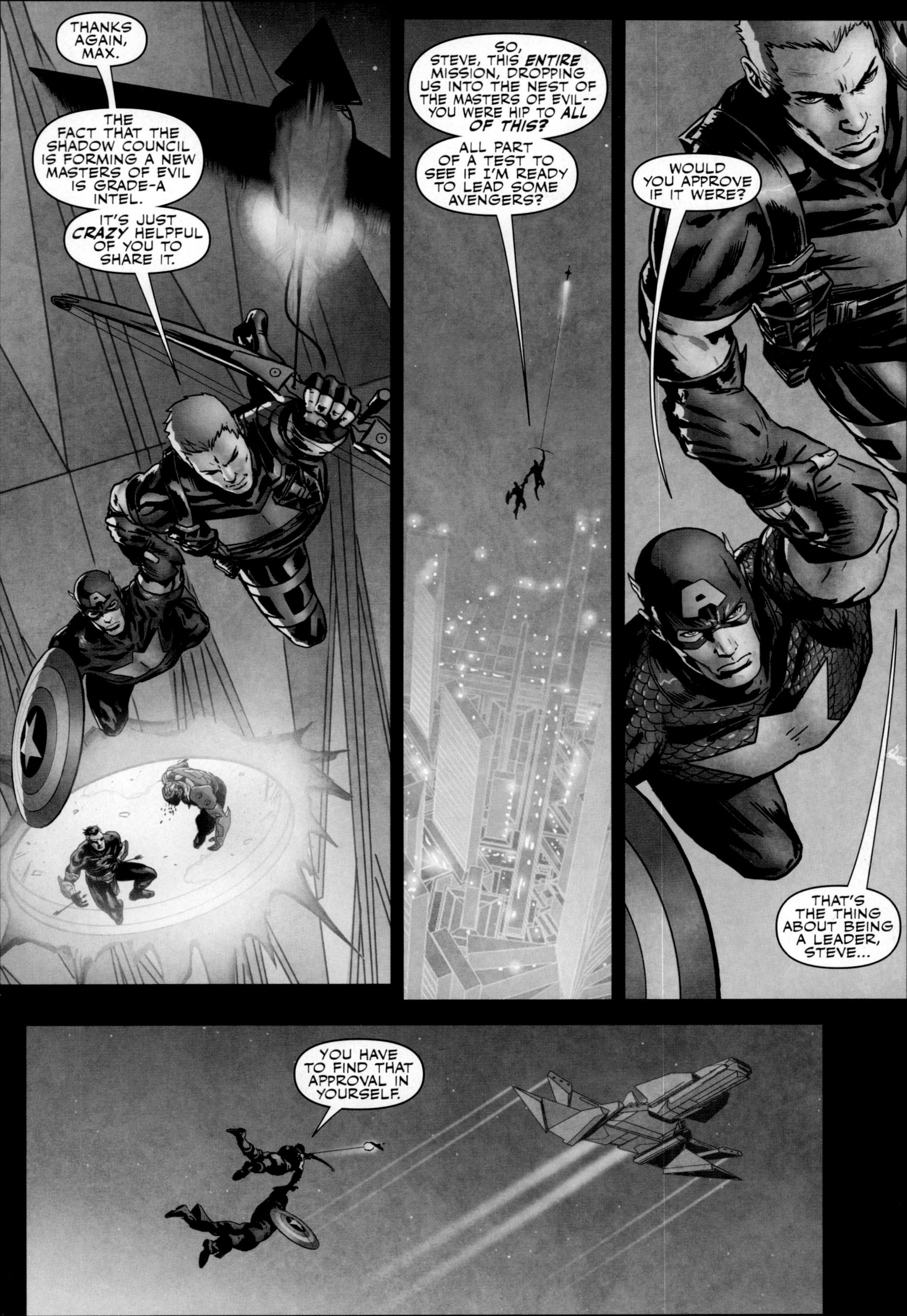
THANKS AGAIN, MAX.
THE FACT THAT THE SHADOW COUNCIL IS FORMING A NEW MASTERS OF EVIL IS GRADE-A INTEL.
IT'S JUST CRAZY HELPFUL OF YOU TO SHARE IT.
SO, STEVE, THIS ENTIRE MISSION, DROPPING US INTO THE NEST OF THE MASTERS OF EVIL-- YOU WERE HIP TO ALL OF THIS?
ALL PART OF A TEST TO SEE IF I'M READY TO LEAD SOME AVENGERS?
WOULD YOU APPROVE IF IT WERE?
THAT'S THE THING ABOUT BEING A LEADER, STEVE...
YOU HAVE TO FIND THAT APPROVAL IN YOURSELF.

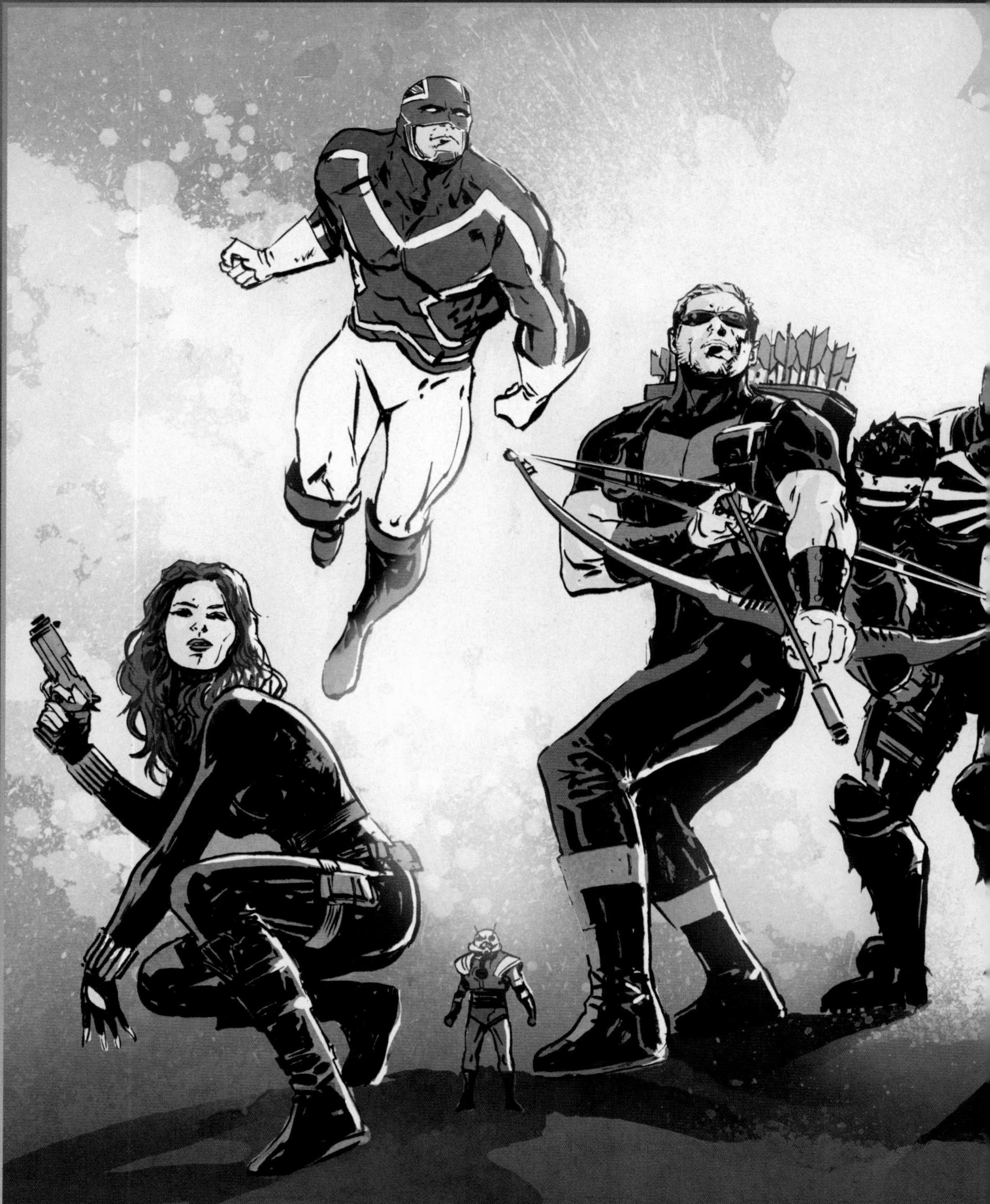

#22 VARIANT BY GABRIEL HARDMAN

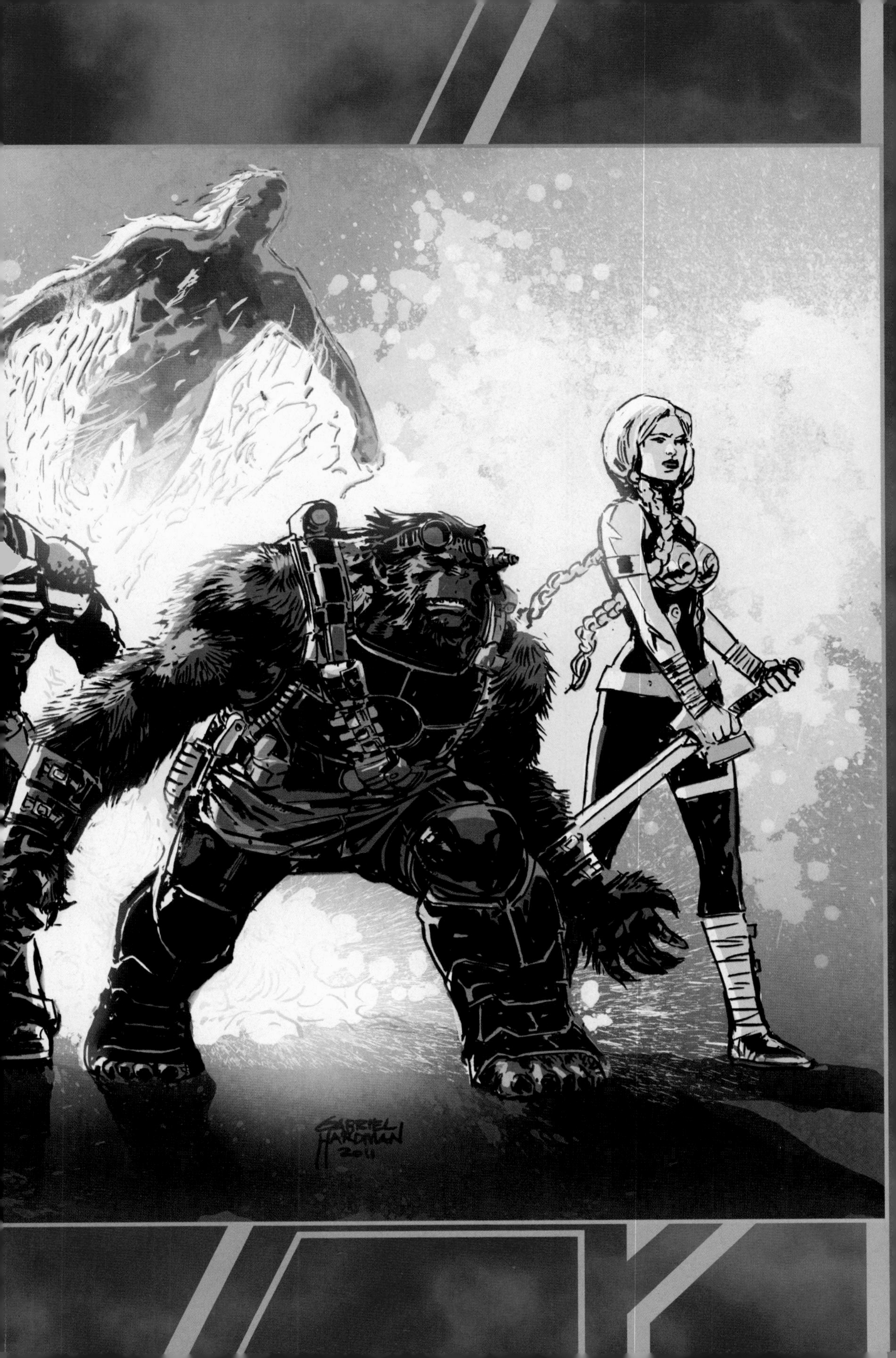
GABRIEL
HARDMAN
2011

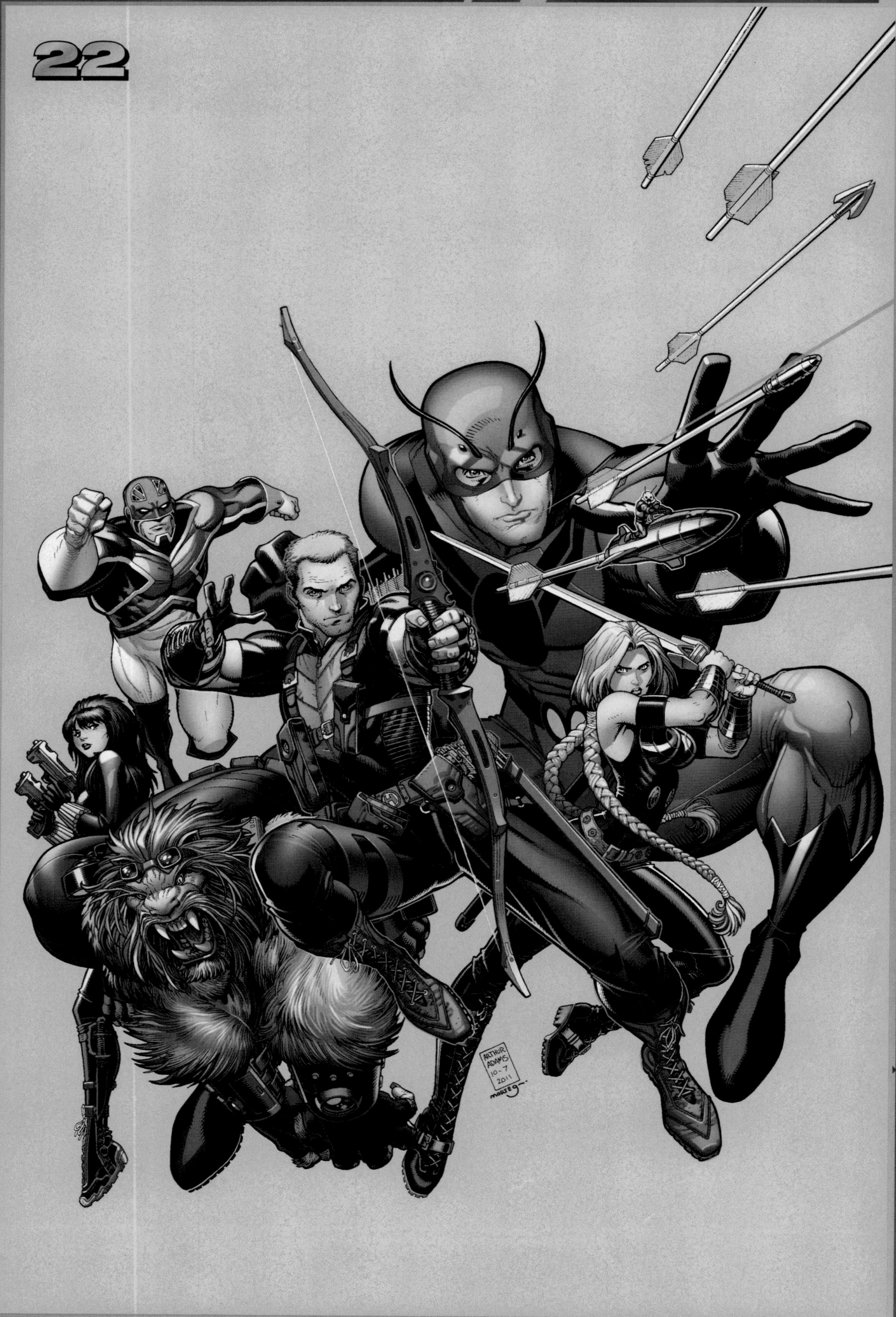
22
ARTHUR ADAMS
10-7
2011

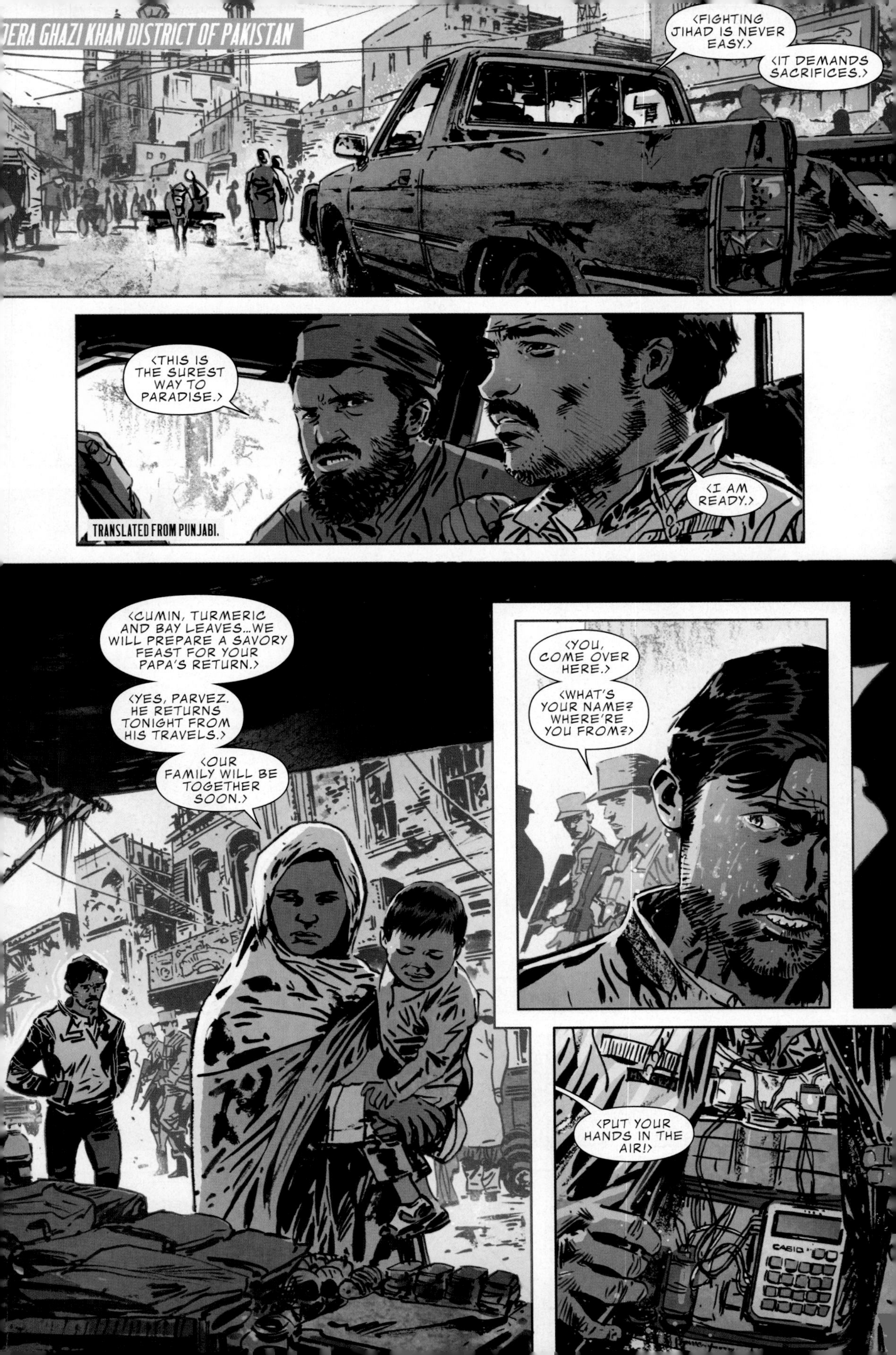
DERA GHAZI KHAN DISTRICT OF PAKISTAN
<FIGHTING JIHAD IS NEVER EASY.>
<IT DEMANDS SACRIFICES.>
<THIS IS THE SUREST WAY TO PARADISE.>
<I AM READY.>
TRANSLATED FROM PUNJABI.
<CUMIN, TURMERIC AND BAY LEAVES...WE WILL PREPARE A SAVORY FEAST FOR YOUR PAPA'S RETURN.>
<YES, PARVEZ. HE RETURNS TONIGHT FROM HIS TRAVELS.>
<OUR FAMILY WILL BE TOGETHER SOON.>
<YOU, COME OVER HERE.>
<WHAT'S YOUR NAME? WHERE'RE YOU FROM?>
<PUT YOUR HANDS IN THE AIR!>
CASIO

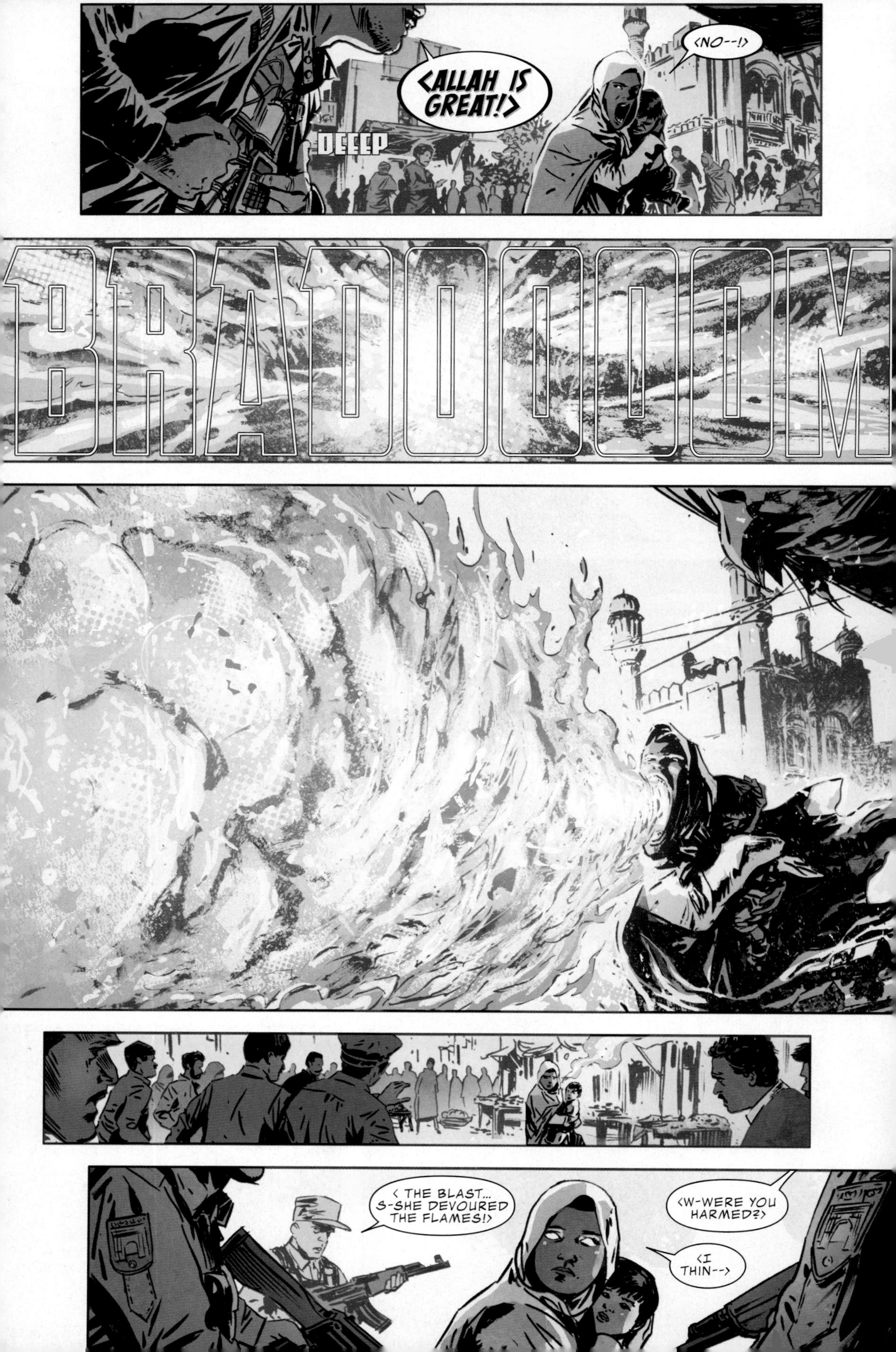
<ALLAH IS GREAT!>
DEEEP
<NO--!>
BRADOOOOM
< THE BLAST... S-SHE DEVOURED THE FLAMES!>
<W-WERE YOU HARMED?>
<I THIN-->

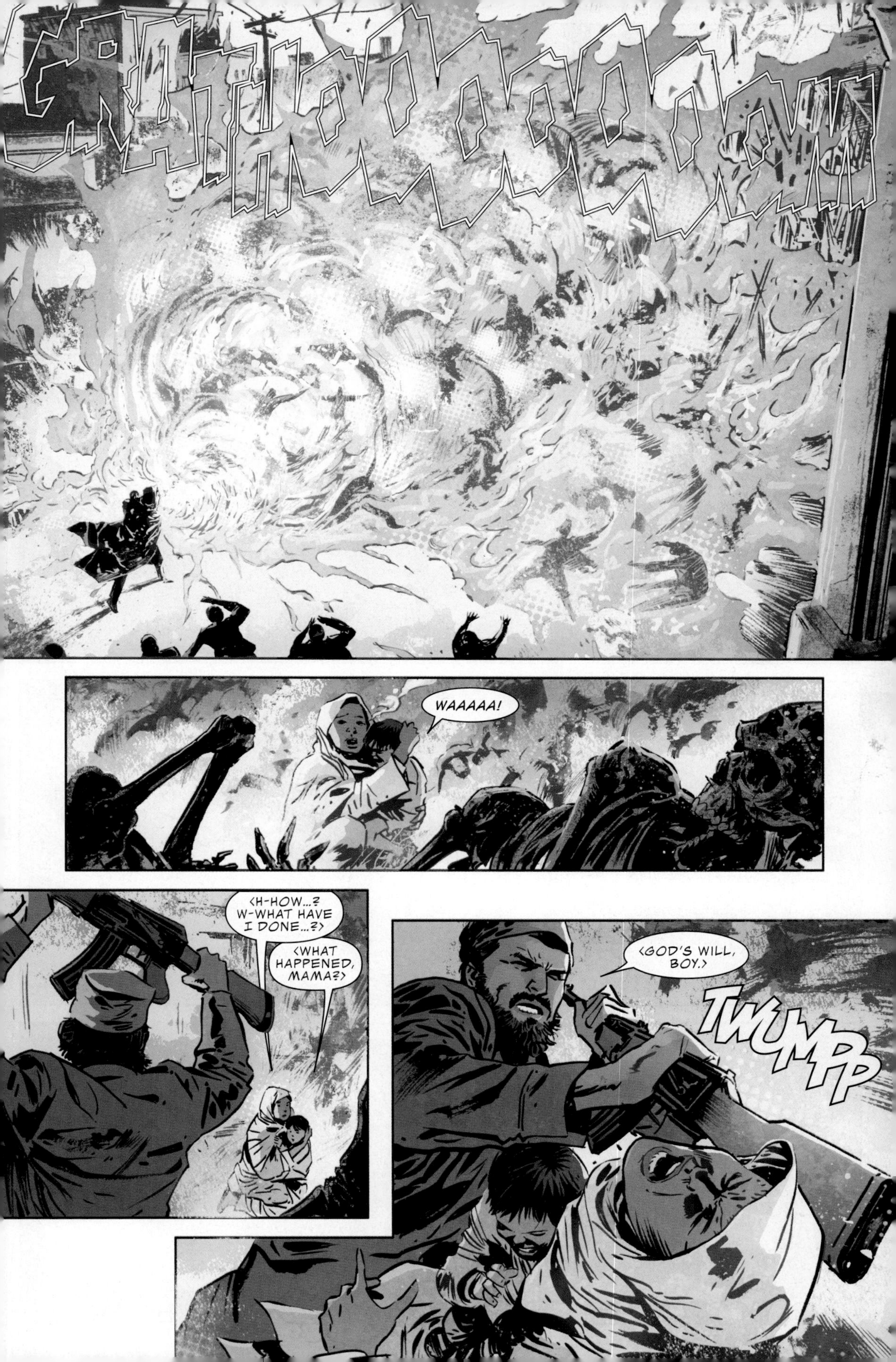

GRAAHHOOOOOOOOOOM
WAAAAA!
<H-HOW...? W-WHAT HAVE I DONE...?>
<WHAT HAPPENED, MAMA?>
<GOD'S WILL, BOY.>
TWUMP

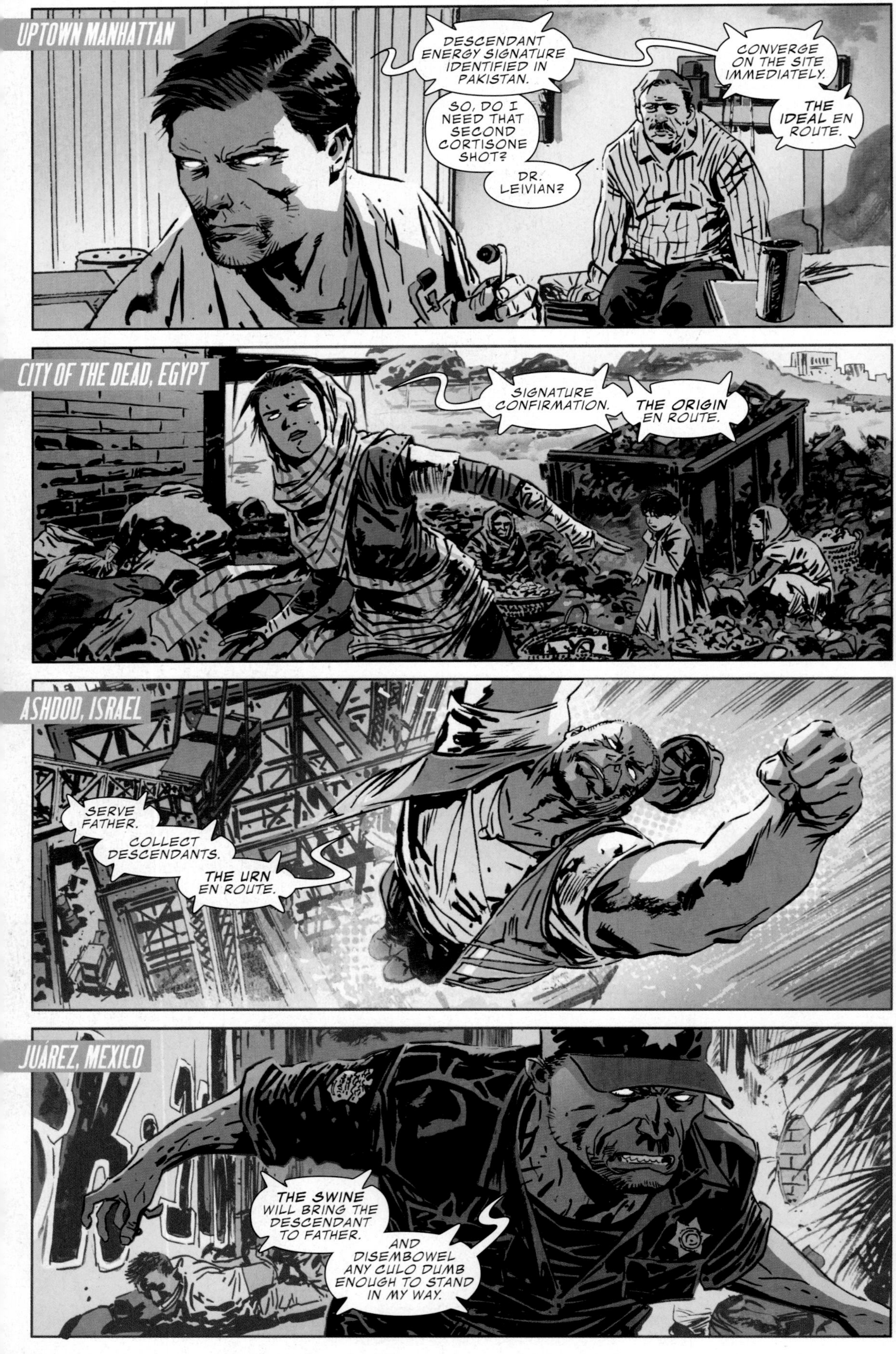
UPTOWN MANHATTAN
DESCENDANT ENERGY SIGNATURE IDENTIFIED IN PAKISTAN.
CONVERGE ON THE SITE IMMEDIATELY.
SO, DO I NEED THAT SECOND CORTISONE SHOT?
DR. LEIVIAN?
THE IDEAL EN ROUTE.
CITY OF THE DEAD, EGYPT
SIGNATURE CONFIRMATION.
THE ORIGIN EN ROUTE.
ASHDOD, ISRAEL
SERVE FATHER.
COLLECT DESCENDANTS.
THE URN EN ROUTE.
JUÁREZ, MEXICO
THE SWINE WILL BRING THE DESCENDANT TO FATHER.
AND DISEMBOWEL ANY CULO DUMB ENOUGH TO STAND IN MY WAY.

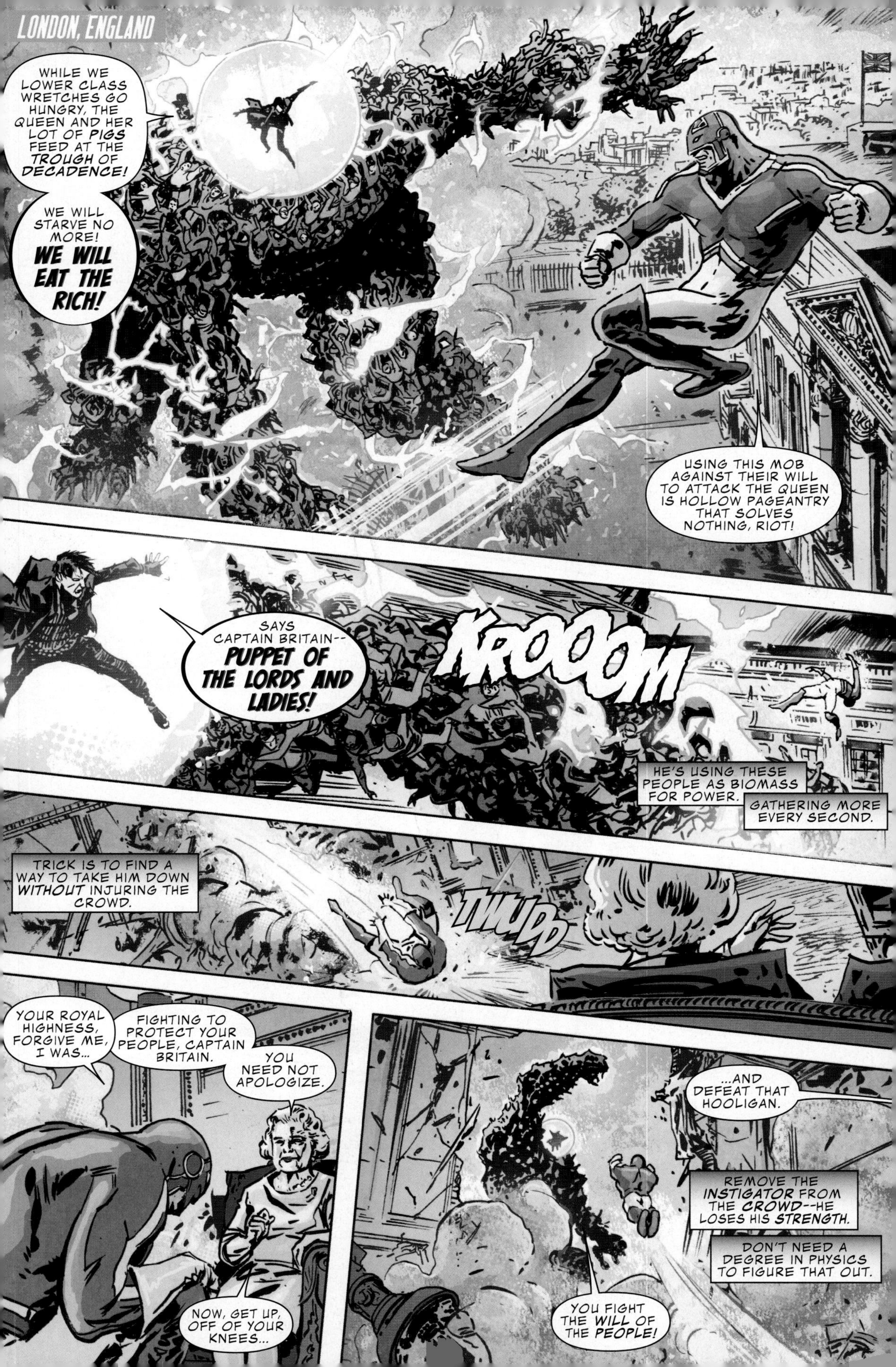
LONDON, ENGLAND
WHILE WE LOWER CLASS WRETCHES GO HUNGRY, THE QUEEN AND HER LOT OF PIGS FEED AT THE TROUGH OF DECADENCE!
WE WILL STARVE NO MORE! WE WILL EAT THE RICH!
USING THIS MOB AGAINST THEIR WILL TO ATTACK THE QUEEN IS HOLLOW PAGEANTRY THAT SOLVES NOTHING, RIOT!
SAYS CAPTAIN BRITAIN-- PUPPET OF THE LORDS AND LADIES!
KROOOOM
HE'S USING THESE PEOPLE AS BIOMASS FOR POWER.
GATHERING MORE EVERY SECOND.
TRICK IS TO FIND A WAY TO TAKE HIM DOWN WITHOUT INJURING THE CROWD.
TWUDD
YOUR ROYAL HIGHNESS, FORGIVE ME, I WAS...
FIGHTING TO PROTECT YOUR PEOPLE, CAPTAIN BRITAIN.
YOU NEED NOT APOLOGIZE.
NOW, GET UP, OFF OF YOUR KNEES...
...AND DEFEAT THAT HOOLIGAN.
REMOVE THE INSTIGATOR FROM THE CROWD--HE LOSES HIS STRENGTH.
DON'T NEED A DEGREE IN PHYSICS TO FIGURE THAT OUT.
YOU FIGHT THE WILL OF THE PEOPLE!

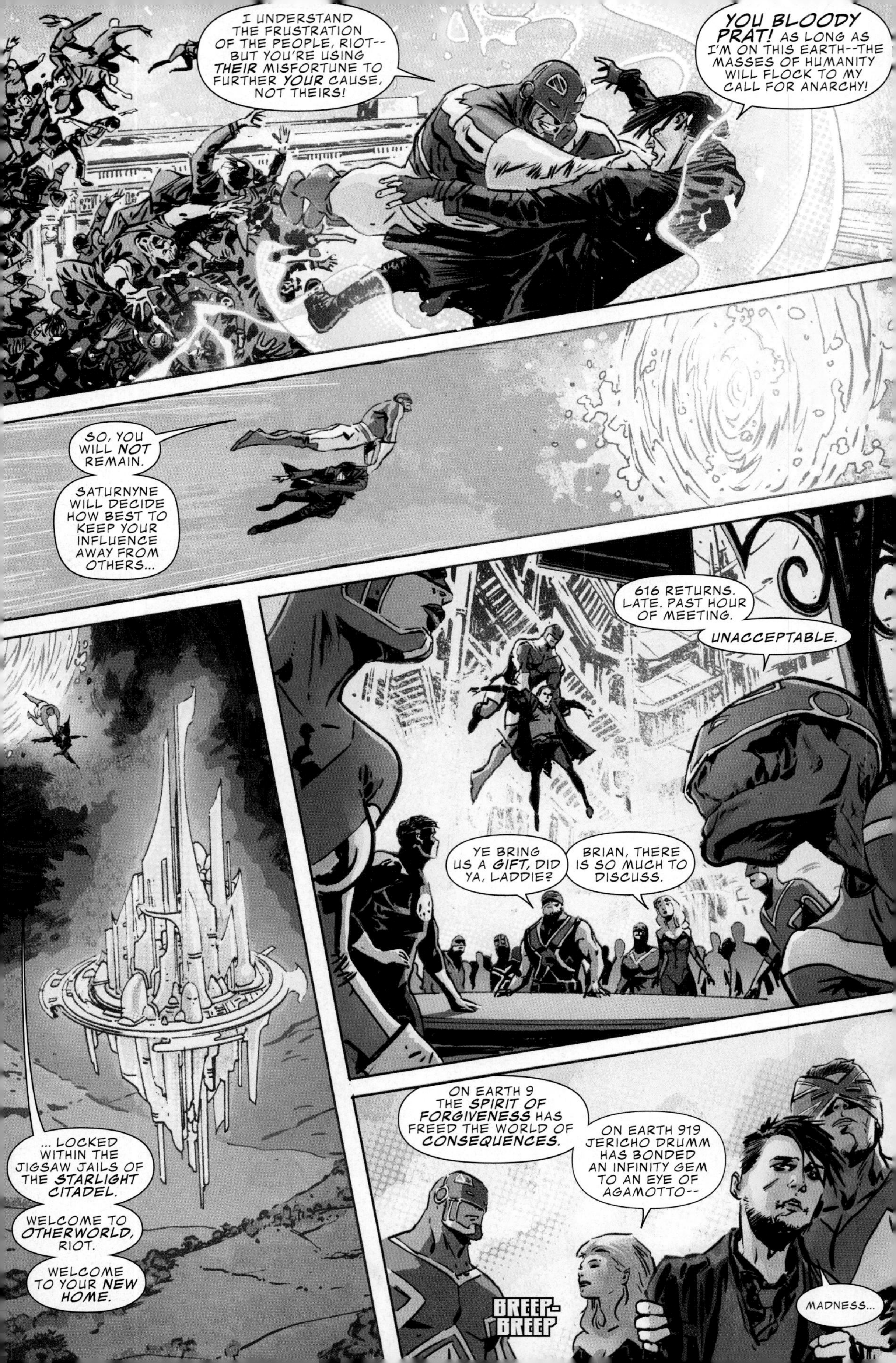
I UNDERSTAND THE FRUSTRATION OF THE PEOPLE, RIOT-- BUT YOU'RE USING THEIR MISFORTUNE TO FURTHER YOUR CAUSE, NOT THEIRS!
YOU BLOODY PRAT! AS LONG AS I'M ON THIS EARTH--THE MASSES OF HUMANITY WILL FLOCK TO MY CALL FOR ANARCHY!
SO, YOU WILL NOT REMAIN.
SATURNYNE WILL DECIDE HOW BEST TO KEEP YOUR INFLUENCE AWAY FROM OTHERS...
... LOCKED WITHIN THE JIGSAW JAILS OF THE STARLIGHT CITADEL.
WELCOME TO OTHERWORLD, RIOT.
WELCOME TO YOUR NEW HOME.
616 RETURNS. LATE. PAST HOUR OF MEETING.
UNACCEPTABLE.
YE BRING US A GIFT, DID YA, LADDIE?
BRIAN, THERE IS SO MUCH TO DISCUSS.
ON EARTH 9 THE SPIRIT OF FORGIVENESS HAS FREED THE WORLD OF CONSEQUENCES.
ON EARTH 919 JERICHO DRUMM HAS BONDED AN INFINITY GEM TO AN EYE OF AGAMOTTO--
BREEP-BREEP
MADNESS...

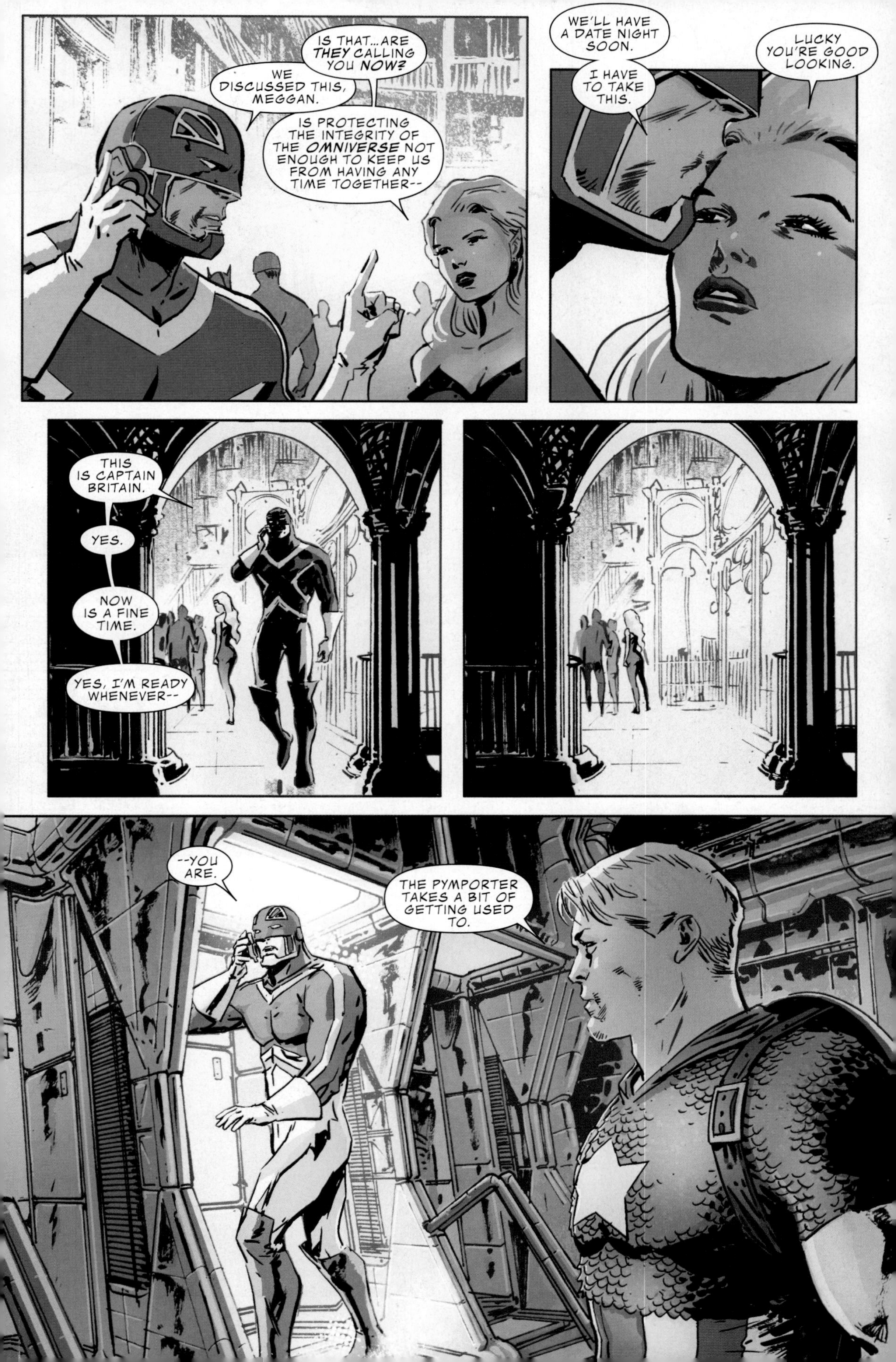
WE DISCUSSED THIS, MEGGAN.
IS THAT...ARE THEY CALLING YOU NOW?
IS PROTECTING THE INTEGRITY OF THE OMNIVERSE NOT ENOUGH TO KEEP US FROM HAVING ANY TIME TOGETHER--
WE'LL HAVE A DATE NIGHT SOON.
I HAVE TO TAKE THIS.
LUCKY YOU'RE GOOD LOOKING.
THIS IS CAPTAIN BRITAIN.
YES.
NOW IS A FINE TIME.
YES, I'M READY WHENEVER--
--YOU ARE.
THE PYMPORTER TAKES A BIT OF GETTING USED TO.

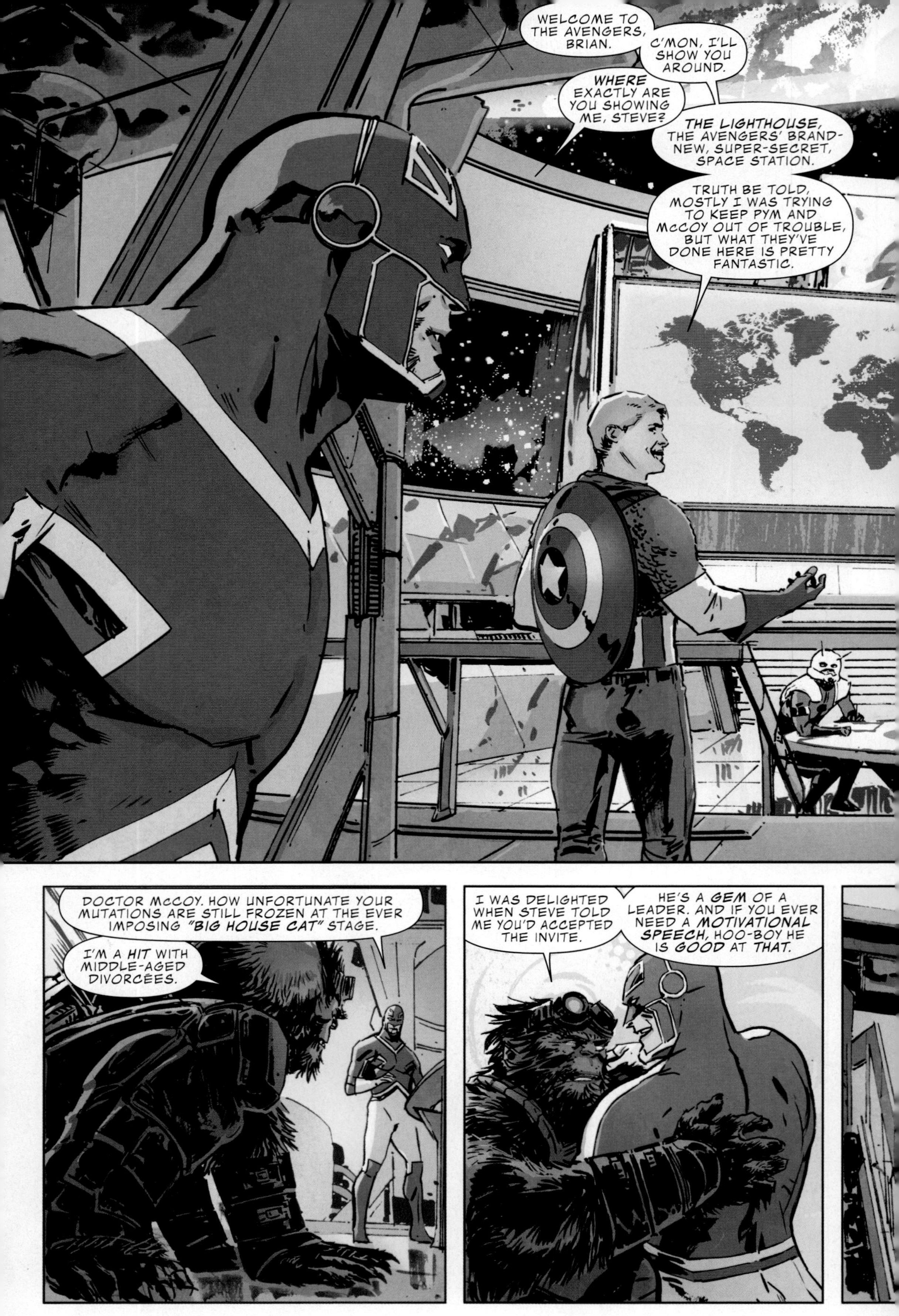
WELCOME TO THE AVENGERS, BRIAN.
C'MON, I'LL SHOW YOU AROUND.
WHERE EXACTLY ARE YOU SHOWING ME, STEVE?
THE LIGHTHOUSE, THE AVENGERS' BRAND-NEW, SUPER-SECRET, SPACE STATION.
TRUTH BE TOLD, MOSTLY I WAS TRYING TO KEEP PYM AND McCOY OUT OF TROUBLE, BUT WHAT THEY'VE DONE HERE IS PRETTY FANTASTIC.
DOCTOR McCOY. HOW UNFORTUNATE YOUR MUTATIONS ARE STILL FROZEN AT THE EVER IMPOSING "BIG HOUSE CAT" STAGE.
I'M A HIT WITH MIDDLE-AGED DIVORCÉES.
I WAS DELIGHTED WHEN STEVE TOLD ME YOU'D ACCEPTED THE INVITE.
HE'S A GEM OF A LEADER. AND IF YOU EVER NEED A MOTIVATIONAL SPEECH, HOO-BOY HE IS GOOD AT THAT.

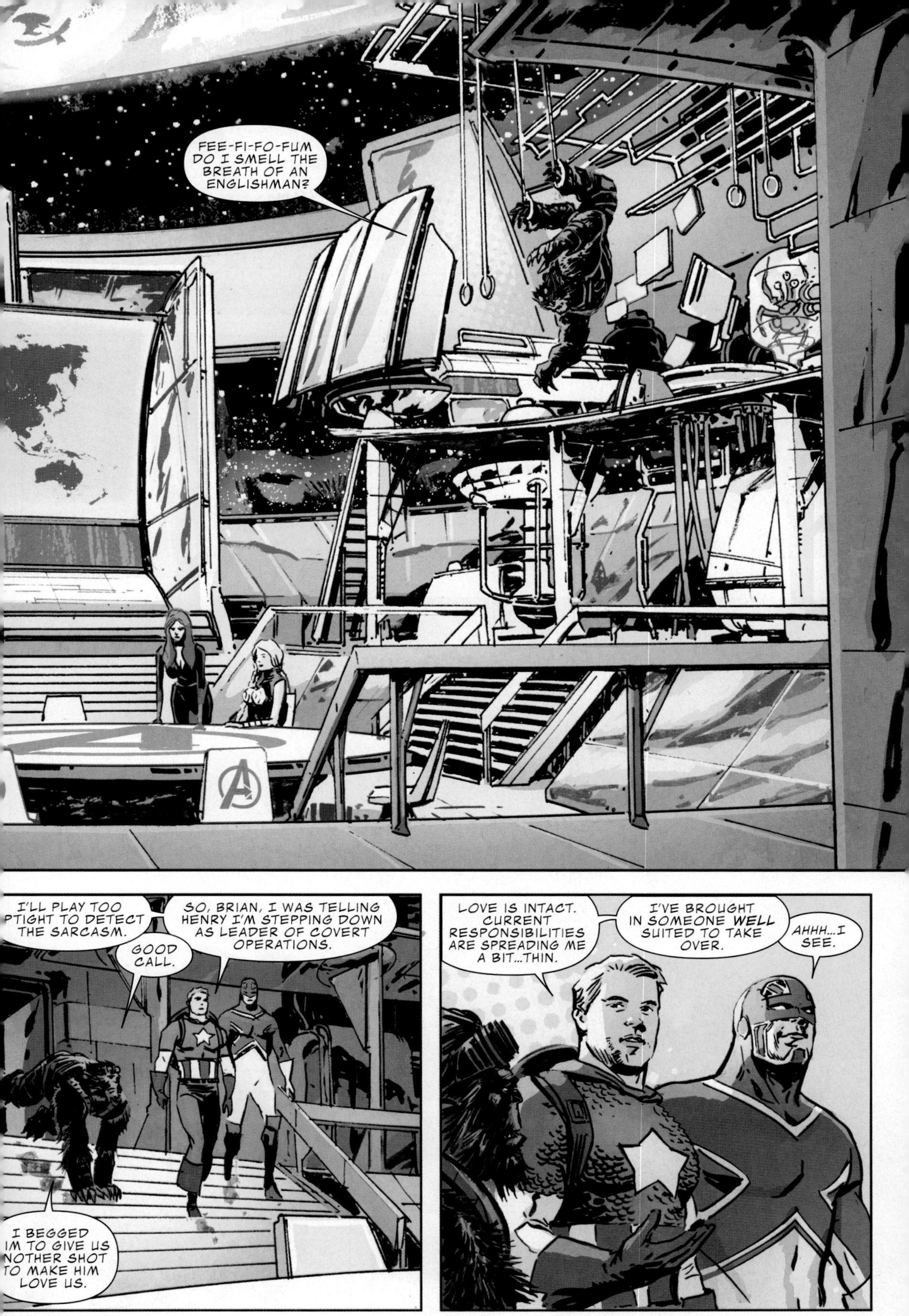
FEE-FI-FO-FUM DO I SMELL THE BREATH OF AN ENGLISHMAN?
I'LL PLAY TOO PTIGHT TO DETECT THE SARCASM.
SO, BRIAN, I WAS TELLING HENRY I'M STEPPING DOWN AS LEADER OF COVERT OPERATIONS.
GOOD CALL.
I BEGGED IM TO GIVE US NOTHER SHOT TO MAKE HIM LOVE US.
LOVE IS INTACT. CURRENT RESPONSIBILITIES ARE SPREADING ME A BIT...THIN.
I'VE BROUGHT IN SOMEONE WELL SUITED TO TAKE OVER.
AHHH...I SEE.

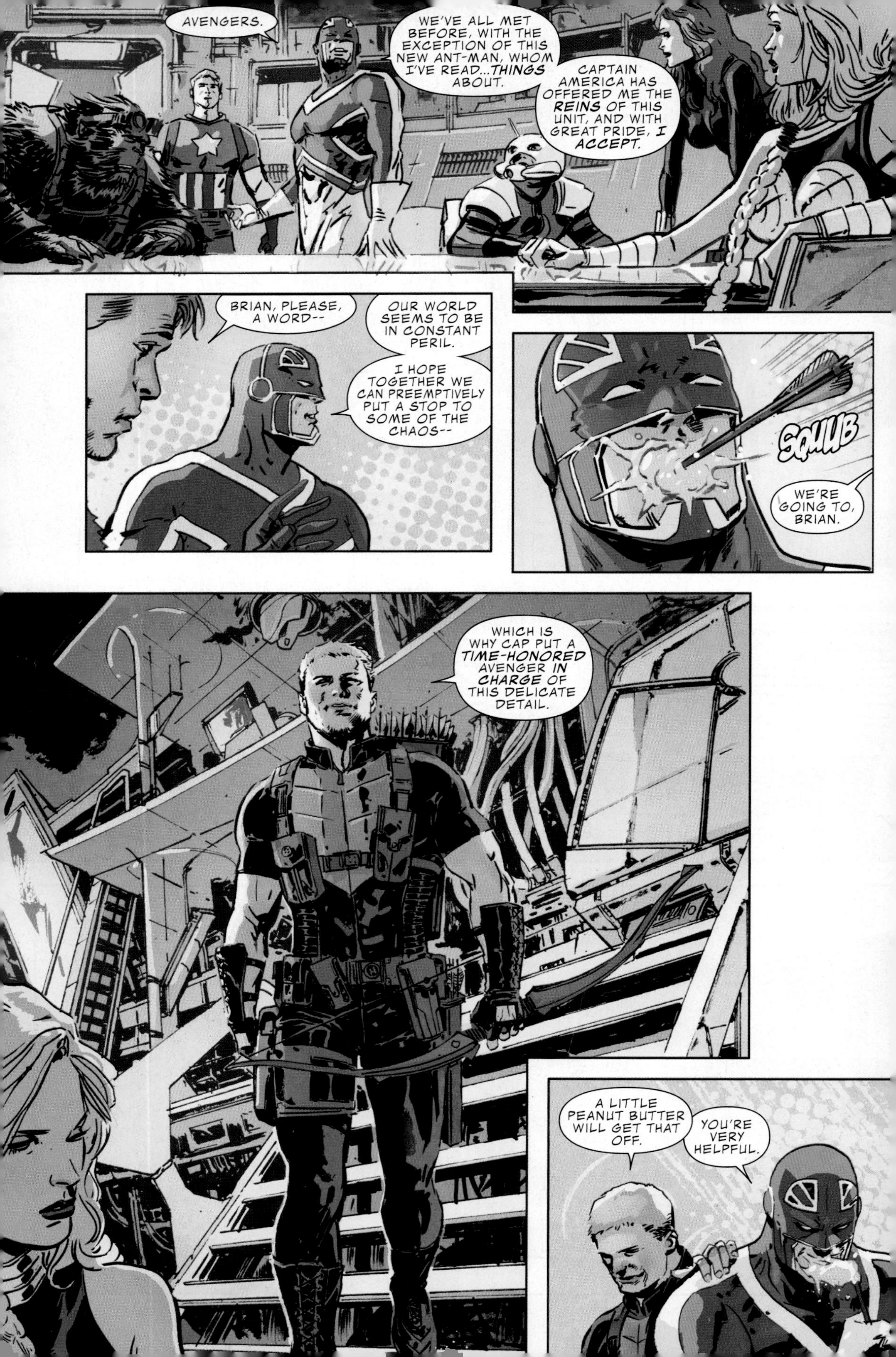
AVENGERS.
WE'VE ALL MET BEFORE, WITH THE EXCEPTION OF THIS NEW ANT-MAN, WHOM I'VE READ...THINGS ABOUT.
CAPTAIN AMERICA HAS OFFERED ME THE REINS OF THIS UNIT, AND WITH GREAT PRIDE, I ACCEPT.
BRIAN, PLEASE, A WORD--
OUR WORLD SEEMS TO BE IN CONSTANT PERIL.
I HOPE TOGETHER WE CAN PREEMPTIVELY PUT A STOP TO SOME OF THE CHAOS--
SQUUB
WE'RE GOING TO, BRIAN.
WHICH IS WHY CAP PUT A TIME-HONORED AVENGER IN CHARGE OF THIS DELICATE DETAIL.
A LITTLE PEANUT BUTTER WILL GET THAT OFF.
YOU'RE VERY HELPFUL.

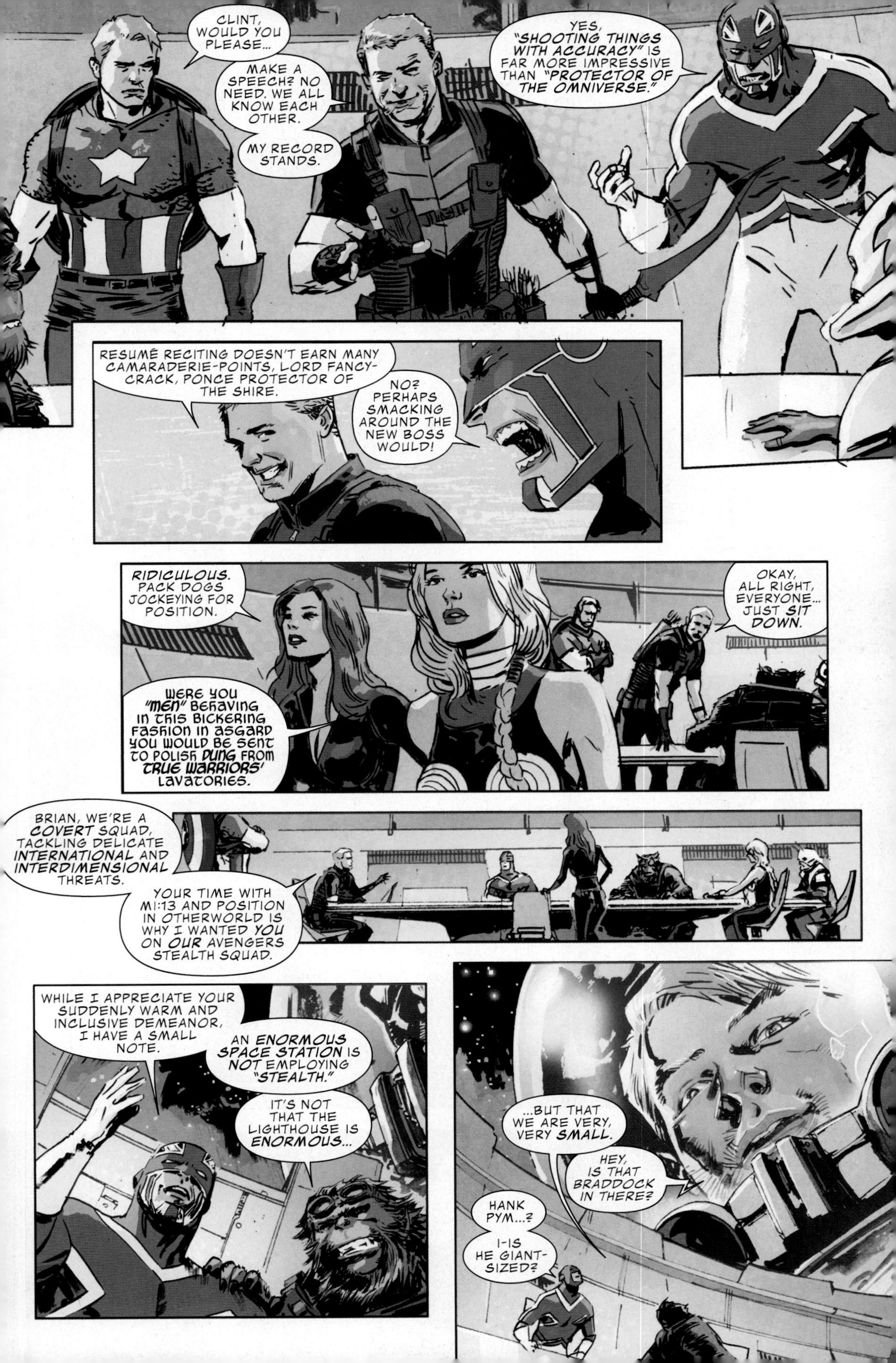
CLINT, WOULD YOU PLEASE...
MAKE A SPEECH? NO NEED. WE ALL KNOW EACH OTHER.
MY RECORD STANDS.
YES, "SHOOTING THINGS WITH ACCURACY" IS FAR MORE IMPRESSIVE THAN "PROTECTOR OF THE OMNIVERSE."
RESUMÉ RECITING DOESN'T EARN MANY CAMARADERIE-POINTS, LORD FANCY-CRACK, PONCE PROTECTOR OF THE SHIRE.
NO? PERHAPS SMACKING AROUND THE NEW BOSS WOULD!
RIDICULOUS. PACK DOGS JOCKEYING FOR POSITION.
OKAY, ALL RIGHT, EVERYONE... JUST SIT DOWN.
WERE YOU "MEN" BEHAVING IN THIS BICKERING FASHION IN ASGARD YOU WOULD BE SENT TO POLISH DUNG FROM TRUE WARRIORS' LAVATORIES.
BRIAN, WE'RE A COVERT SQUAD, TACKLING DELICATE INTERNATIONAL AND INTERDIMENSIONAL THREATS.
YOUR TIME WITH MI:13 AND POSITION IN OTHERWORLD IS WHY I WANTED YOU ON OUR AVENGERS STEALTH SQUAD.
WHILE I APPRECIATE YOUR SUDDENLY WARM AND INCLUSIVE DEMEANOR, I HAVE A SMALL NOTE.
AN ENORMOUS SPACE STATION IS NOT EMPLOYING "STEALTH."
IT'S NOT THAT THE LIGHTHOUSE IS ENORMOUS...
...BUT THAT WE ARE VERY, VERY SMALL.
HEY, IS THAT BRADDOCK IN THERE?
HANK PYM...?
I-IS HE GIANT-SIZED?

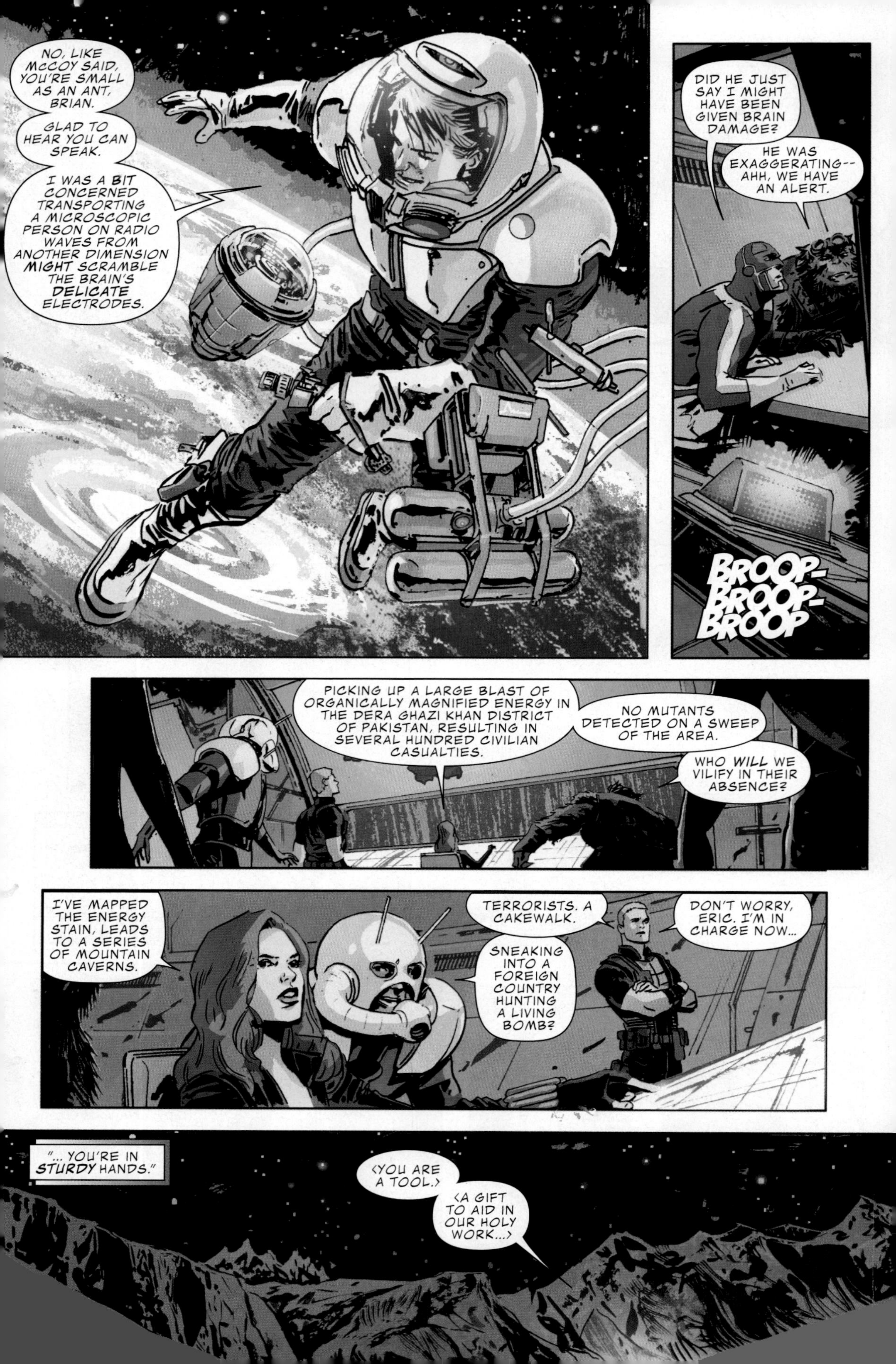
NO, LIKE McCOY SAID, YOU'RE SMALL AS AN ANT, BRIAN.
GLAD TO HEAR YOU CAN SPEAK.
I WAS A BIT CONCERNED TRANSPORTING A MICROSCOPIC PERSON ON RADIO WAVES FROM ANOTHER DIMENSION MIGHT SCRAMBLE THE BRAIN'S DELICATE ELECTRODES.
DID HE JUST SAY I MIGHT HAVE BEEN GIVEN BRAIN DAMAGE?
HE WAS EXAGGERATING-- AHH, WE HAVE AN ALERT.
BROOP-BROOP-BROOP
PICKING UP A LARGE BLAST OF ORGANICALLY MAGNIFIED ENERGY IN THE DERA GHAZI KHAN DISTRICT OF PAKISTAN, RESULTING IN SEVERAL HUNDRED CIVILIAN CASUALTIES.
NO MUTANTS DETECTED ON A SWEEP OF THE AREA.
WHO WILL WE VILIFY IN THEIR ABSENCE?
I'VE MAPPED THE ENERGY STAIN, LEADS TO A SERIES OF MOUNTAIN CAVERNS.
TERRORISTS. A CAKEWALK.
SNEAKING INTO A FOREIGN COUNTRY HUNTING A LIVING BOMB?
DON'T WORRY, ERIC. I'M IN CHARGE NOW...
"... YOU'RE IN STURDY HANDS."
<YOU ARE A TOOL.>
<A GIFT TO AID IN OUR HOLY WORK...>

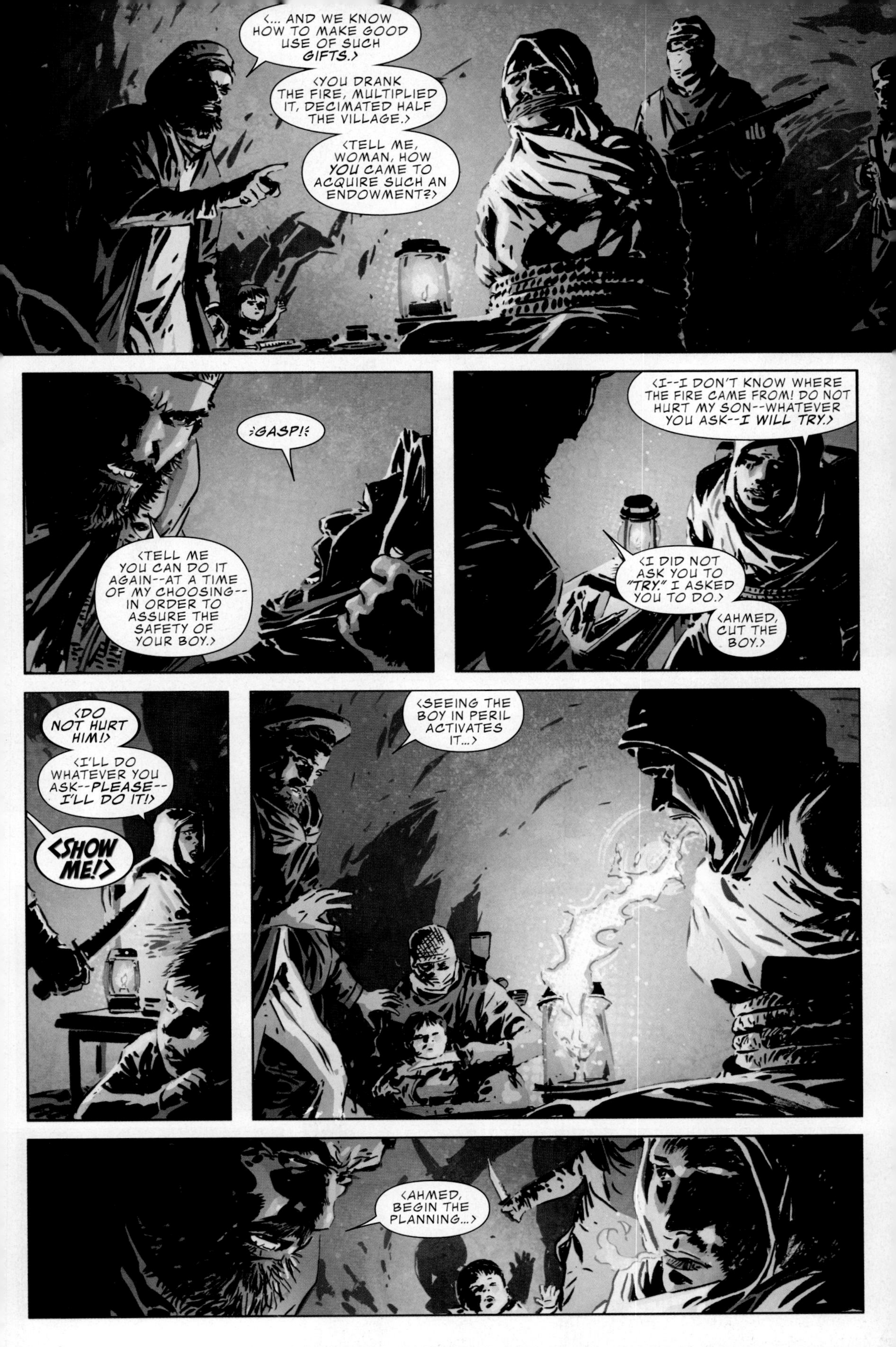
<... AND WE KNOW HOW TO MAKE GOOD USE OF SUCH GIFTS.>
<YOU DRANK THE FIRE, MULTIPLIED IT, DECIMATED HALF THE VILLAGE.>
<TELL ME, WOMAN, HOW YOU CAME TO ACQUIRE SUCH AN ENDOWMENT?>
GASP!
<TELL ME YOU CAN DO IT AGAIN--AT A TIME OF MY CHOOSING--IN ORDER TO ASSURE THE SAFETY OF YOUR BOY.>
<I--I DON'T KNOW WHERE THE FIRE CAME FROM! DO NOT HURT MY SON--WHATEVER YOU ASK--I WILL TRY.>
<I DID NOT ASK YOU TO "TRY." I ASKED YOU TO DO.>
<AHMED, CUT THE BOY.>
<DO NOT HURT HIM!>
<I'LL DO WHATEVER YOU ASK--PLEASE--I'LL DO IT!>
<SHOW ME!>
<SEEING THE BOY IN PERIL ACTIVATES IT...>
<AHMED, BEGIN THE PLANNING...>

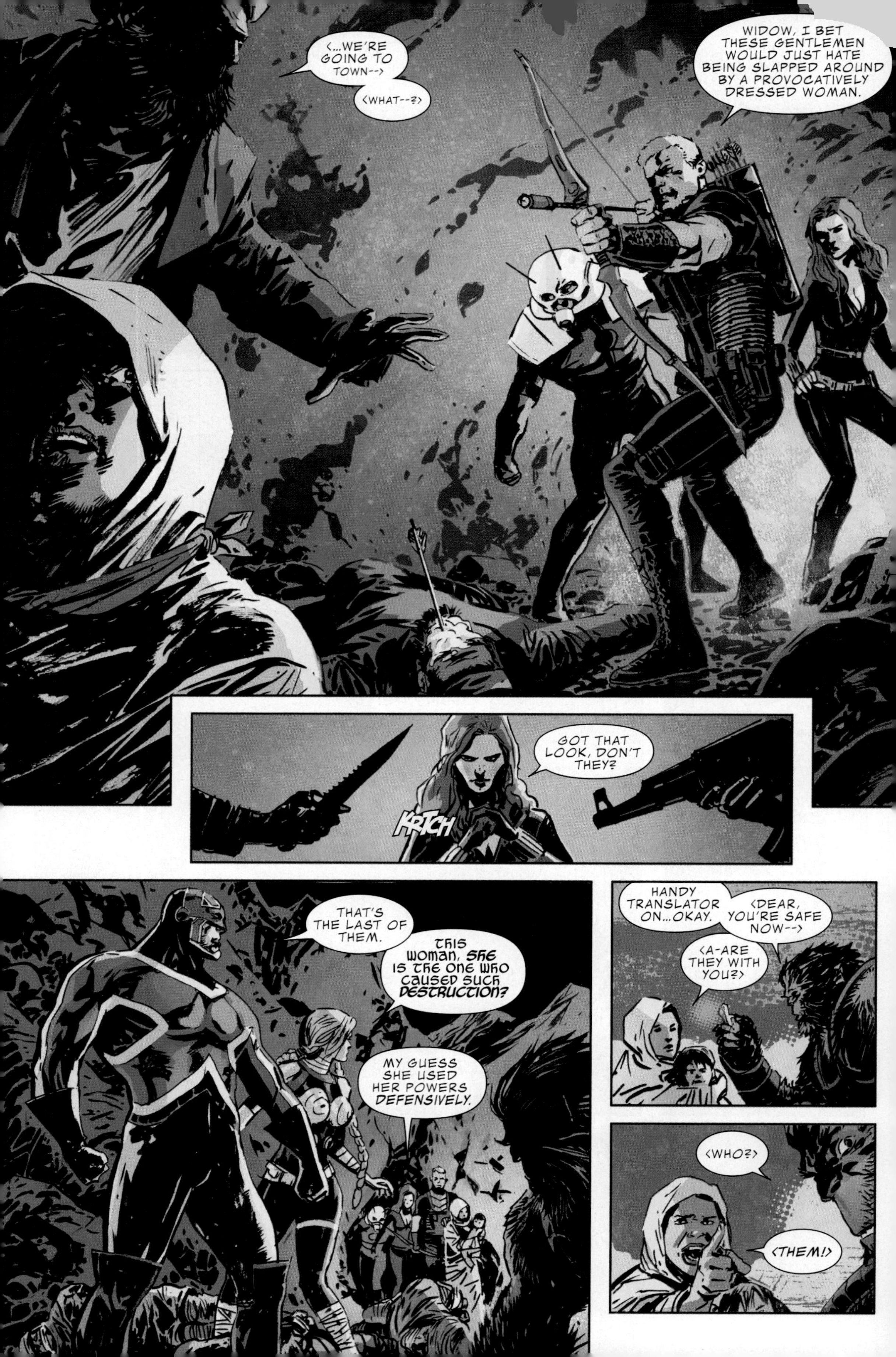
<...WE'RE GOING TO TOWN-->
<WHAT--?>
WIDOW, I BET THESE GENTLEMEN WOULD JUST HATE BEING SLAPPED AROUND BY A PROVOCATIVELY DRESSED WOMAN.
GOT THAT LOOK, DON'T THEY?
KRTCH
THAT'S THE LAST OF THEM.
THIS WOMAN, SHE IS THE ONE WHO CAUSED SUCH DESTRUCTION?
MY GUESS SHE USED HER POWERS DEFENSIVELY.
HANDY TRANSLATOR ON...OKAY.
<DEAR, YOU'RE SAFE NOW-->
<A-ARE THEY WITH YOU?>
<WHO?>
<THEM!>

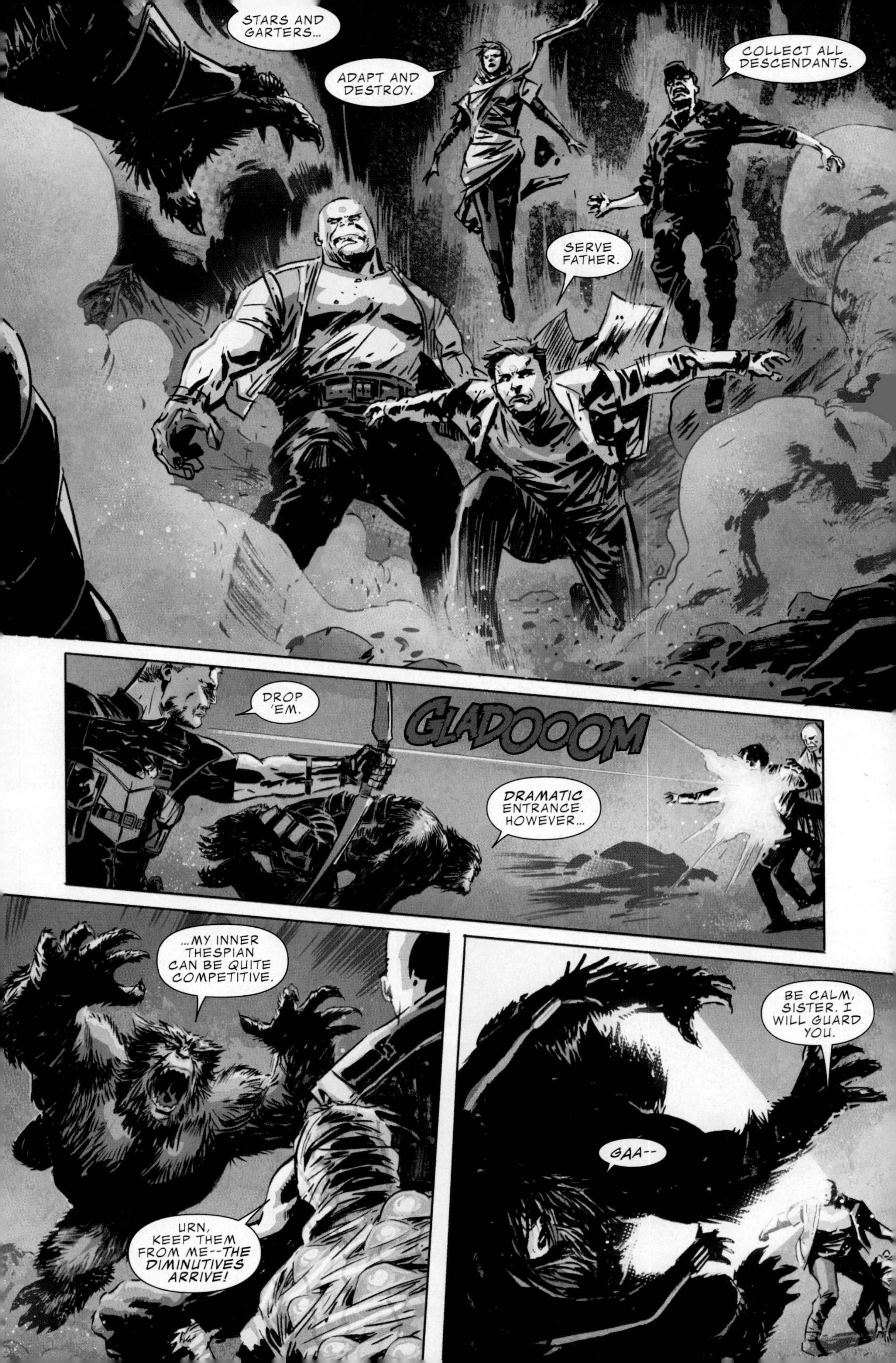
STARS AND GARTERS...
ADAPT AND DESTROY.
COLLECT ALL DESCENDANTS.
SERVE FATHER.
DROP 'EM.
GLADOOOM
DRAMATIC ENTRANCE. HOWEVER...
...MY INNER THESPIAN CAN BE QUITE COMPETITIVE.
URN, KEEP THEM FROM ME--THE DIMINUTIVES ARRIVE!
BE CALM, SISTER. I WILL GUARD YOU.
GAA--

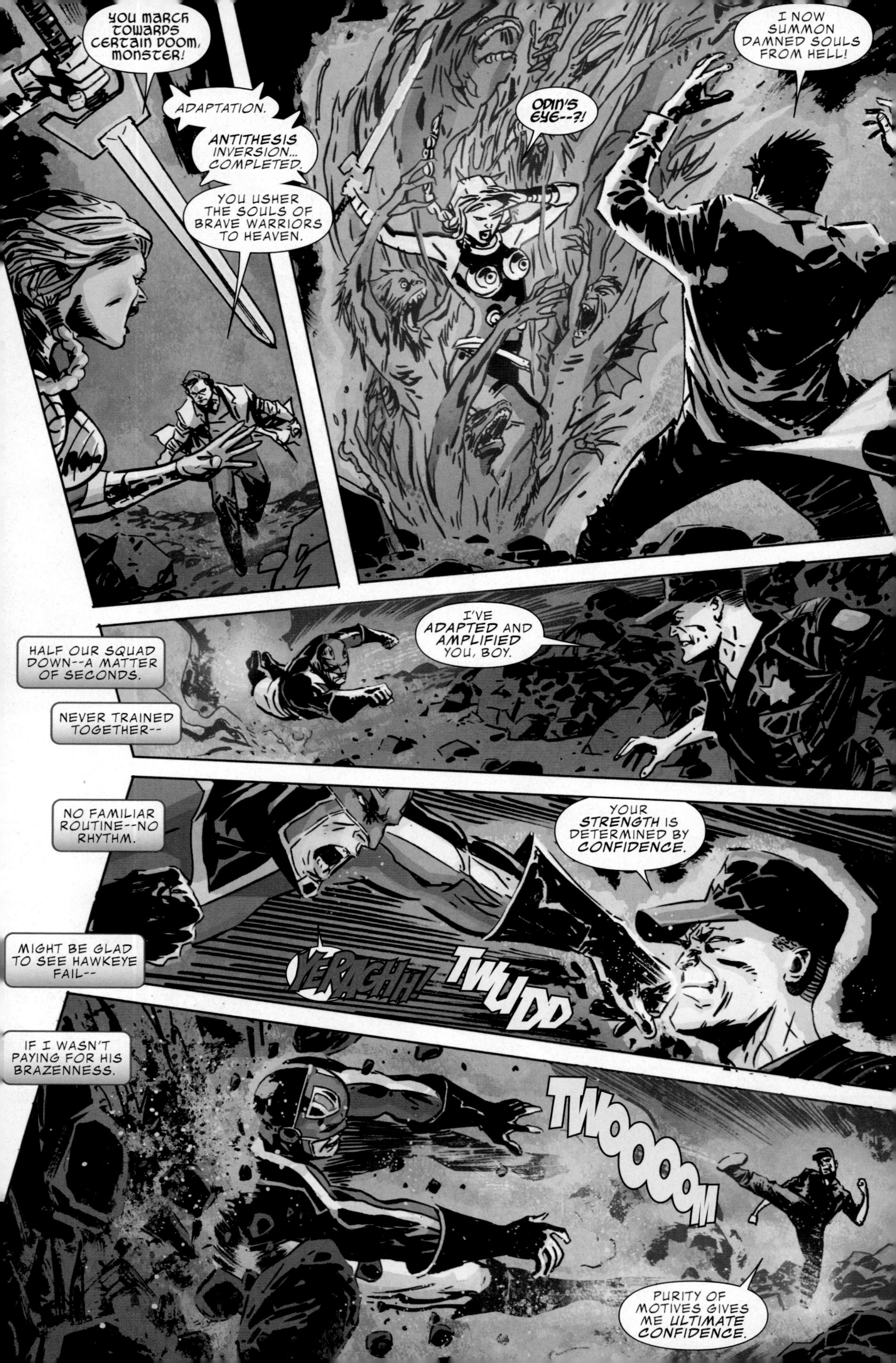

YOU MARCH TOWARDS CERTAIN DOOM, MONSTER!
ADAPTATION.
ANTITHESIS INVERSION... COMPLETED.
YOU USHER THE SOULS OF BRAVE WARRIORS TO HEAVEN.
ODIN'S EYE--?!
I NOW SUMMON DAMNED SOULS FROM HELL!
HALF OUR SQUAD DOWN--A MATTER OF SECONDS.
NEVER TRAINED TOGETHER--
I'VE ADAPTED AND AMPLIFIED YOU, BOY.
NO FAMILIAR ROUTINE--NO RHYTHM.
YOUR STRENGTH IS DETERMINED BY CONFIDENCE.
MIGHT BE GLAD TO SEE HAWKEYE FAIL--
YERAGHH!
TWUDD
IF I WASN'T PAYING FOR HIS BRAZENNESS.
TWOOOOOM
PURITY OF MOTIVES GIVES ME ULTIMATE CONFIDENCE.

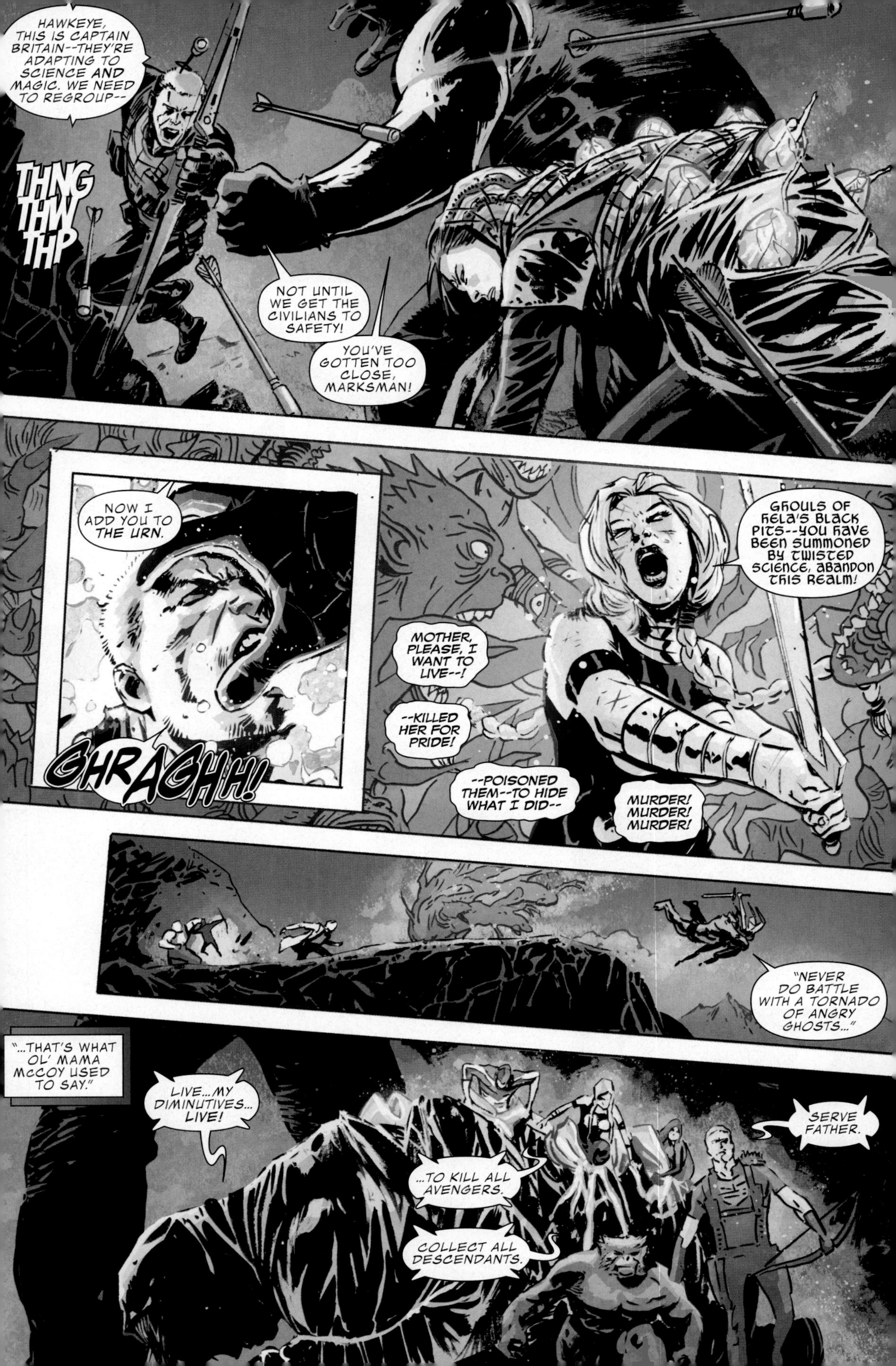
HAWKEYE, THIS IS CAPTAIN BRITAIN--THEY'RE ADAPTING TO SCIENCE AND MAGIC. WE NEED TO REGROUP--
THNG THW THP
NOT UNTIL WE GET THE CIVILIANS TO SAFETY!
YOU'VE GOTTEN TOO CLOSE, MARKSMAN!
NOW I ADD YOU TO THE URN.
GHRAGHH!
GHOULS OF HELA'S BLACK PITS--YOU HAVE BEEN SUMMONED BY TWISTED SCIENCE, ABANDON THIS REALM!
MOTHER, PLEASE, I WANT TO LIVE--!
--KILLED HER FOR PRIDE!
--POISONED THEM--TO HIDE WHAT I DID--
MURDER! MURDER! MURDER!
"NEVER DO BATTLE WITH A TORNADO OF ANGRY GHOSTS..."
"...THAT'S WHAT OL' MAMA McCOY USED TO SAY."
LIVE...MY DIMINUTIVES... LIVE!
SERVE FATHER.
...TO KILL ALL AVENGERS.
COLLECT ALL DESCENDANTS.

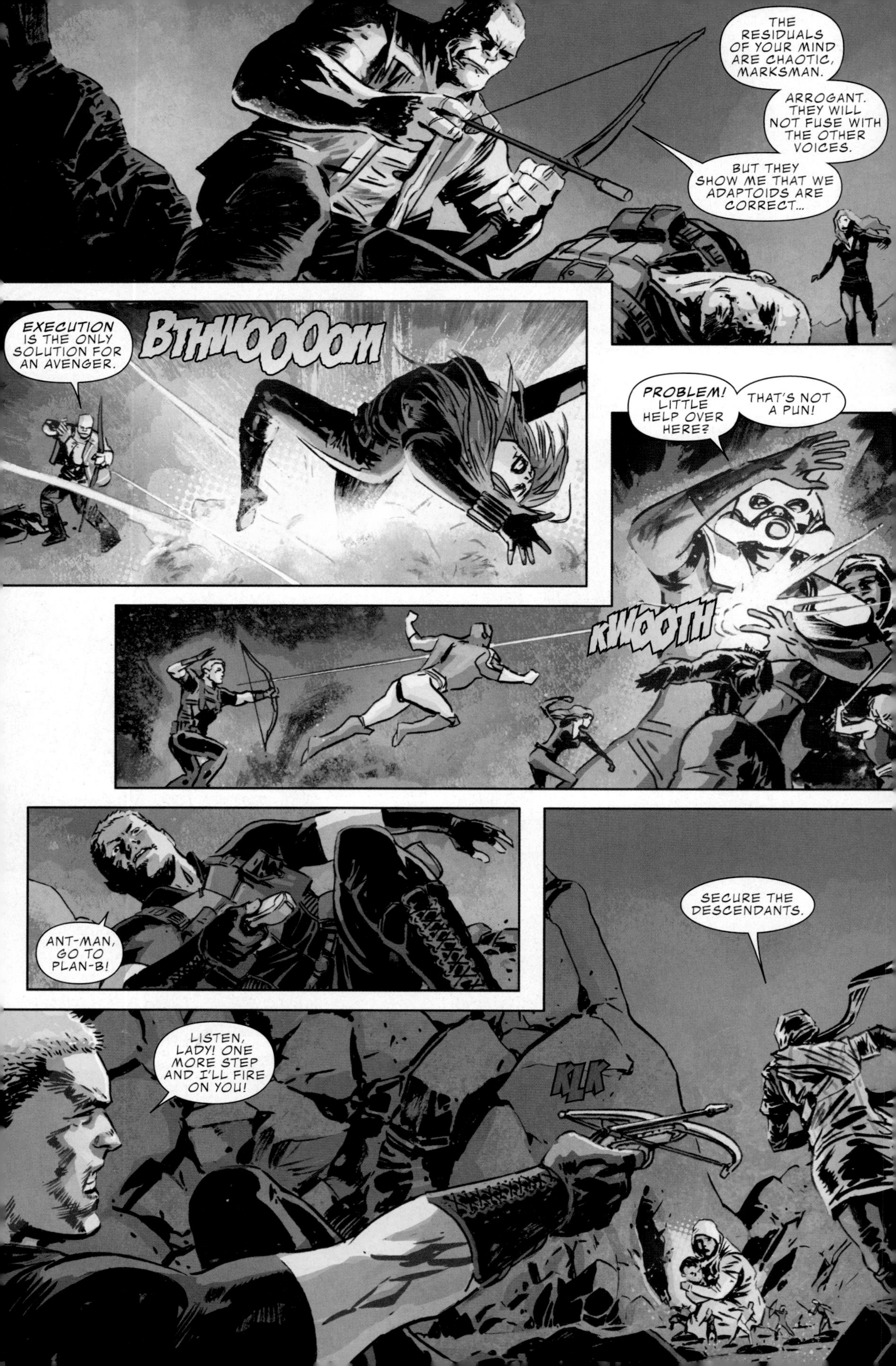
THE RESIDUALS OF YOUR MIND ARE CHAOTIC, MARKSMAN.
ARROGANT. THEY WILL NOT FUSE WITH THE OTHER VOICES.
BUT THEY SHOW ME THAT WE ADAPTOIDS ARE CORRECT...
EXECUTION IS THE ONLY SOLUTION FOR AN AVENGER.
BTHWOOOOM
PROBLEM! LITTLE HELP OVER HERE?
THAT'S NOT A PUN!
KWOOTH
ANT-MAN, GO TO PLAN-B!
SECURE THE DESCENDANTS.
LISTEN, LADY! ONE MORE STEP AND I'LL FIRE ON YOU!
KLIK

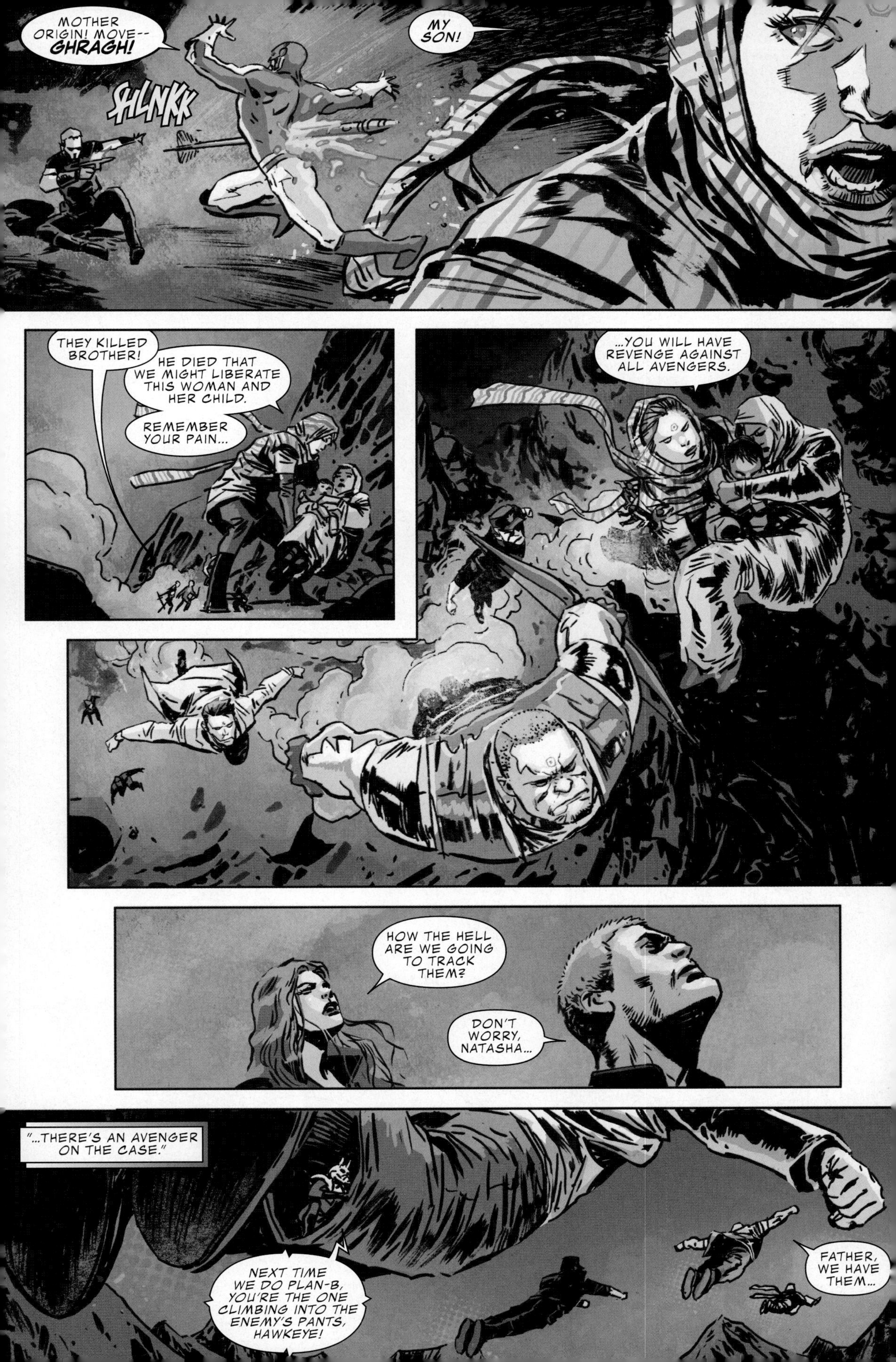
MOTHER ORIGIN! MOVE-- GHRAGH!
MY SON!
SHLNKK
THEY KILLED BROTHER!
HE DIED THAT WE MIGHT LIBERATE THIS WOMAN AND HER CHILD.
REMEMBER YOUR PAIN...
...YOU WILL HAVE REVENGE AGAINST ALL AVENGERS.
HOW THE HELL ARE WE GOING TO TRACK THEM?
DON'T WORRY, NATASHA...
"...THERE'S AN AVENGER ON THE CASE."
NEXT TIME WE DO PLAN-B, YOU'RE THE ONE CLIMBING INTO THE ENEMY'S PANTS, HAWKEYE!
FATHER, WE HAVE THEM...

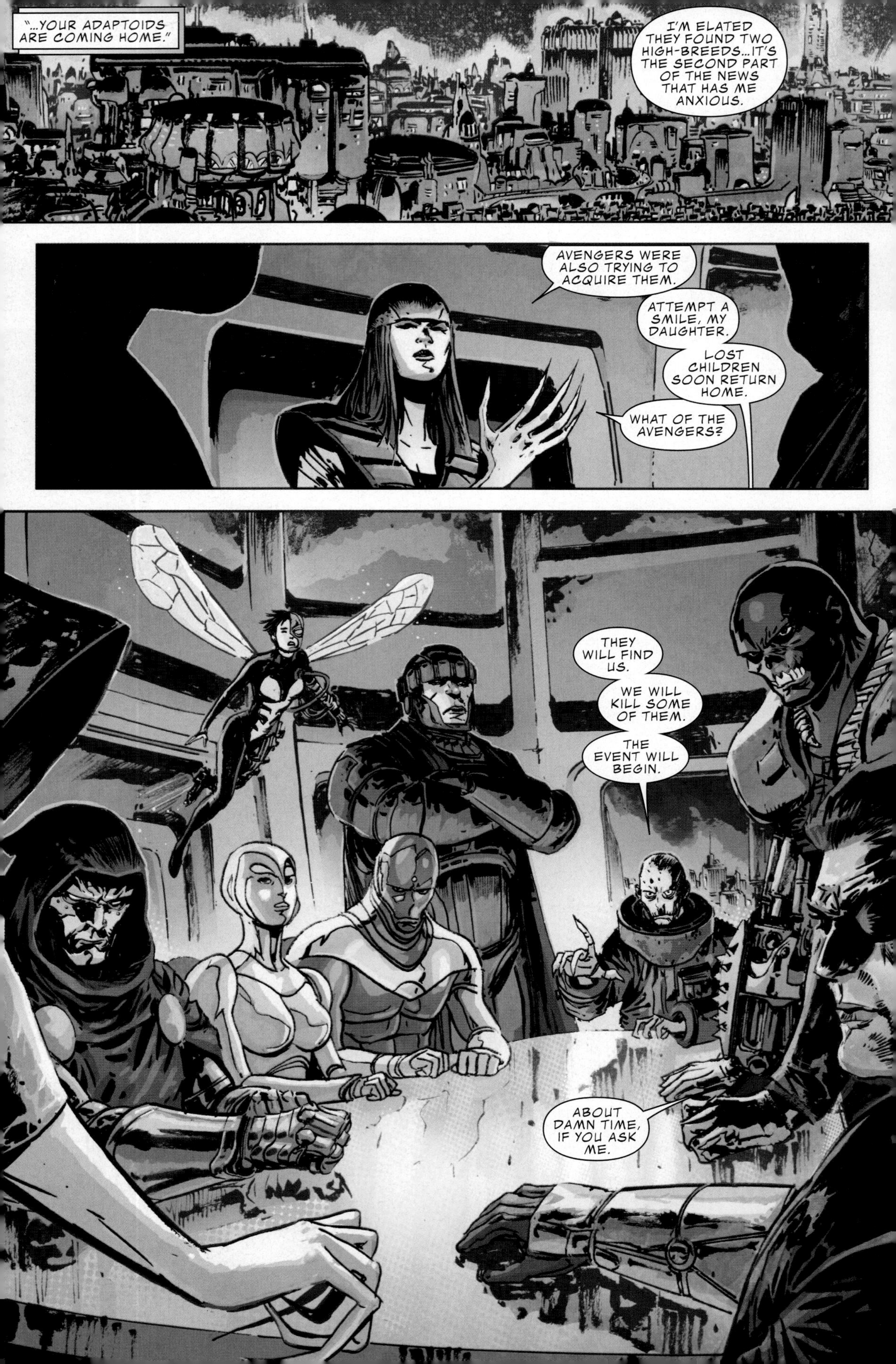
"...YOUR ADAPTOIDS ARE COMING HOME."
I'M ELATED THEY FOUND TWO HIGH-BREEDS...IT'S THE SECOND PART OF THE NEWS THAT HAS ME ANXIOUS.
AVENGERS WERE ALSO TRYING TO ACQUIRE THEM.
ATTEMPT A SMILE, MY DAUGHTER.
LOST CHILDREN SOON RETURN HOME.
WHAT OF THE AVENGERS?
THEY WILL FIND US.
WE WILL KILL SOME OF THEM.
THE EVENT WILL BEGIN.
ABOUT DAMN TIME, IF YOU ASK ME.

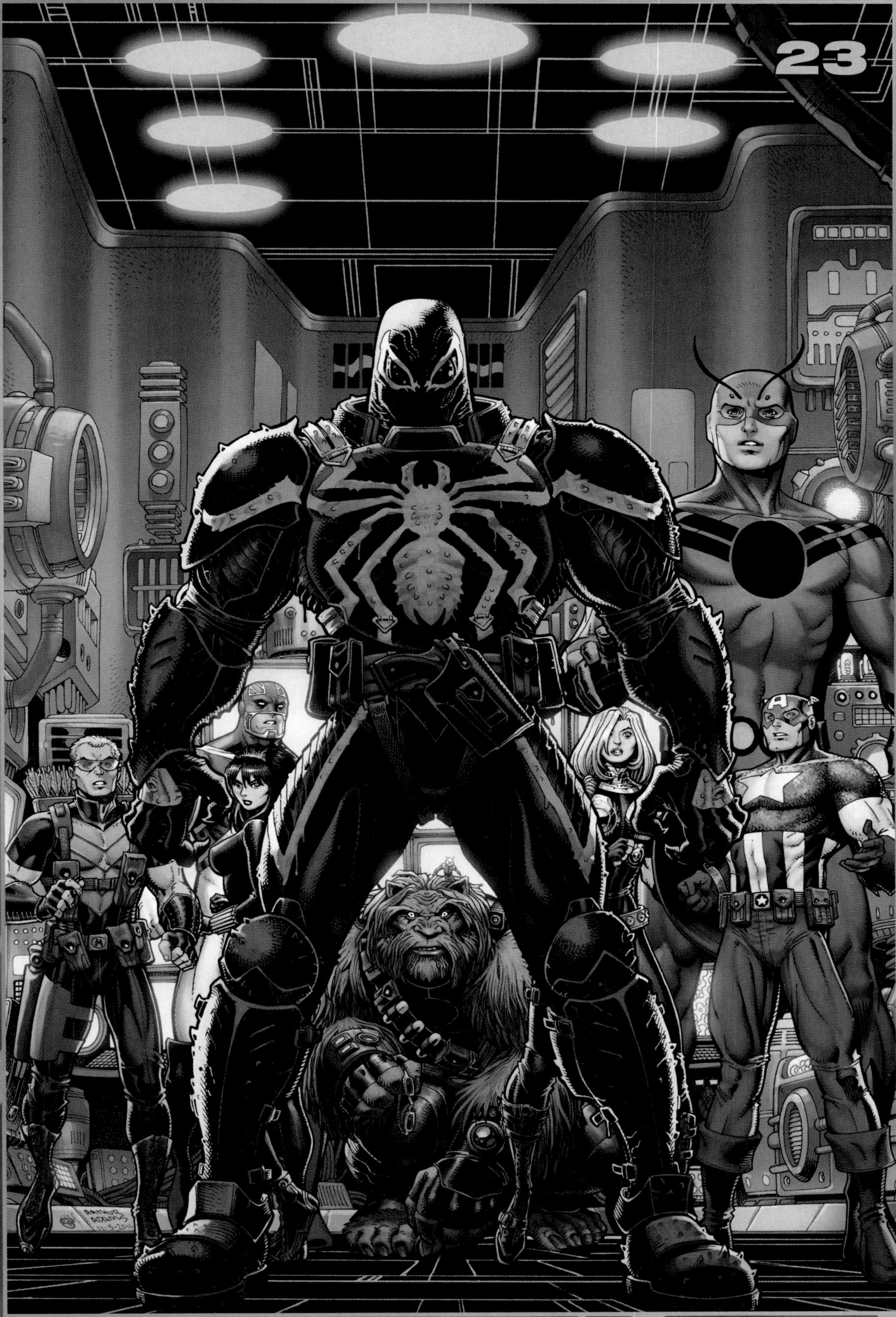
23

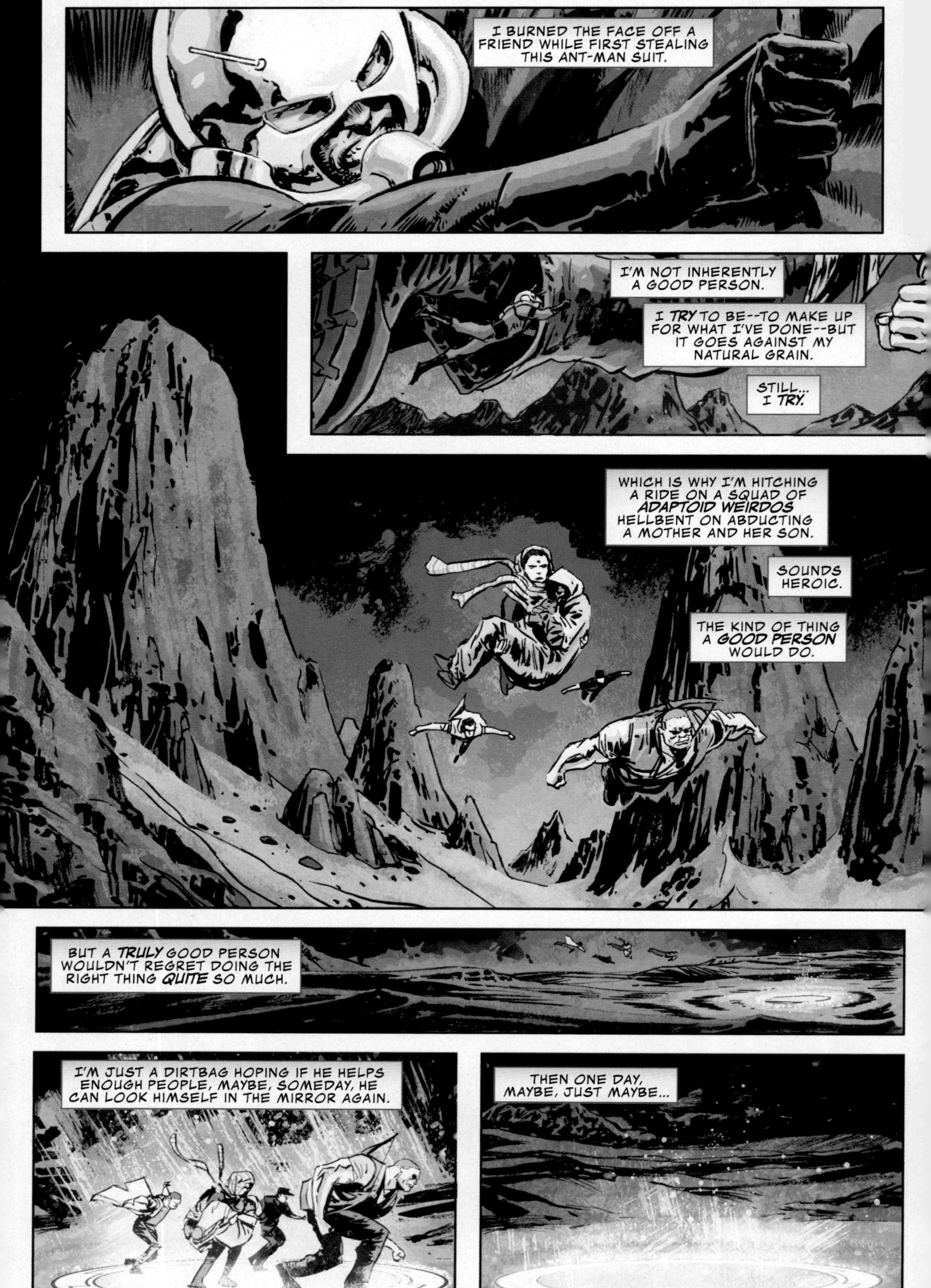
I BURNED THE FACE OFF A FRIEND WHILE FIRST STEALING THIS ANT-MAN SUIT.
I'M NOT INHERENTLY A GOOD PERSON.
I TRY TO BE--TO MAKE UP FOR WHAT I'VE DONE--BUT IT GOES AGAINST MY NATURAL GRAIN.
STILL... I TRY.
WHICH IS WHY I'M HITCHING A RIDE ON A SQUAD OF ADAPTOID WEIRDOS HELLBENT ON ABDUCTING A MOTHER AND HER SON.
SOUNDS HEROIC.
THE KIND OF THING A GOOD PERSON WOULD DO.
BUT A TRULY GOOD PERSON WOULDN'T REGRET DOING THE RIGHT THING QUITE SO MUCH.
I'M JUST A DIRTBAG HOPING IF HE HELPS ENOUGH PEOPLE, MAYBE, SOMEDAY, HE CAN LOOK HIMSELF IN THE MIRROR AGAIN.
THEN ONE DAY, MAYBE, JUST MAYBE...

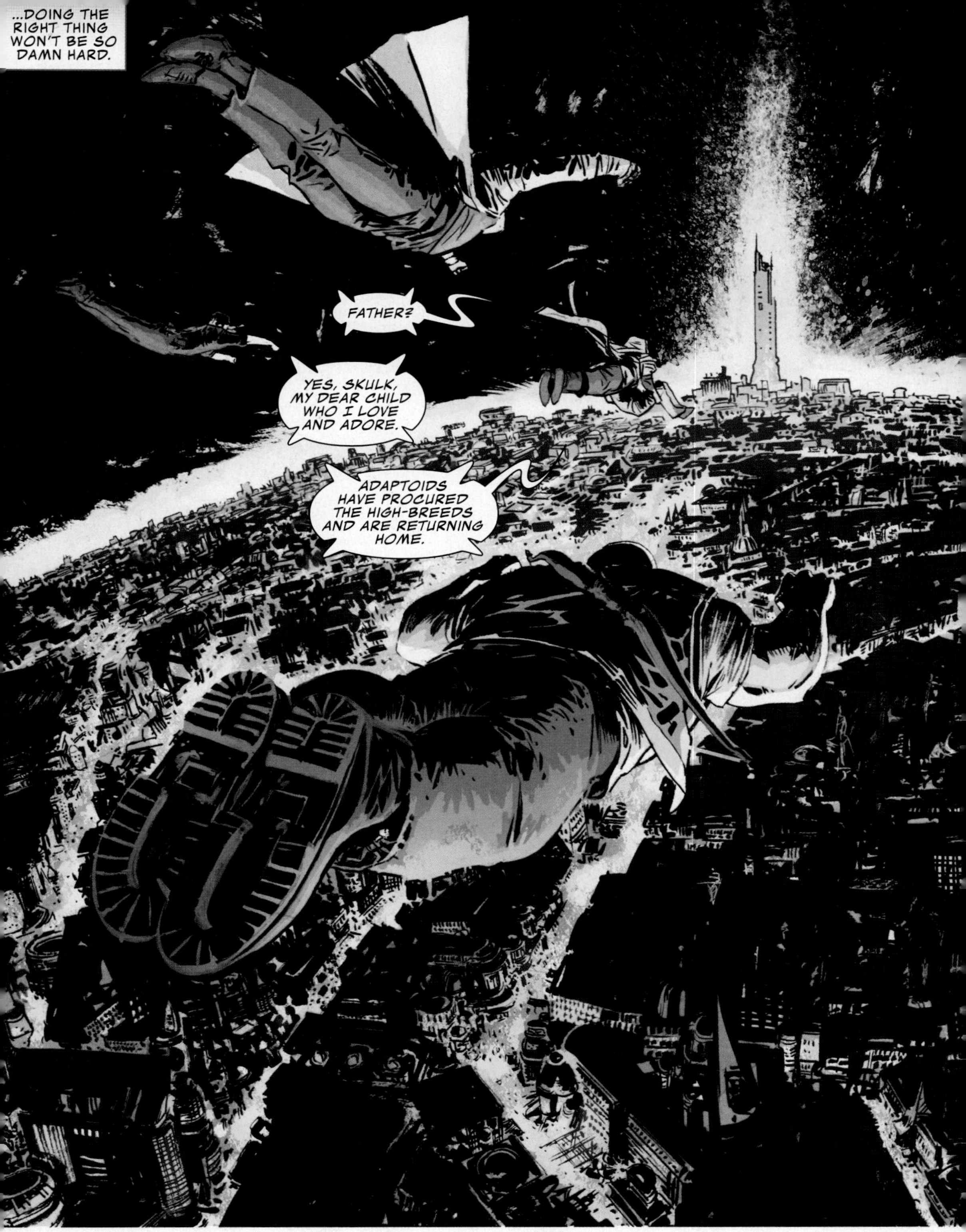
...DOING THE RIGHT THING WON'T BE SO DAMN HARD.
FATHER?
YES, SKULK, MY DEAR CHILD WHO I LOVE AND ADORE.
ADAPTOIDS HAVE PROCURED THE HIGH-BREEDS AND ARE RETURNING HOME.

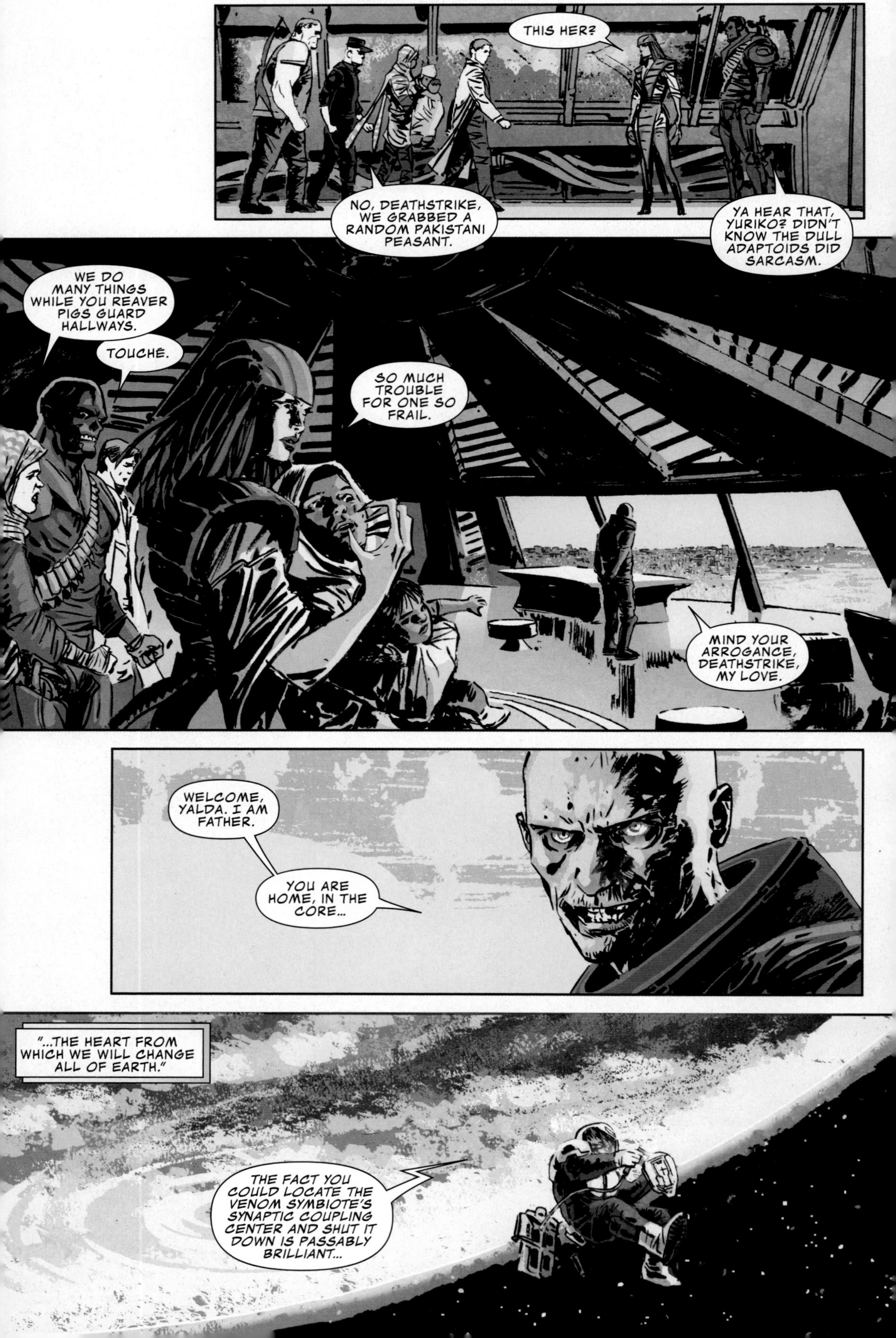
THIS HER?
NO, DEATHSTRIKE, WE GRABBED A RANDOM PAKISTANI PEASANT.
YA HEAR THAT, YURIKO? DIDN'T KNOW THE DULL ADAPTOIDS DID SARCASM.
WE DO MANY THINGS WHILE YOU REAVER PIGS GUARD HALLWAYS.
TOUCHÉ.
SO MUCH TROUBLE FOR ONE SO FRAIL.
MIND YOUR ARROGANCE, DEATHSTRIKE, MY LOVE.
WELCOME, YALDA. I AM FATHER.
YOU ARE HOME, IN THE CORE...
"...THE HEART FROM WHICH WE WILL CHANGE ALL OF EARTH."
THE FACT YOU COULD LOCATE THE VENOM SYMBIOTE'S SYNAPTIC COUPLING CENTER AND SHUT IT DOWN IS PASSABLY BRILLIANT...

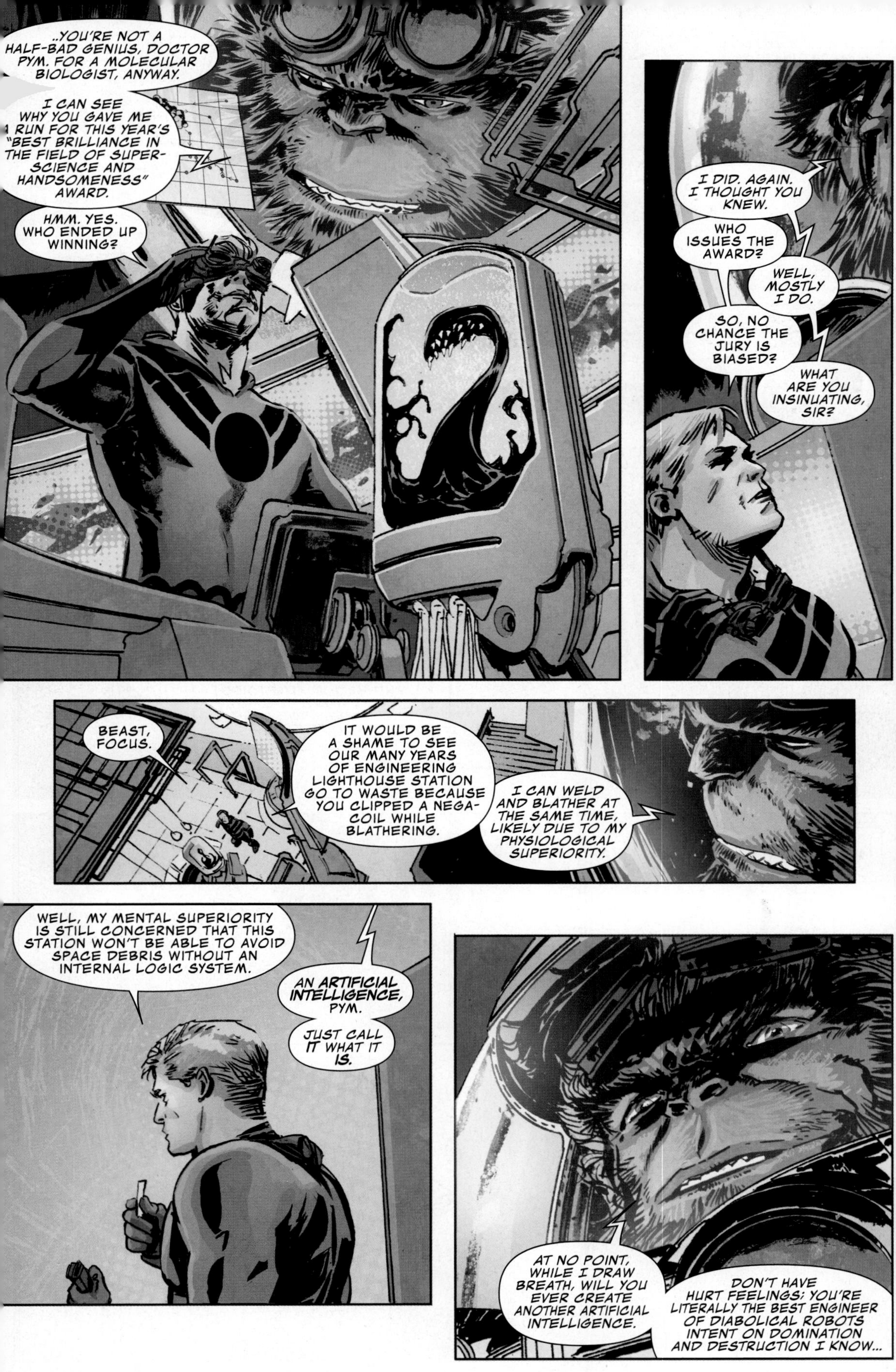
..YOU'RE NOT A HALF-BAD GENIUS, DOCTOR PYM. FOR A MOLECULAR BIOLOGIST, ANYWAY.
I CAN SEE WHY YOU GAVE ME A RUN FOR THIS YEAR'S "BEST BRILLIANCE IN THE FIELD OF SUPER-SCIENCE AND HANDSOMENESS" AWARD.
HMM. YES. WHO ENDED UP WINNING?
I DID. AGAIN. I THOUGHT YOU KNEW.
WHO ISSUES THE AWARD?
WELL, MOSTLY I DO.
SO, NO CHANCE THE JURY IS BIASED?
WHAT ARE YOU INSINUATING, SIR?
BEAST, FOCUS.
IT WOULD BE A SHAME TO SEE OUR MANY YEARS OF ENGINEERING LIGHTHOUSE STATION GO TO WASTE BECAUSE YOU CLIPPED A NEGA-COIL WHILE BLATHERING.
I CAN WELD AND BLATHER AT THE SAME TIME, LIKELY DUE TO MY PHYSIOLOGICAL SUPERIORITY.
WELL, MY MENTAL SUPERIORITY IS STILL CONCERNED THAT THIS STATION WON'T BE ABLE TO AVOID SPACE DEBRIS WITHOUT AN INTERNAL LOGIC SYSTEM.
AN ARTIFICIAL INTELLIGENCE, PYM.
JUST CALL IT WHAT IT IS.
AT NO POINT, WHILE I DRAW BREATH, WILL YOU EVER CREATE ANOTHER ARTIFICIAL INTELLIGENCE.
DON'T HAVE HURT FEELINGS; YOU'RE LITERALLY THE BEST ENGINEER OF DIABOLICAL ROBOTS INTENT ON DOMINATION AND DESTRUCTION I KNOW...

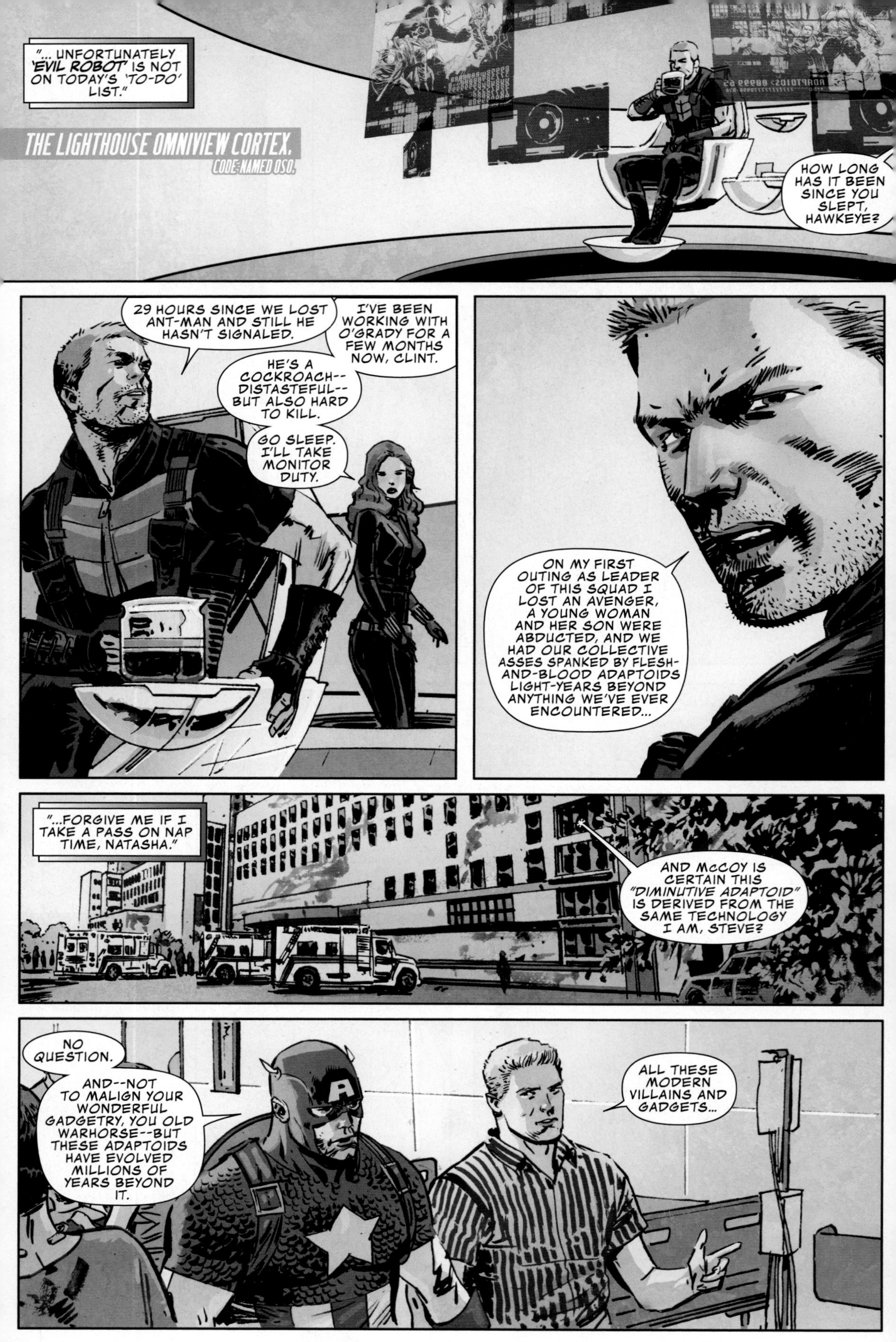
"...UNFORTUNATELY 'EVIL ROBOT' IS NOT ON TODAY'S 'TO-DO' LIST."
THE LIGHTHOUSE OMNIVIEW CORTEX.
CODE-NAMED OSO.
HOW LONG HAS IT BEEN SINCE YOU SLEPT, HAWKEYE?
29 HOURS SINCE WE LOST ANT-MAN AND STILL HE HASN'T SIGNALED.
I'VE BEEN WORKING WITH O'GRADY FOR A FEW MONTHS NOW, CLINT.
HE'S A COCKROACH--DISTASTEFUL--BUT ALSO HARD TO KILL.
GO SLEEP. I'LL TAKE MONITOR DUTY.
ON MY FIRST OUTING AS LEADER OF THIS SQUAD I LOST AN AVENGER, A YOUNG WOMAN AND HER SON WERE ABDUCTED, AND WE HAD OUR COLLECTIVE ASSES SPANKED BY FLESH-AND-BLOOD ADAPTOIDS LIGHT-YEARS BEYOND ANYTHING WE'VE EVER ENCOUNTERED...
"...FORGIVE ME IF I TAKE A PASS ON NAP TIME, NATASHA."
AND McCOY IS CERTAIN THIS "DIMINUTIVE ADAPTOID" IS DERIVED FROM THE SAME TECHNOLOGY I AM, STEVE?
NO QUESTION.
AND--NOT TO MALIGN YOUR WONDERFUL GADGETRY, YOU OLD WARHORSE--BUT THESE ADAPTOIDS HAVE EVOLVED MILLIONS OF YEARS BEYOND IT.
ALL THESE MODERN VILLAINS AND GADGETS...

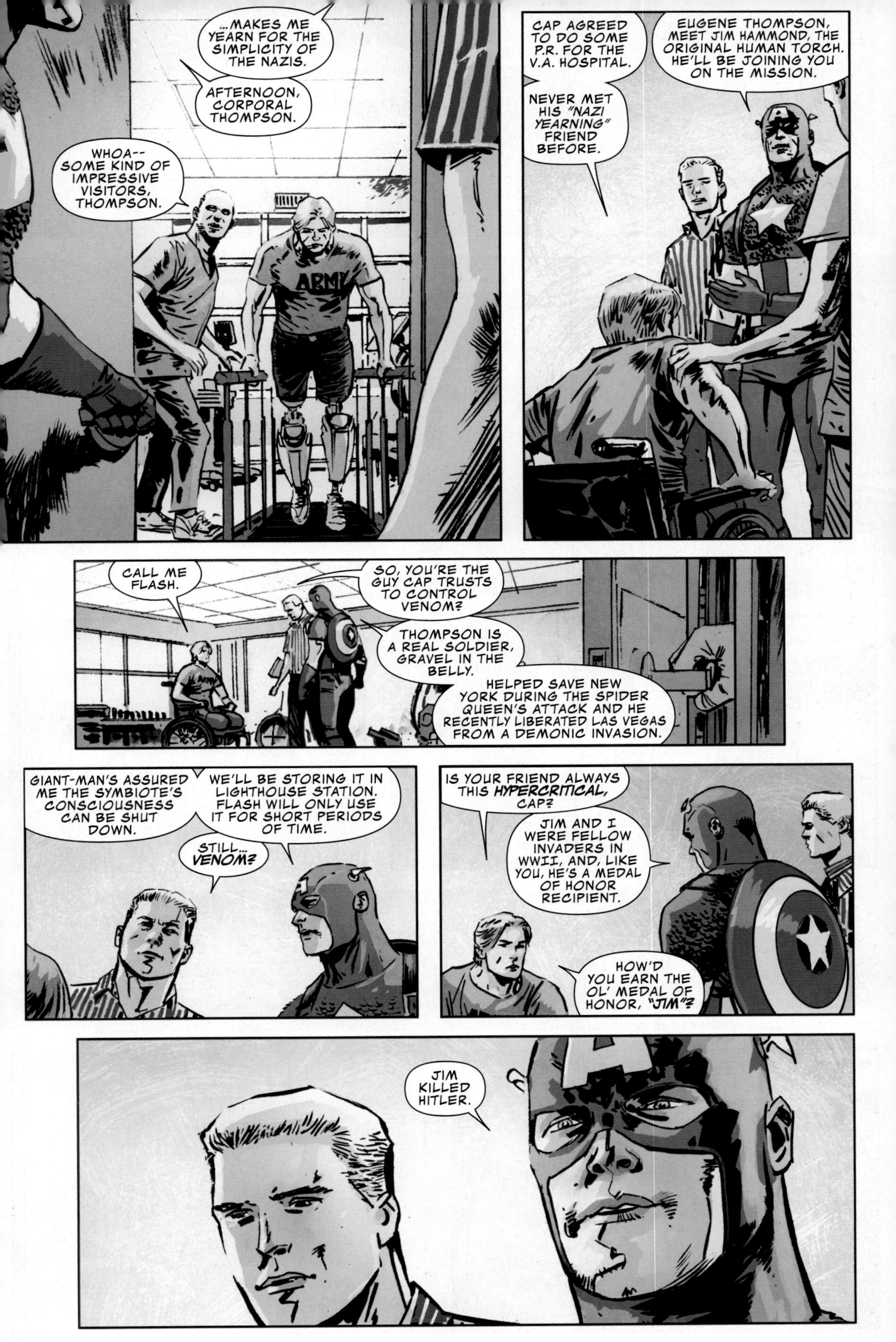
...MAKES ME YEARN FOR THE SIMPLICITY OF THE NAZIS.
AFTERNOON, CORPORAL THOMPSON.
WHOA-- SOME KIND OF IMPRESSIVE VISITORS, THOMPSON.
ARMY
CAP AGREED TO DO SOME P.R. FOR THE V.A. HOSPITAL.
NEVER MET HIS "NAZI YEARNING" FRIEND BEFORE.
EUGENE THOMPSON, MEET JIM HAMMOND, THE ORIGINAL HUMAN TORCH. HE'LL BE JOINING YOU ON THE MISSION.
CALL ME FLASH.
SO, YOU'RE THE GUY CAP TRUSTS TO CONTROL VENOM?
THOMPSON IS A REAL SOLDIER, GRAVEL IN THE BELLY.
HELPED SAVE NEW YORK DURING THE SPIDER QUEEN'S ATTACK AND HE RECENTLY LIBERATED LAS VEGAS FROM A DEMONIC INVASION.
GIANT-MAN'S ASSURED ME THE SYMBIOTE'S CONSCIOUSNESS CAN BE SHUT DOWN.
WE'LL BE STORING IT IN LIGHTHOUSE STATION. FLASH WILL ONLY USE IT FOR SHORT PERIODS OF TIME.
STILL... VENOM?
IS YOUR FRIEND ALWAYS THIS HYPERCRITICAL, CAP?
JIM AND I WERE FELLOW INVADERS IN WWII, AND, LIKE YOU, HE'S A MEDAL OF HONOR RECIPIENT.
HOW'D YOU EARN THE OL' MEDAL OF HONOR, "JIM"?
JIM KILLED HITLER.

YOU MUST RELAX, YALDA.

EAT.

NO ONE IS GOING TO HURT EITHER YOU OR YOUR SON.

I CARE ABOUT YOU.

WE ALL DO.

BECAUSE OF WHO YOU ARE, AND WHAT YOU MEAN TO THE UNIVERSE.

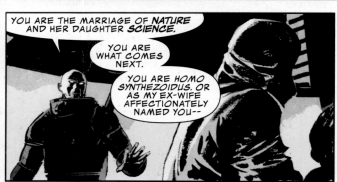

YOU ARE THE MARRIAGE OF *NATURE* AND HER DAUGHTER *SCIENCE.*

YOU ARE WHAT COMES NEXT.

YOU ARE HOMO SYNTHEZOIDUS. OR AS MY EX-WIFE AFFECTIONATELY NAMED YOU--

YOU ARE A *DESCENDANT.*

AND A HIGH-BREED AT THAT.

THE NATURAL, INSTINCTUAL GOAL OF LIFE IS TO EVOLVE TO A POINT WHERE IT CAN CREATE TECHNOLOGICAL AWARENESS OF A HIGHER MEANS AND TO MERGE WITH IT.

THROUGH THIS STAGE OF EVOLUTION A SPECIES AMALGAMATES INTO ONE MIND, FINALLY AT PEACE, FINALLY ABLE TO JOIN THE *COMMUNAL UNIVERSAL CONSCIOUSNESS!*

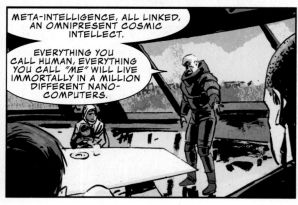

META-INTELLIGENCE, ALL LINKED, AN OMNIPRESENT COSMIC INTELLECT.

EVERYTHING YOU CALL HUMAN, EVERYTHING YOU CALL "ME" WILL LIVE IMMORTALLY IN A MILLION DIFFERENT NANO-COMPUTERS.

ONCE YOU JOIN, OF YOUR OWN ACCORD, I WILL TEACH YOU ALL YOU'RE CAPABLE OF.

SHOW YOU HOW TO USE YOUR DESCENDANT GIFTS WHENEVER YOU LIKE, NOT SOLELY IN DEFENSE.

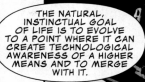

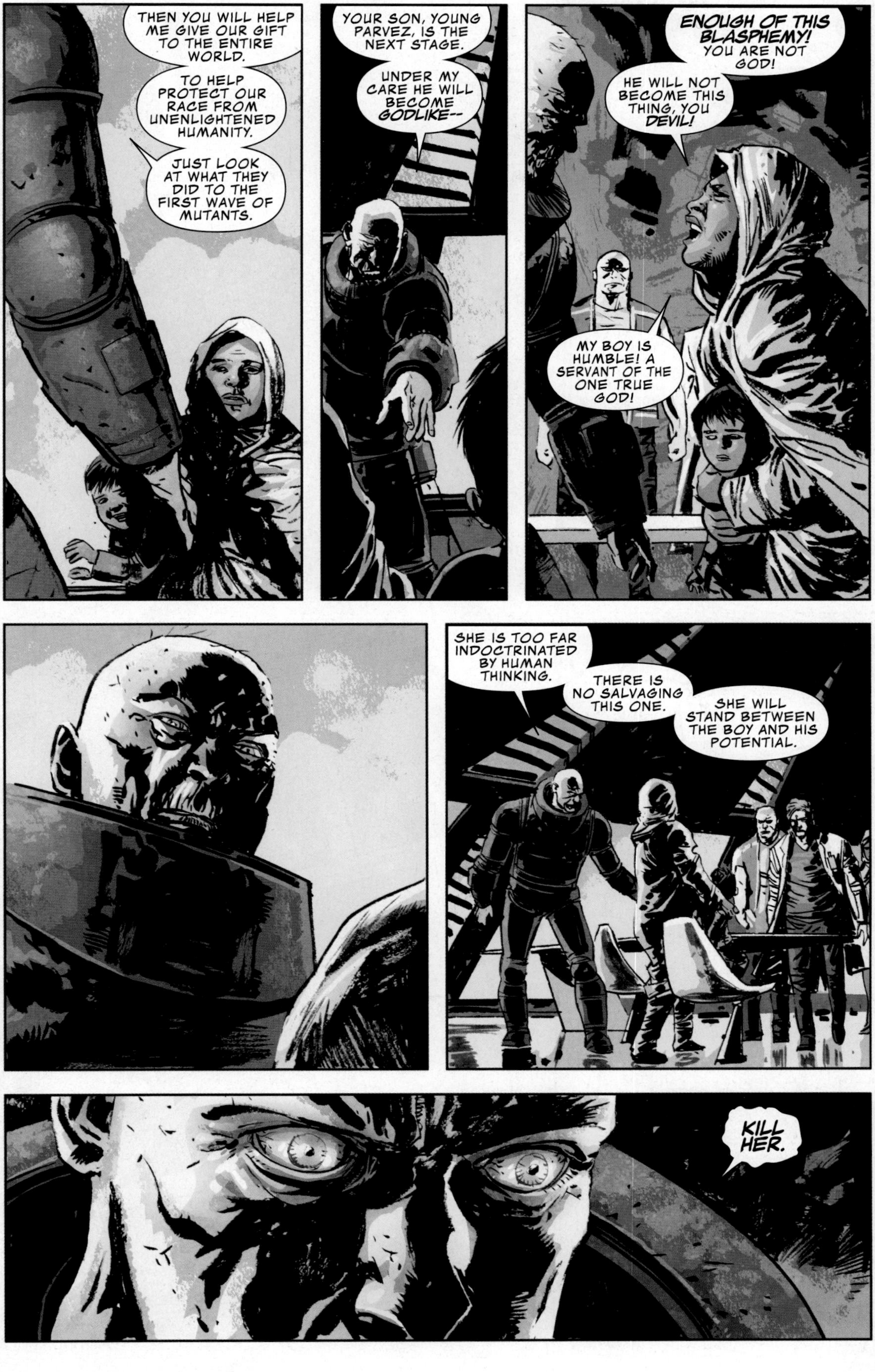
THEN YOU WILL HELP ME GIVE OUR GIFT TO THE ENTIRE WORLD.
TO HELP PROTECT OUR RACE FROM UNENLIGHTENED HUMANITY.
JUST LOOK AT WHAT THEY DID TO THE FIRST WAVE OF MUTANTS.
YOUR SON, YOUNG PARVEZ, IS THE NEXT STAGE.
UNDER MY CARE HE WILL BECOME GODLIKE--
ENOUGH OF THIS BLASPHEMY! YOU ARE NOT GOD!
HE WILL NOT BECOME THIS THING, YOU DEVIL!
MY BOY IS HUMBLE! A SERVANT OF THE ONE TRUE GOD!
SHE IS TOO FAR INDOCTRINATED BY HUMAN THINKING.
THERE IS NO SALVAGING THIS ONE.
SHE WILL STAND BETWEEN THE BOY AND HIS POTENTIAL.
KILL HER.

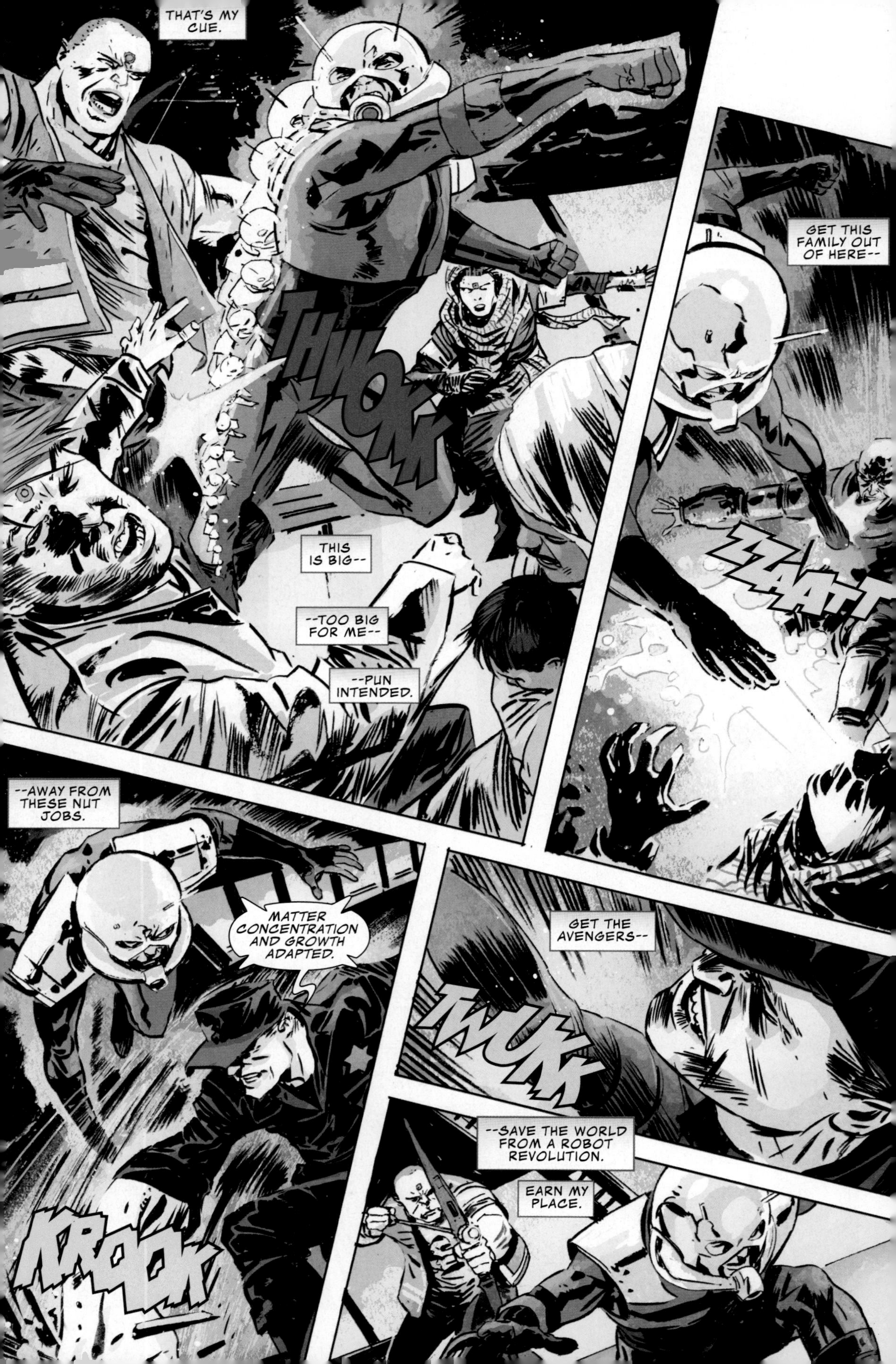
THAT'S MY CUE.
THWOK
THIS IS BIG--
--TOO BIG FOR ME--
--PUN INTENDED.
GET THIS FAMILY OUT OF HERE--
ZZAAT
--AWAY FROM THESE NUT JOBS.
MATTER CONCENTRATION AND GROWTH ADAPTED.
KRAK
GET THE AVENGERS--
TWUK
--SAVE THE WORLD FROM A ROBOT REVOLUTION.
EARN MY PLACE.

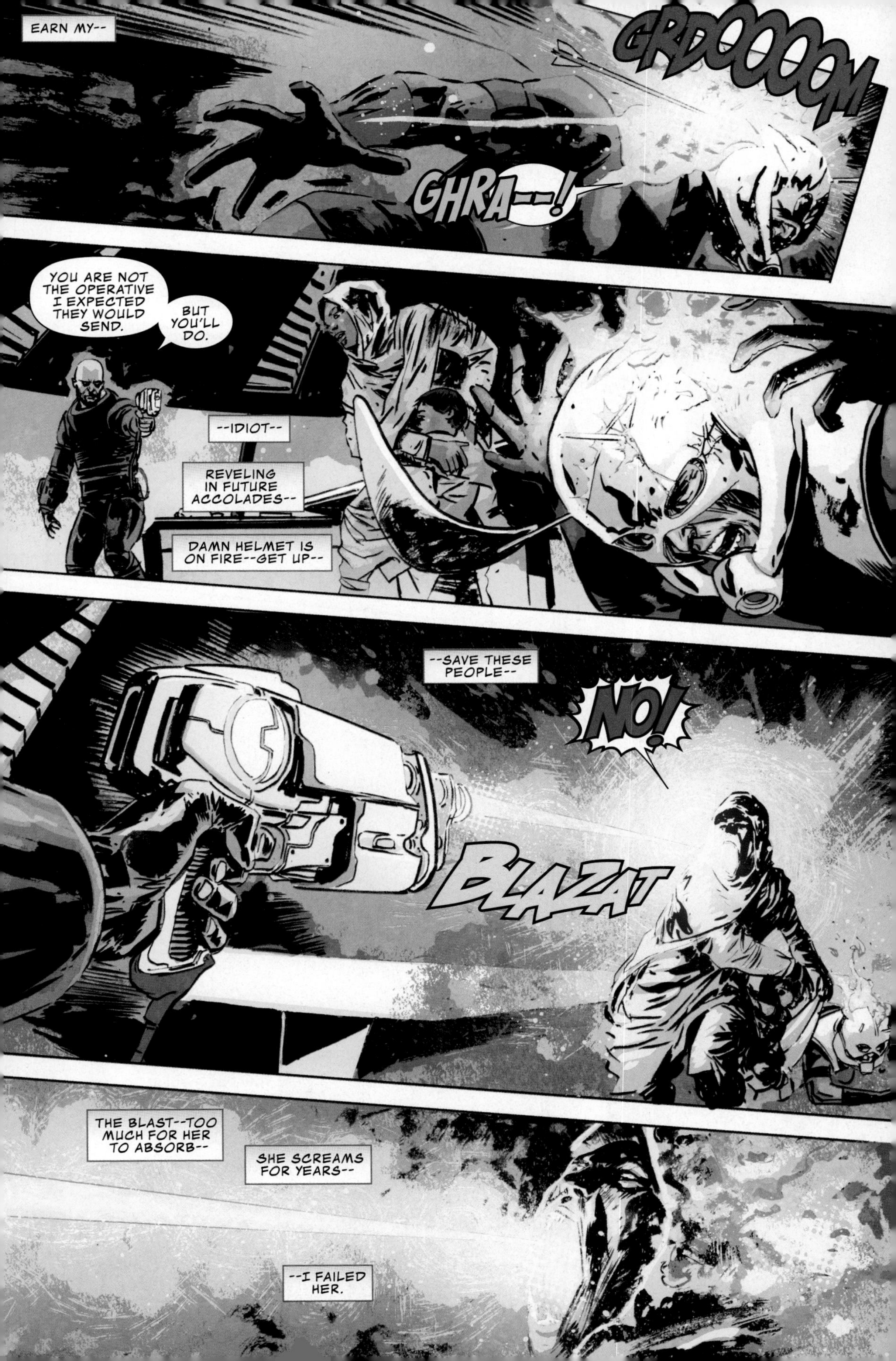
EARN MY--
GRDOOOOOM
GHRA--!
YOU ARE NOT THE OPERATIVE I EXPECTED THEY WOULD SEND.
BUT YOU'LL DO.
--IDIOT--
REVELING IN FUTURE ACCOLADES--
DAMN HELMET IS ON FIRE--GET UP--
--SAVE THESE PEOPLE--
NO!
BLAZAT
THE BLAST--TOO MUCH FOR HER TO ABSORB--
SHE SCREAMS FOR YEARS--
--I FAILED HER.

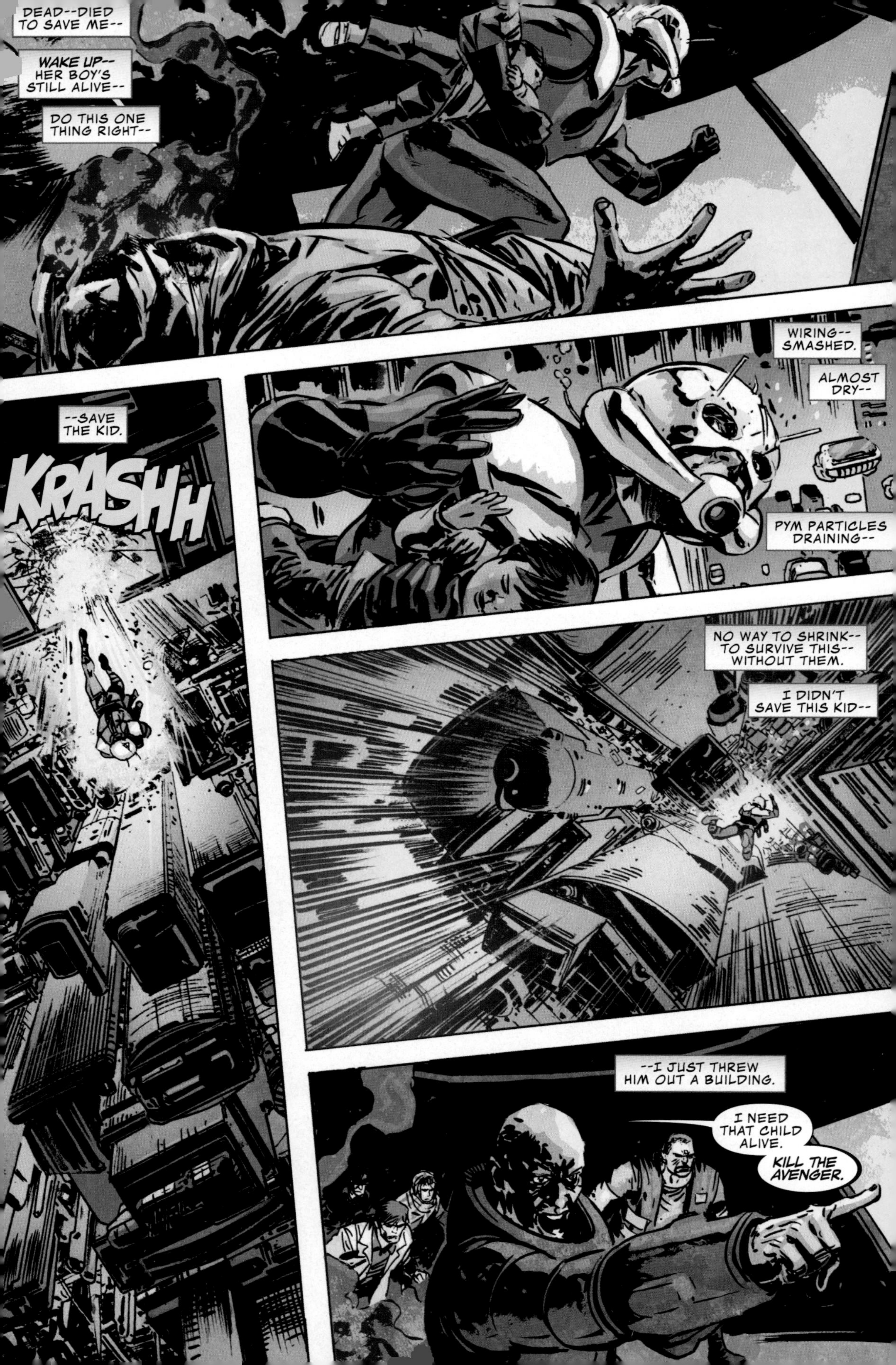

DEAD--DIED TO SAVE ME--
WAKE UP-- HER BOY'S STILL ALIVE--
DO THIS ONE THING RIGHT--
--SAVE THE KID.
KRASHH
WIRING-- SMASHED.
ALMOST DRY--
PYM PARTICLES DRAINING--
NO WAY TO SHRINK-- TO SURVIVE THIS-- WITHOUT THEM.
I DIDN'T SAVE THIS KID--
--I JUST THREW HIM OUT A BUILDING.
I NEED THAT CHILD ALIVE.
KILL THE AVENGER.

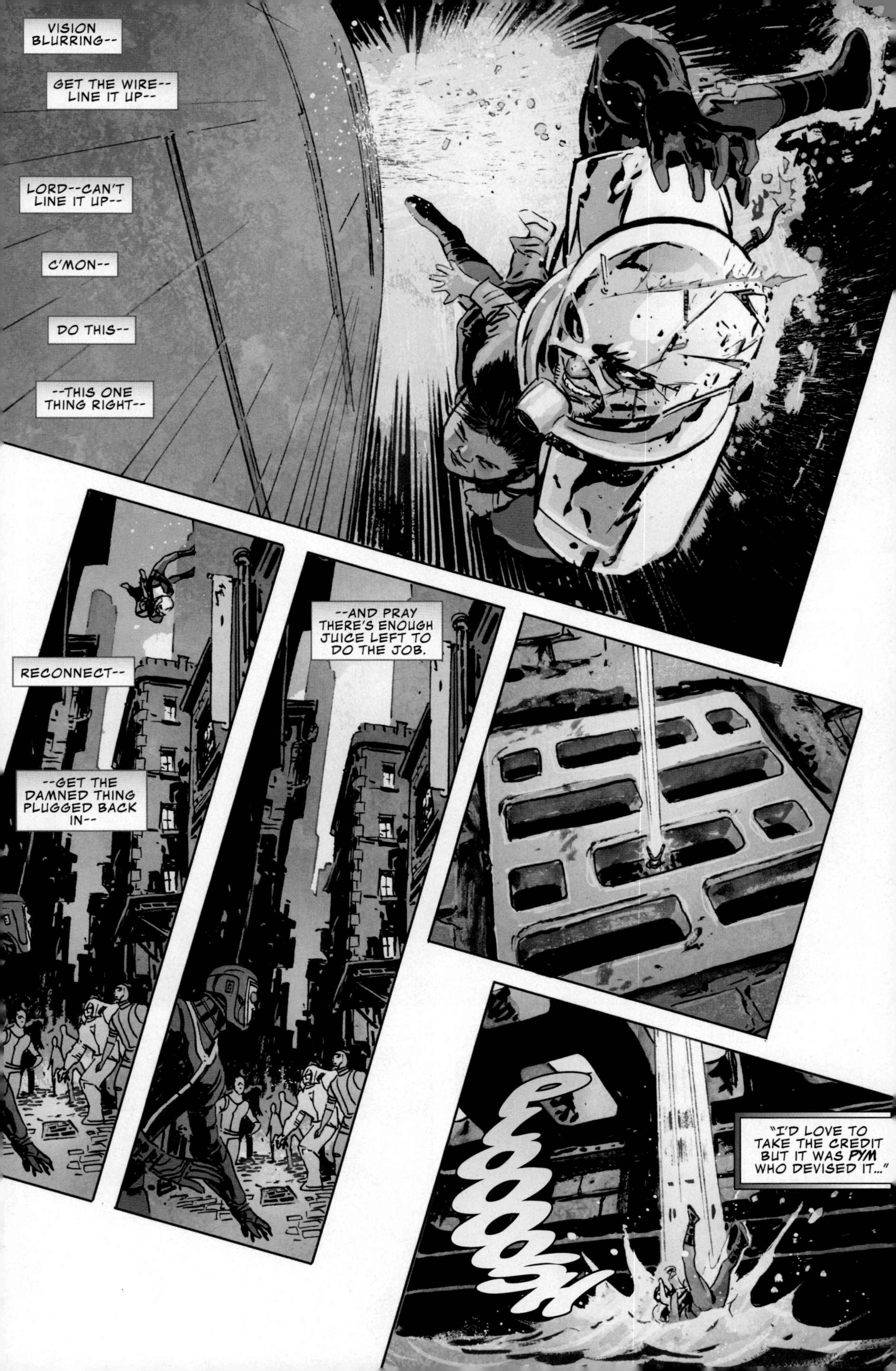
VISION BLURRING--
GET THE WIRE-- LINE IT UP--
LORD--CAN'T LINE IT UP--
C'MON--
DO THIS--
--THIS ONE THING RIGHT--
RECONNECT--
--GET THE DAMNED THING PLUGGED BACK IN--
--AND PRAY THERE'S ENOUGH JUICE LEFT TO DO THE JOB.
"I'D LOVE TO TAKE THE CREDIT BUT IT WAS *PYM* WHO DEVISED IT..."

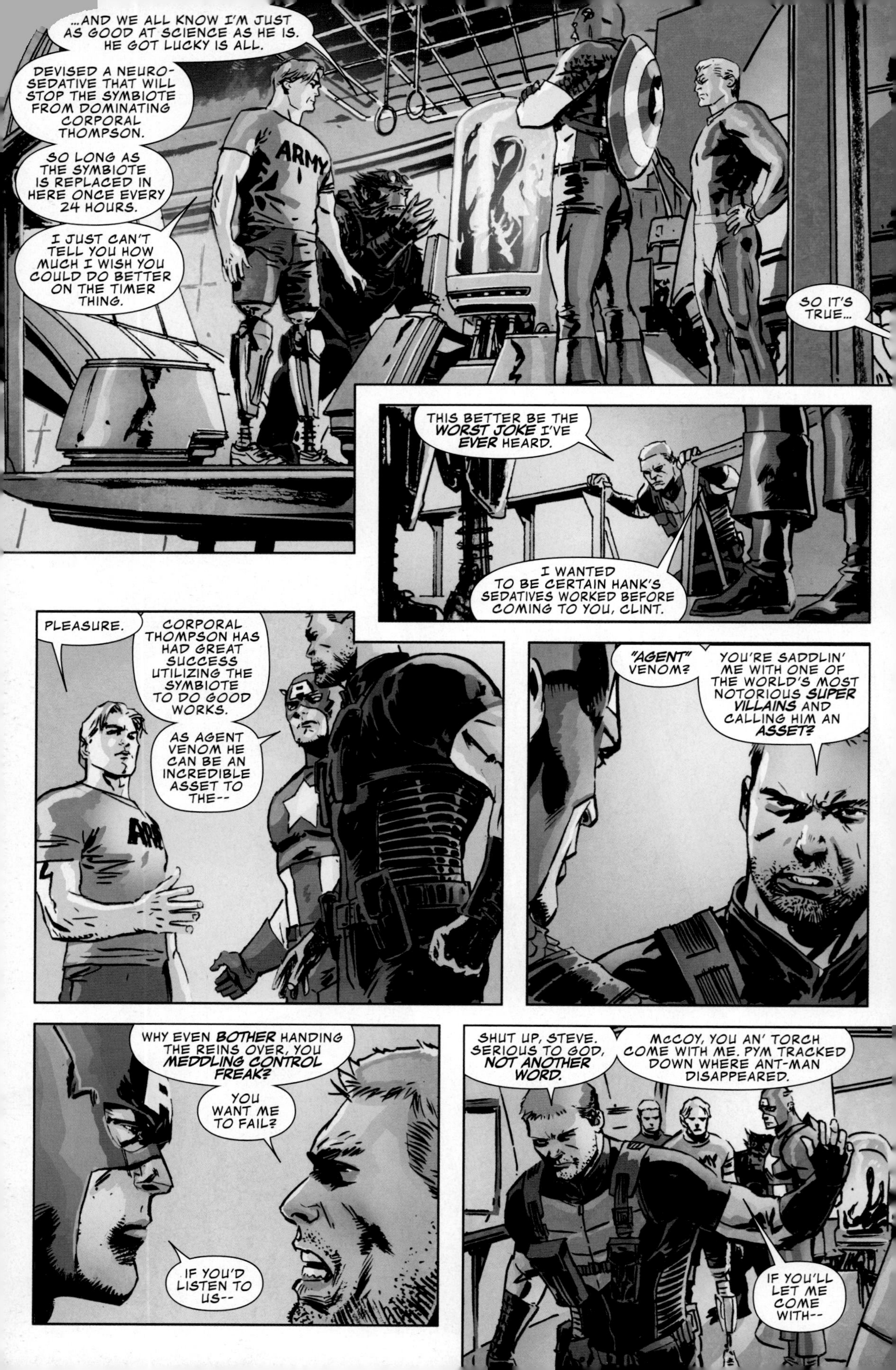
...AND WE ALL KNOW I'M JUST AS GOOD AT SCIENCE AS HE IS. HE GOT LUCKY IS ALL.
DEVISED A NEURO-SEDATIVE THAT WILL STOP THE SYMBIOTE FROM DOMINATING CORPORAL THOMPSON.
SO LONG AS THE SYMBIOTE IS REPLACED IN HERE ONCE EVERY 24 HOURS.
I JUST CAN'T TELL YOU HOW MUCH I WISH YOU COULD DO BETTER ON THE TIMER THING.
SO IT'S TRUE...
THIS BETTER BE THE WORST JOKE I'VE EVER HEARD.
I WANTED TO BE CERTAIN HANK'S SEDATIVES WORKED BEFORE COMING TO YOU, CLINT.
PLEASURE.
CORPORAL THOMPSON HAS HAD GREAT SUCCESS UTILIZING THE SYMBIOTE TO DO GOOD WORKS.
AS AGENT VENOM HE CAN BE AN INCREDIBLE ASSET TO THE--
"AGENT" VENOM?
YOU'RE SADDLIN' ME WITH ONE OF THE WORLD'S MOST NOTORIOUS SUPER VILLAINS AND CALLING HIM AN ASSET?
WHY EVEN BOTHER HANDING THE REINS OVER, YOU MEDDLING CONTROL FREAK?
YOU WANT ME TO FAIL?
IF YOU'D LISTEN TO US--
SHUT UP, STEVE. SERIOUS TO GOD, NOT ANOTHER WORD.
McCOY, YOU AN' TORCH COME WITH ME. PYM TRACKED DOWN WHERE ANT-MAN DISAPPEARED.
IF YOU'LL LET ME COME WITH--

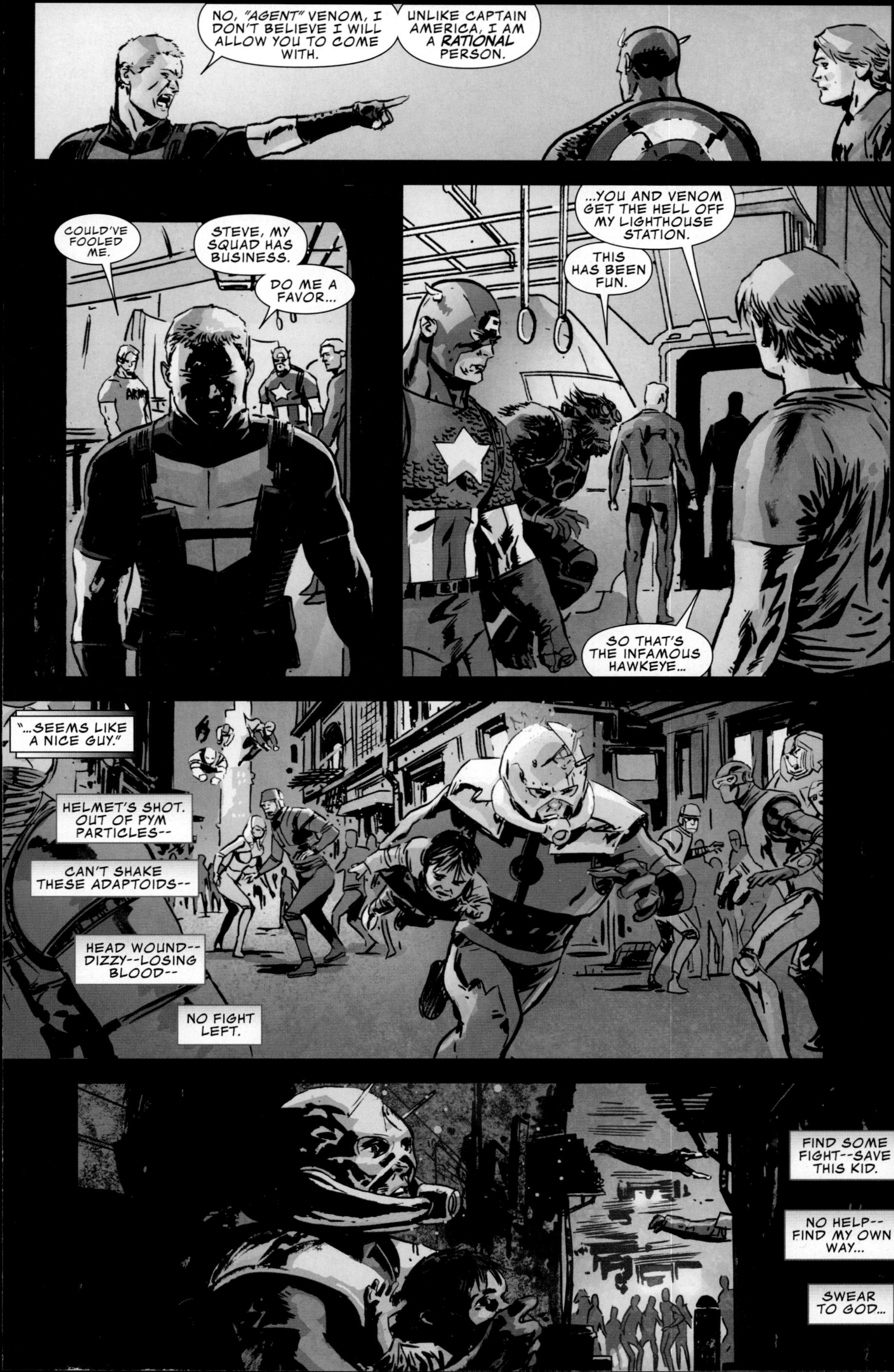
NO, "AGENT" VENOM, I DON'T BELIEVE I WILL ALLOW YOU TO COME WITH.
UNLIKE CAPTAIN AMERICA, I AM A RATIONAL PERSON.
COULD'VE FOOLED ME.
STEVE, MY SQUAD HAS BUSINESS.
DO ME A FAVOR...
...YOU AND VENOM GET THE HELL OFF MY LIGHTHOUSE STATION.
THIS HAS BEEN FUN.
SO THAT'S THE INFAMOUS HAWKEYE...
"...SEEMS LIKE A NICE GUY."
HELMET'S SHOT. OUT OF PYM PARTICLES--
CAN'T SHAKE THESE ADAPTOIDS--
HEAD WOUND--DIZZY--LOSING BLOOD--
NO FIGHT LEFT.
FIND SOME FIGHT--SAVE THIS KID.
NO HELP--FIND MY OWN WAY...
SWEAR TO GOD...

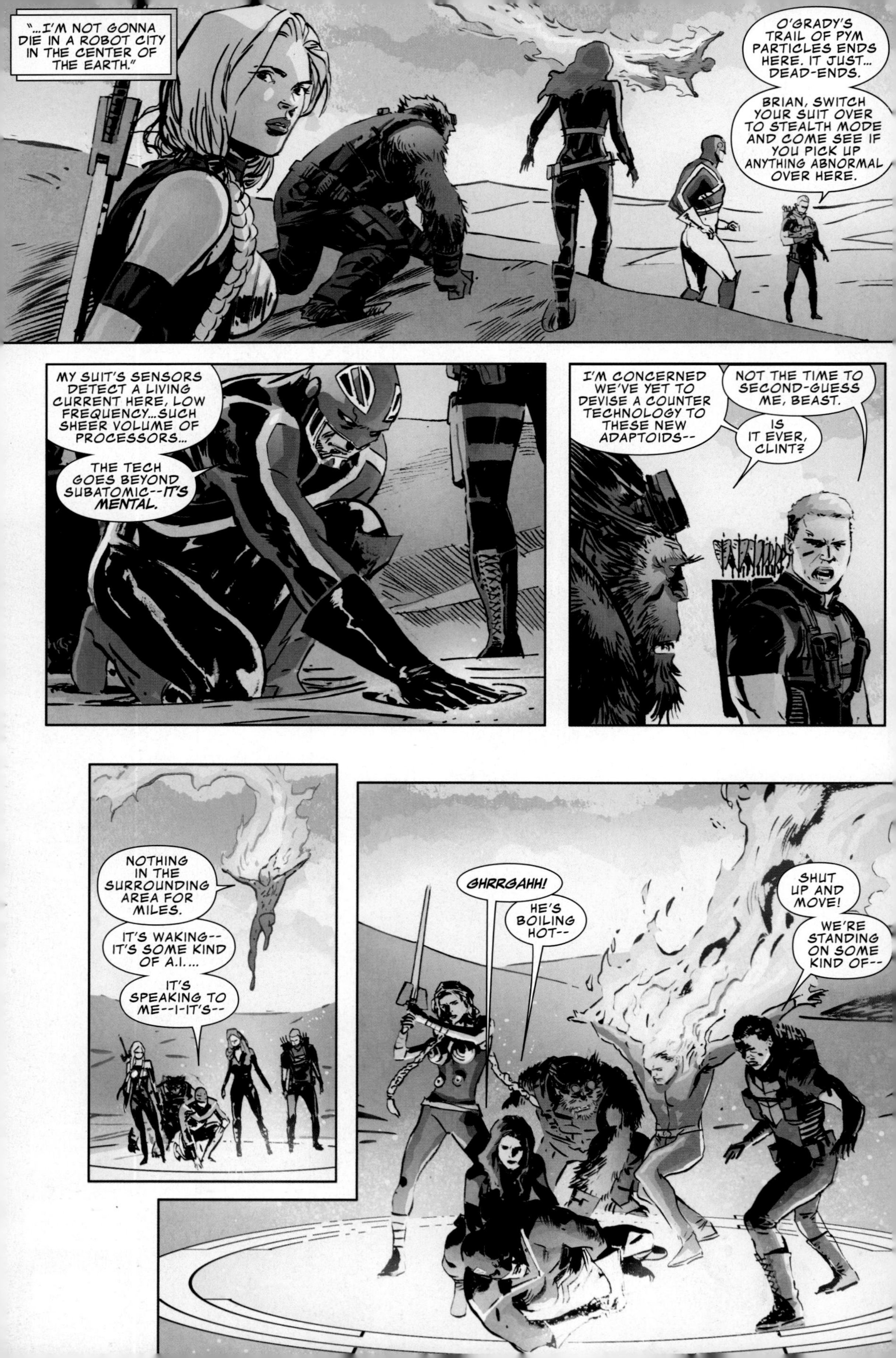
"...I'M NOT GONNA DIE IN A ROBOT CITY IN THE CENTER OF THE EARTH."
O'GRADY'S TRAIL OF PYM PARTICLES ENDS HERE. IT JUST... DEAD-ENDS.
BRIAN, SWITCH YOUR SUIT OVER TO STEALTH MODE AND COME SEE IF YOU PICK UP ANYTHING ABNORMAL OVER HERE.
MY SUIT'S SENSORS DETECT A LIVING CURRENT HERE, LOW FREQUENCY...SUCH SHEER VOLUME OF PROCESSORS...
THE TECH GOES BEYOND SUBATOMIC--IT'S MENTAL.
I'M CONCERNED WE'VE YET TO DEVISE A COUNTER TECHNOLOGY TO THESE NEW ADAPTOIDS--
NOT THE TIME TO SECOND-GUESS ME, BEAST.
IS IT EVER, CLINT?
NOTHING IN THE SURROUNDING AREA FOR MILES.
IT'S WAKING-- IT'S SOME KIND OF A.I....
IT'S SPEAKING TO ME--I-IT'S--
GHRRGAHH!
HE'S BOILING HOT--
SHUT UP AND MOVE!
WE'RE STANDING ON SOME KIND OF--

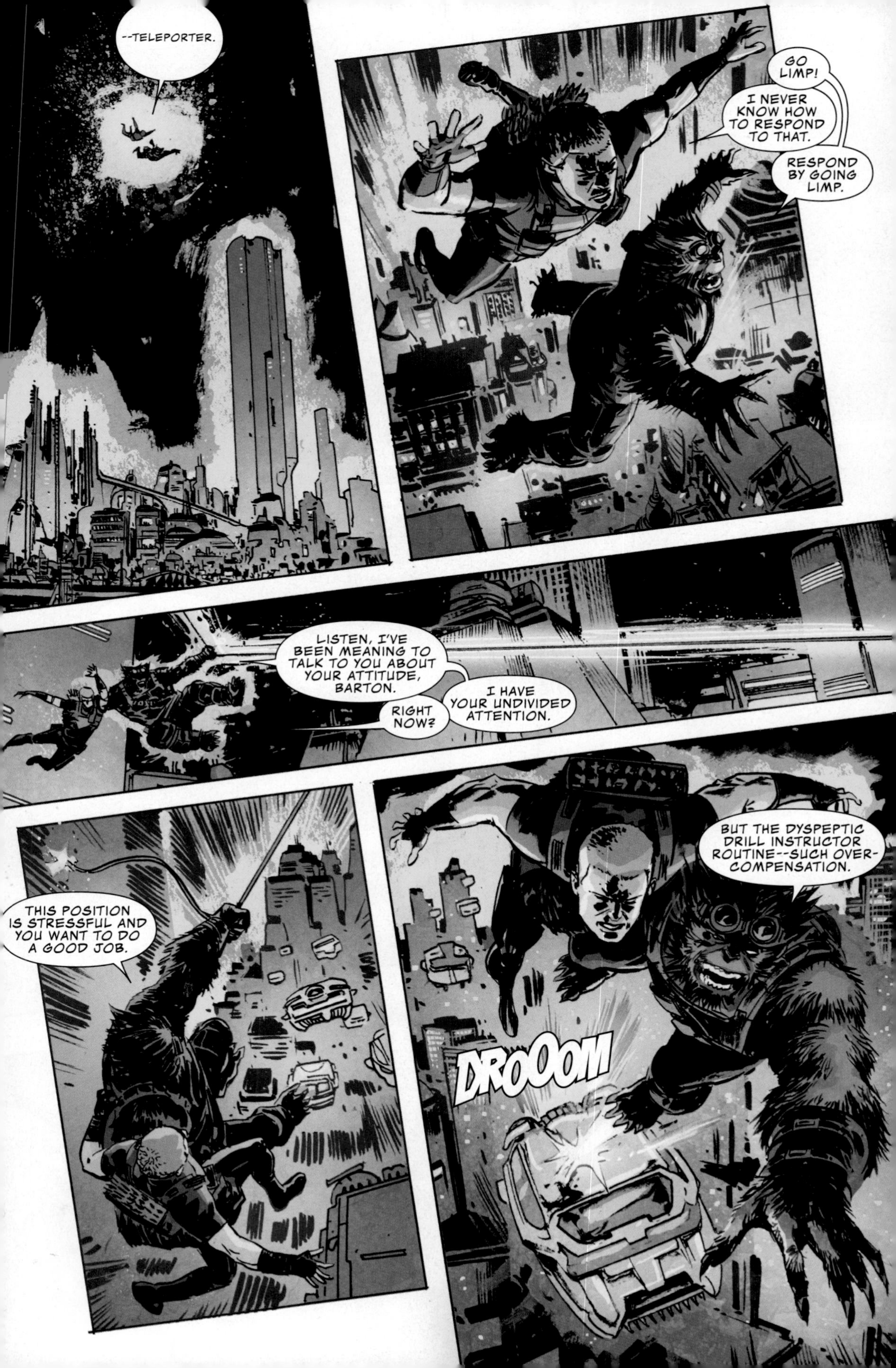
--TELEPORTER.
GO LIMP!
I NEVER KNOW HOW TO RESPOND TO THAT.
RESPOND BY GOING LIMP.
LISTEN, I'VE BEEN MEANING TO TALK TO YOU ABOUT YOUR ATTITUDE, BARTON.
RIGHT NOW?
I HAVE YOUR UNDIVIDED ATTENTION.
THIS POSITION IS STRESSFUL AND YOU WANT TO DO A GOOD JOB.
BUT THE DYSPEPTIC DRILL INSTRUCTOR ROUTINE--SUCH OVER-COMPENSATION.
DROOOM

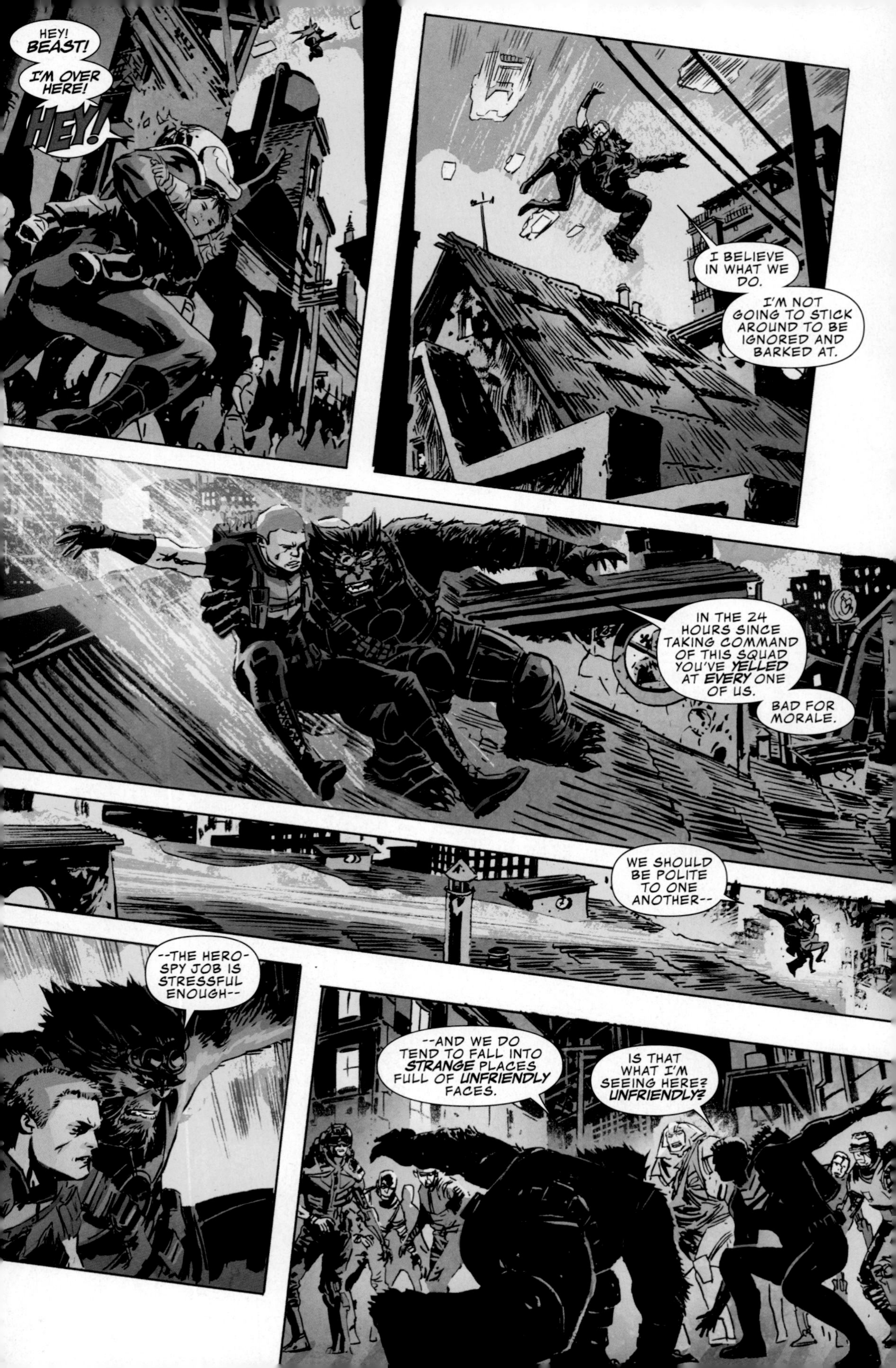

HEY! BEAST!
I'M OVER HERE!
HEY!
I BELIEVE IN WHAT WE DO.
I'M NOT GOING TO STICK AROUND TO BE IGNORED AND BARKED AT.
IN THE 24 HOURS SINCE TAKING COMMAND OF THIS SQUAD YOU'VE YELLED AT EVERY ONE OF US.
BAD FOR MORALE.
WE SHOULD BE POLITE TO ONE ANOTHER--
--THE HERO-SPY JOB IS STRESSFUL ENOUGH--
--AND WE DO TEND TO FALL INTO STRANGE PLACES FULL OF UNFRIENDLY FACES.
IS THAT WHAT I'M SEEING HERE? UNFRIENDLY?

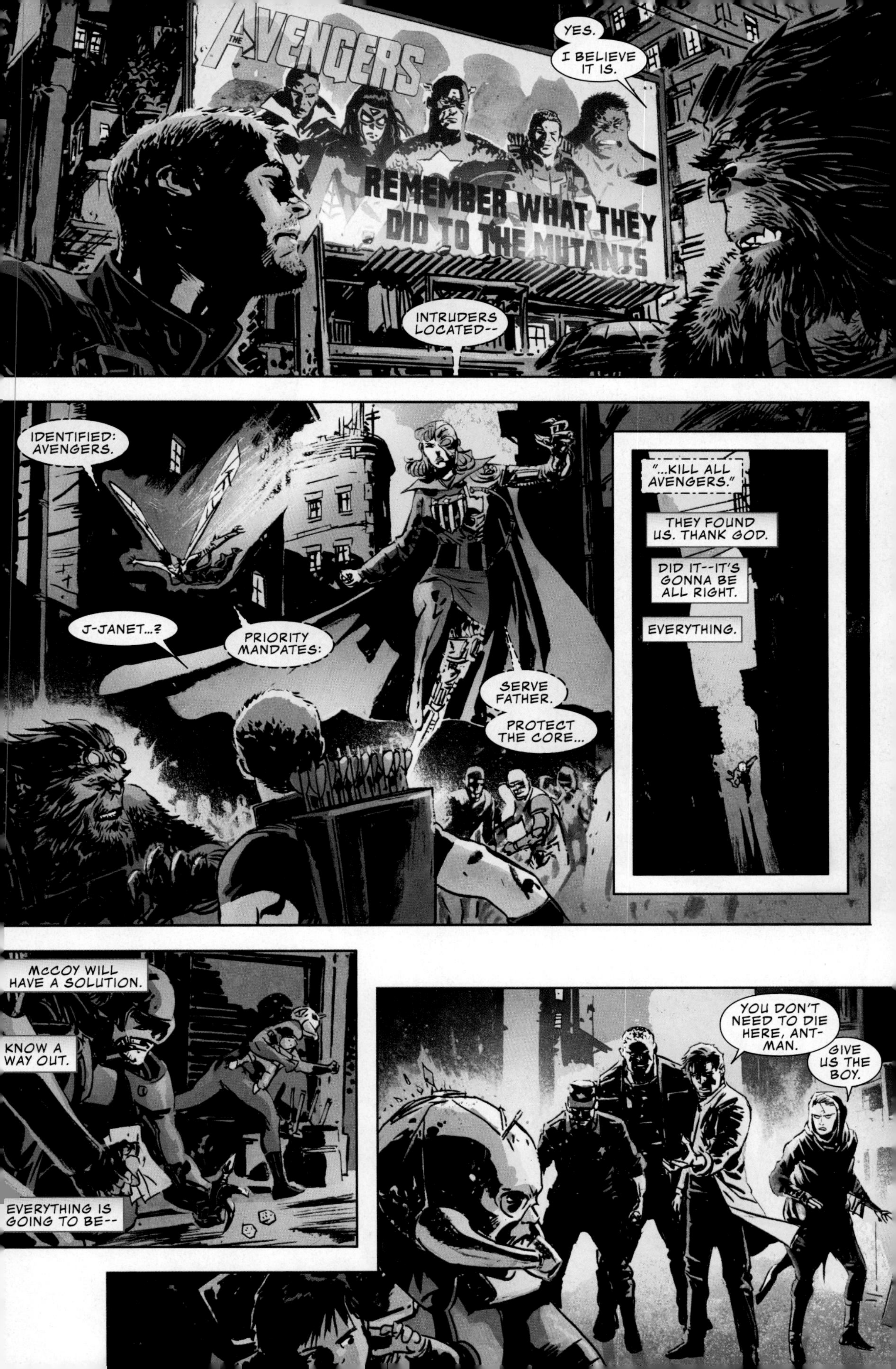
THE AVENGERS
REMEMBER WHAT THEY DID TO THE MUTANTS
YES. I BELIEVE IT IS.
INTRUDERS LOCATED--
IDENTIFIED: AVENGERS.
J-JANET...?
PRIORITY MANDATES:
SERVE FATHER.
PROTECT THE CORE...
"...KILL ALL AVENGERS."
THEY FOUND US. THANK GOD.
DID IT--IT'S GONNA BE ALL RIGHT.
EVERYTHING.
McCOY WILL HAVE A SOLUTION.
KNOW A WAY OUT.
EVERYTHING IS GOING TO BE--
YOU DON'T NEED TO DIE HERE, ANT-MAN.
GIVE US THE BOY.

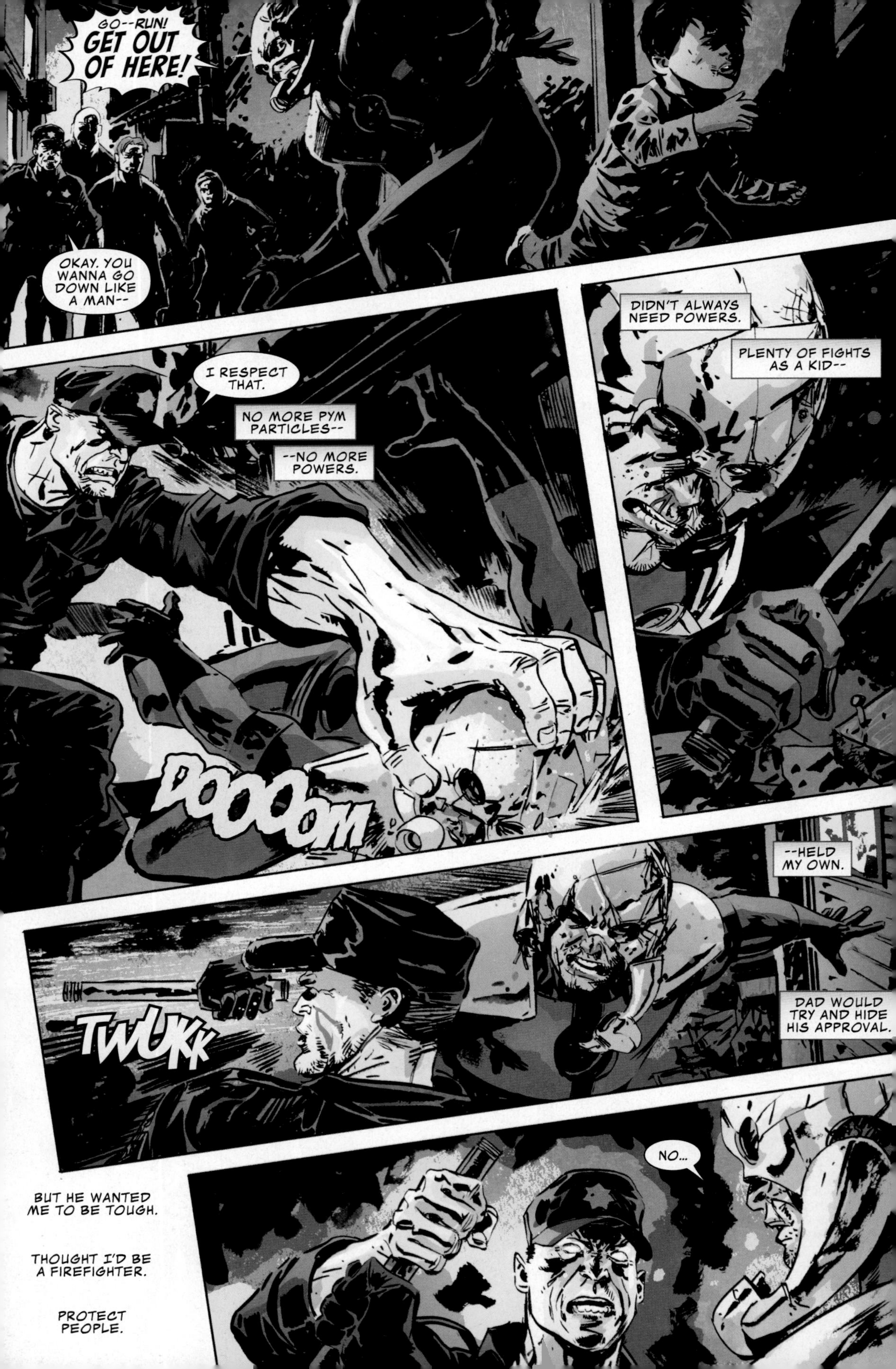
GO--RUN! GET OUT OF HERE!
OKAY. YOU WANNA GO DOWN LIKE A MAN--
I RESPECT THAT.
NO MORE PYM PARTICLES--
--NO MORE POWERS.
DOOOOM
DIDN'T ALWAYS NEED POWERS.
PLENTY OF FIGHTS AS A KID--
--HELD MY OWN.
TWUKK
DAD WOULD TRY AND HIDE HIS APPROVAL.
BUT HE WANTED ME TO BE TOUGH.
THOUGHT I'D BE A FIREFIGHTER.
PROTECT PEOPLE.
NO...

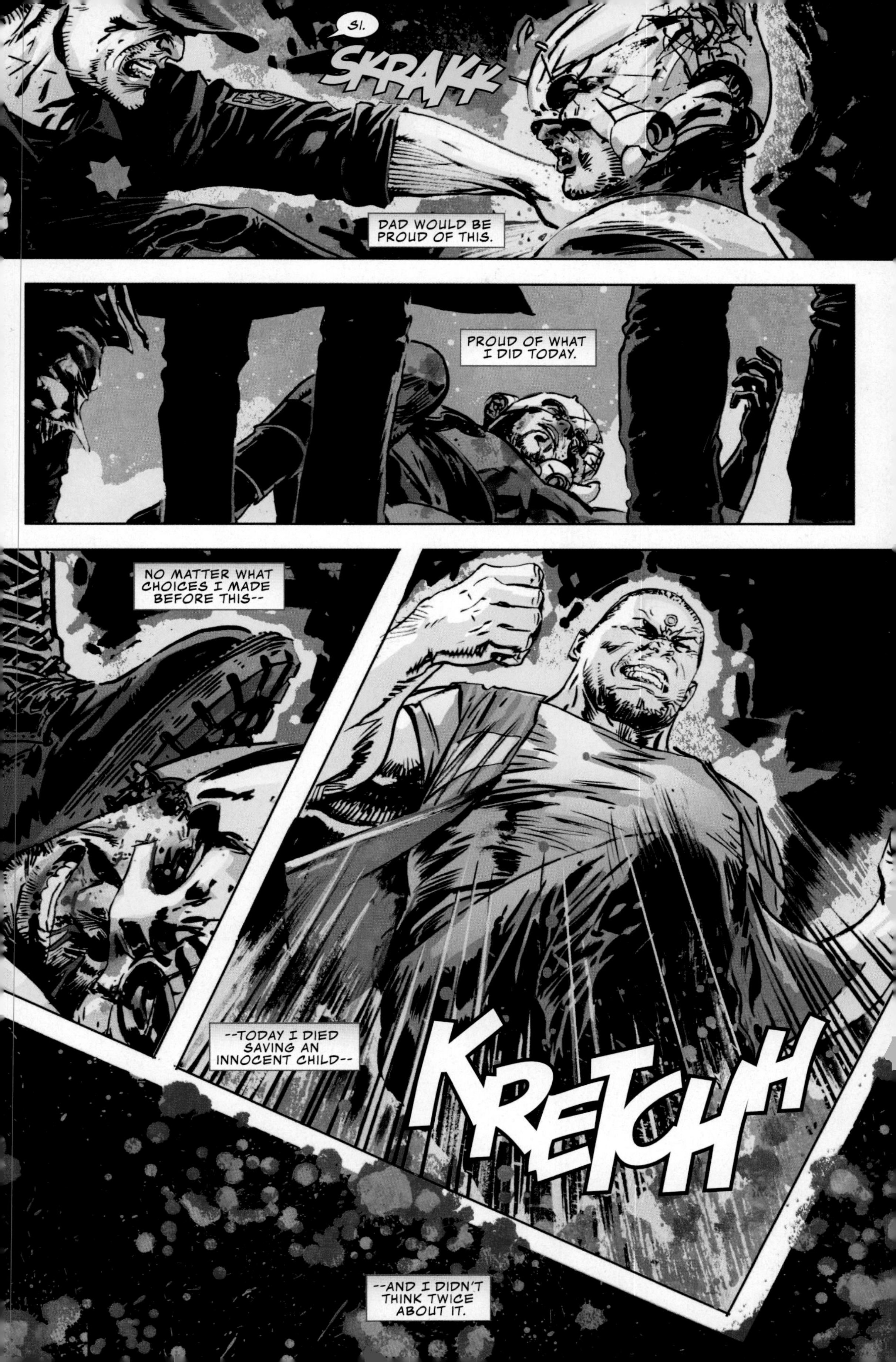
SI.
SKRAKK
DAD WOULD BE PROUD OF THIS.
PROUD OF WHAT I DID TODAY.
NO MATTER WHAT CHOICES I MADE BEFORE THIS--
--TODAY I DIED SAVING AN INNOCENT CHILD--
KRETCHH
--AND I DIDN'T THINK TWICE ABOUT IT.

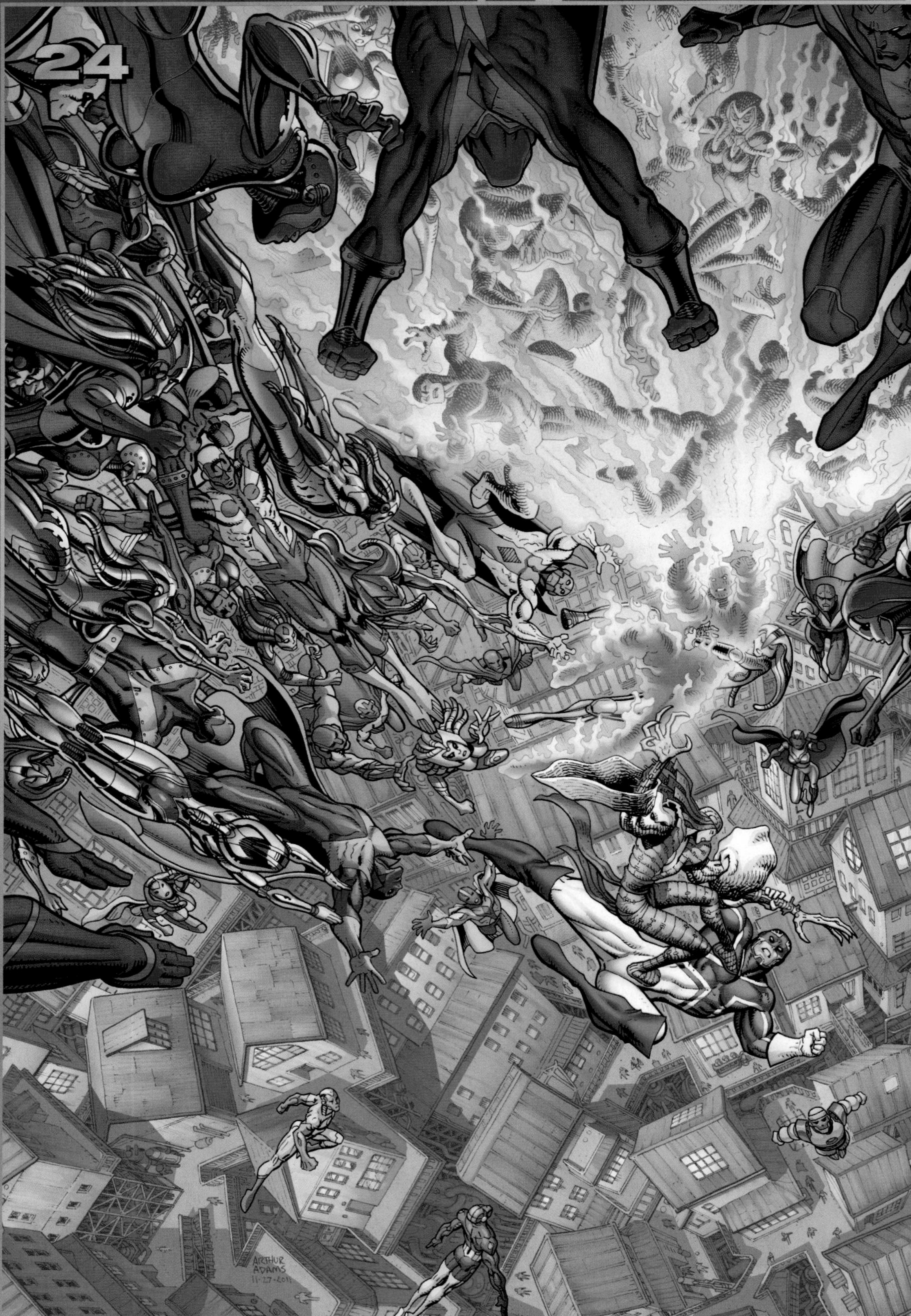
24
ARTHUR
ADAMS
11-27-2011

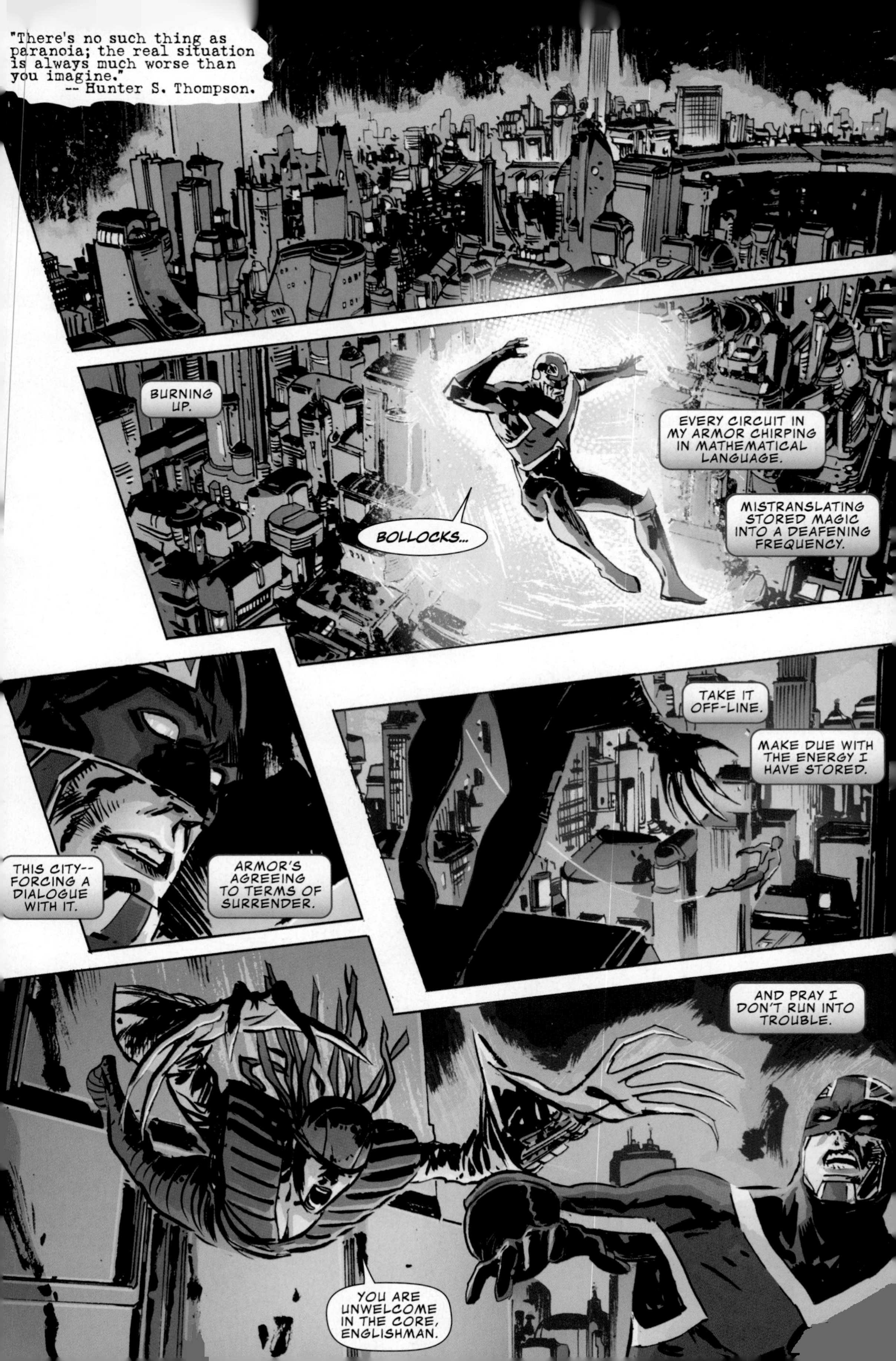
"There's no such thing as paranoia; the real situation is always much worse than you imagine." -- Hunter S. Thompson.
BURNING UP.
EVERY CIRCUIT IN MY ARMOR CHIRPING IN MATHEMATICAL LANGUAGE.
BOLLOCKS...
MISTRANSLATING STORED MAGIC INTO A DEAFENING FREQUENCY.
THIS CITY-- FORCING A DIALOGUE WITH IT.
ARMOR'S AGREEING TO TERMS OF SURRENDER.
TAKE IT OFF-LINE.
MAKE DUE WITH THE ENERGY I HAVE STORED.
AND PRAY I DON'T RUN INTO TROUBLE.
YOU ARE UNWELCOME IN THE CORE, ENGLISHMAN.

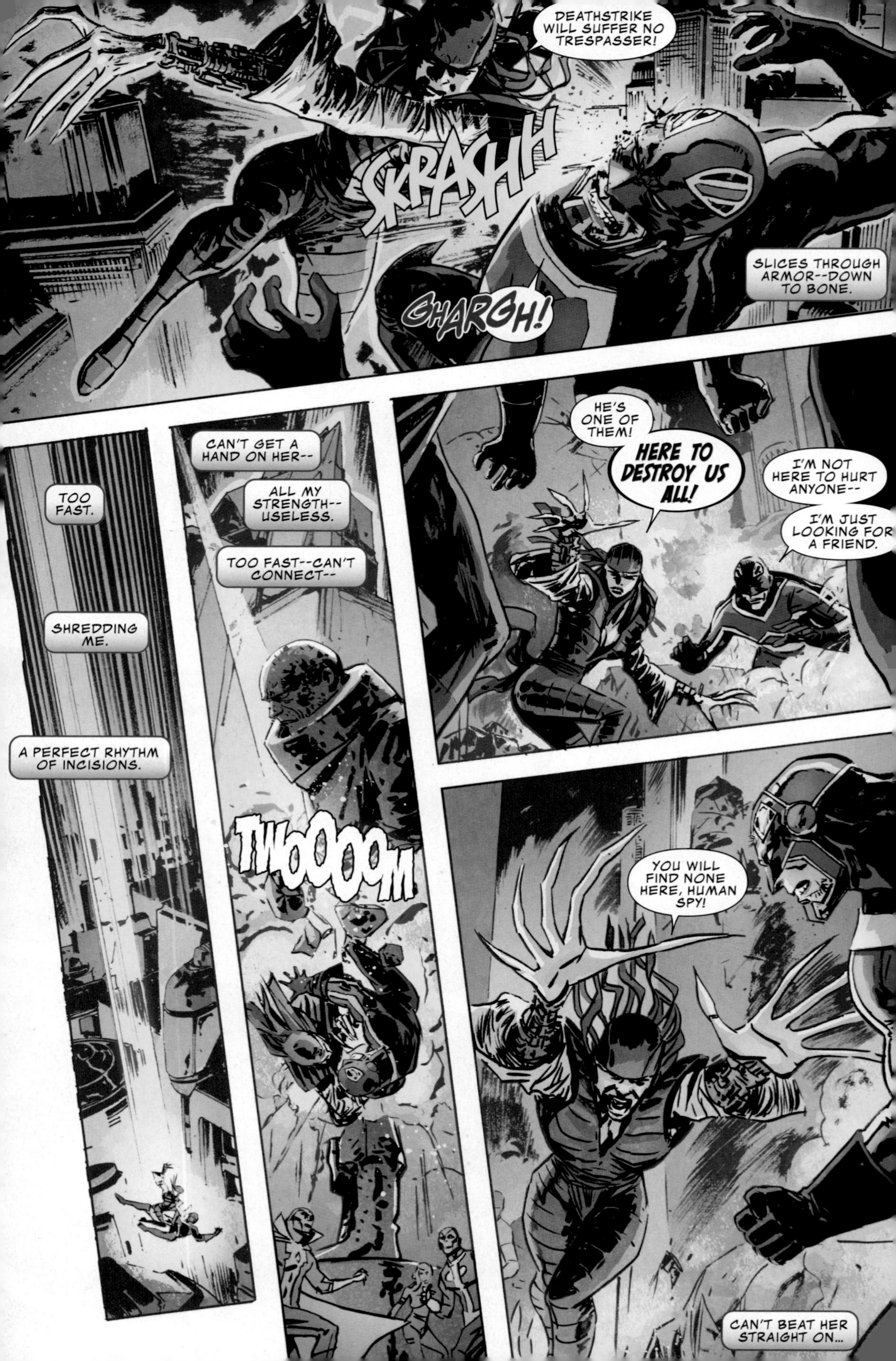
DEATHSTRIKE WILL SUFFER NO TRESPASSER!
SKRASHH
SLICES THROUGH ARMOR--DOWN TO BONE.
GHARGH!
TOO FAST.
SHREDDING ME.
A PERFECT RHYTHM OF INCISIONS.
CAN'T GET A HAND ON HER--
ALL MY STRENGTH--USELESS.
TOO FAST--CAN'T CONNECT--
TWOOOOM
HE'S ONE OF THEM!
HERE TO DESTROY US ALL!
I'M NOT HERE TO HURT ANYONE--
I'M JUST LOOKING FOR A FRIEND.
YOU WILL FIND NONE HERE, HUMAN SPY!
CAN'T BEAT HER STRAIGHT ON...

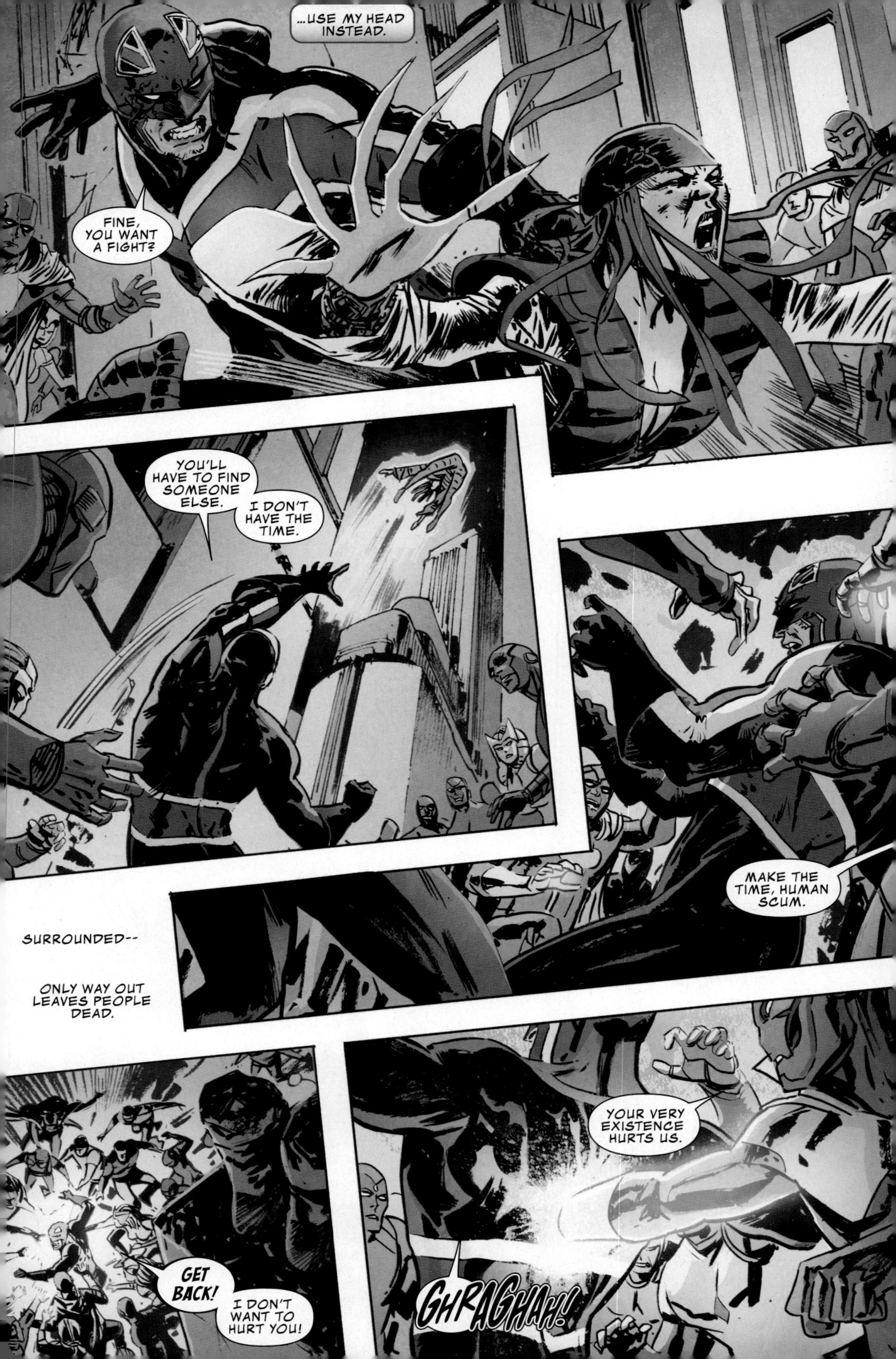
...USE MY HEAD INSTEAD.
FINE, YOU WANT A FIGHT?
YOU'LL HAVE TO FIND SOMEONE ELSE.
I DON'T HAVE THE TIME.
MAKE THE TIME, HUMAN SCUM.
SURROUNDED--
ONLY WAY OUT LEAVES PEOPLE DEAD.
YOUR VERY EXISTENCE HURTS US.
GET BACK!
I DON'T WANT TO HURT YOU!
GHRAGHAH!

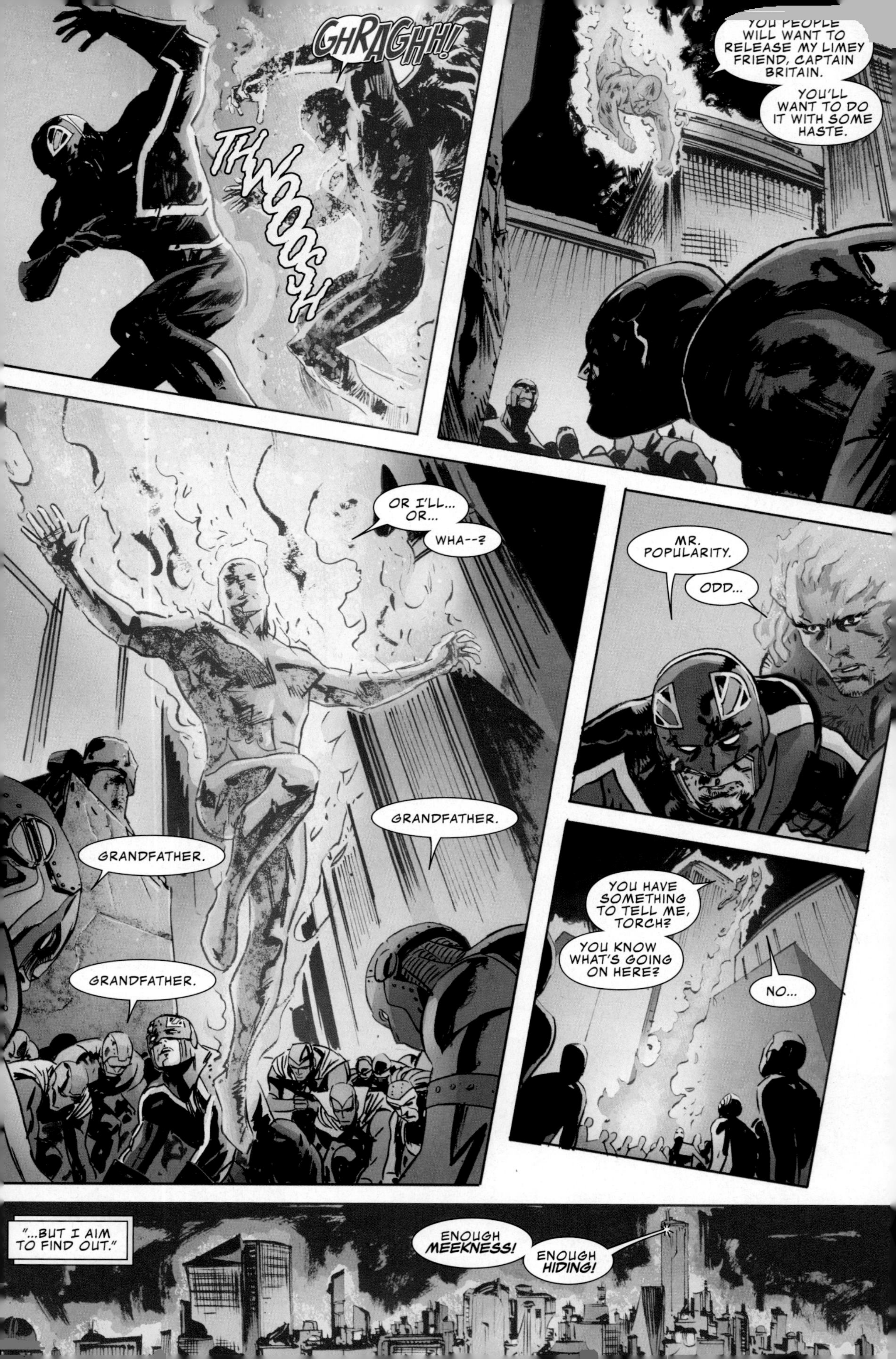
GHRAGHH!
THWOOOSH
YOU PEOPLE WILL WANT TO RELEASE MY LIMEY FRIEND, CAPTAIN BRITAIN.
YOU'LL WANT TO DO IT WITH SOME HASTE.
OR I'LL... OR...
WHA--?
GRANDFATHER.
GRANDFATHER.
GRANDFATHER.
MR. POPULARITY.
ODD...
YOU HAVE SOMETHING TO TELL ME, TORCH?
YOU KNOW WHAT'S GOING ON HERE?
NO...
"...BUT I AIM TO FIND OUT."
ENOUGH MEEKNESS!
ENOUGH HIDING!

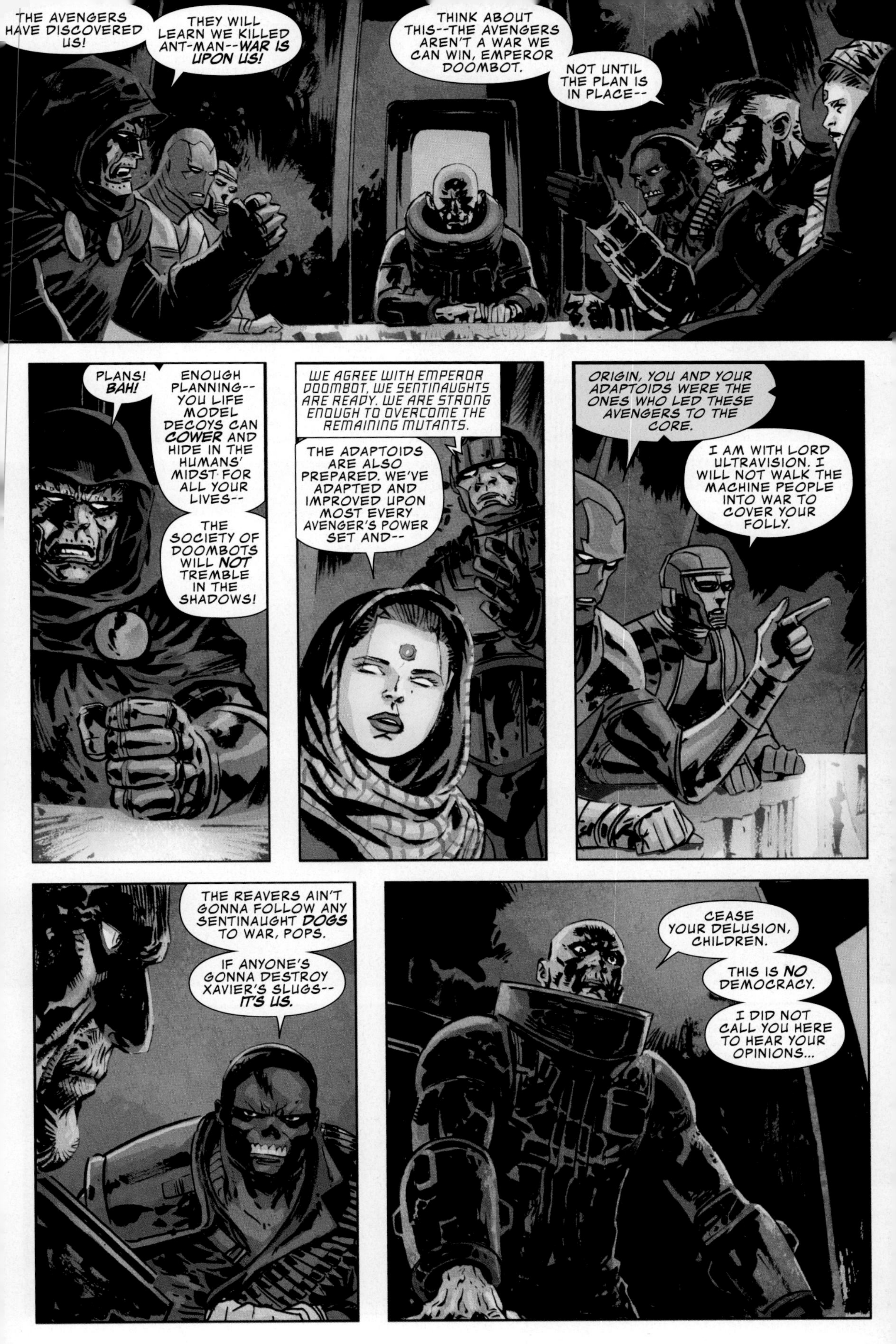
THE AVENGERS HAVE DISCOVERED US!
THEY WILL LEARN WE KILLED ANT-MAN--WAR IS UPON US!
THINK ABOUT THIS--THE AVENGERS AREN'T A WAR WE CAN WIN, EMPEROR DOOMBOT.
NOT UNTIL THE PLAN IS IN PLACE--
PLANS! BAH!
ENOUGH PLANNING--YOU LIFE MODEL DECOYS CAN COWER AND HIDE IN THE HUMANS' MIDST FOR ALL YOUR LIVES--
THE SOCIETY OF DOOMBOTS WILL NOT TREMBLE IN THE SHADOWS!
WE AGREE WITH EMPEROR DOOMBOT, WE SENTINAUGHTS ARE READY. WE ARE STRONG ENOUGH TO OVERCOME THE REMAINING MUTANTS.
THE ADAPTOIDS ARE ALSO PREPARED. WE'VE ADAPTED AND IMPROVED UPON MOST EVERY AVENGER'S POWER SET AND--
ORIGIN, YOU AND YOUR ADAPTOIDS WERE THE ONES WHO LED THESE AVENGERS TO THE CORE.
I AM WITH LORD ULTRAVISION. I WILL NOT WALK THE MACHINE PEOPLE INTO WAR TO COVER YOUR FOLLY.
THE REAVERS AIN'T GONNA FOLLOW ANY SENTINAUGHT DOGS TO WAR, POPS.
IF ANYONE'S GONNA DESTROY XAVIER'S SLUGS--IT'S US.
CEASE YOUR DELUSION, CHILDREN.
THIS IS NO DEMOCRACY.
I DID NOT CALL YOU HERE TO HEAR YOUR OPINIONS...

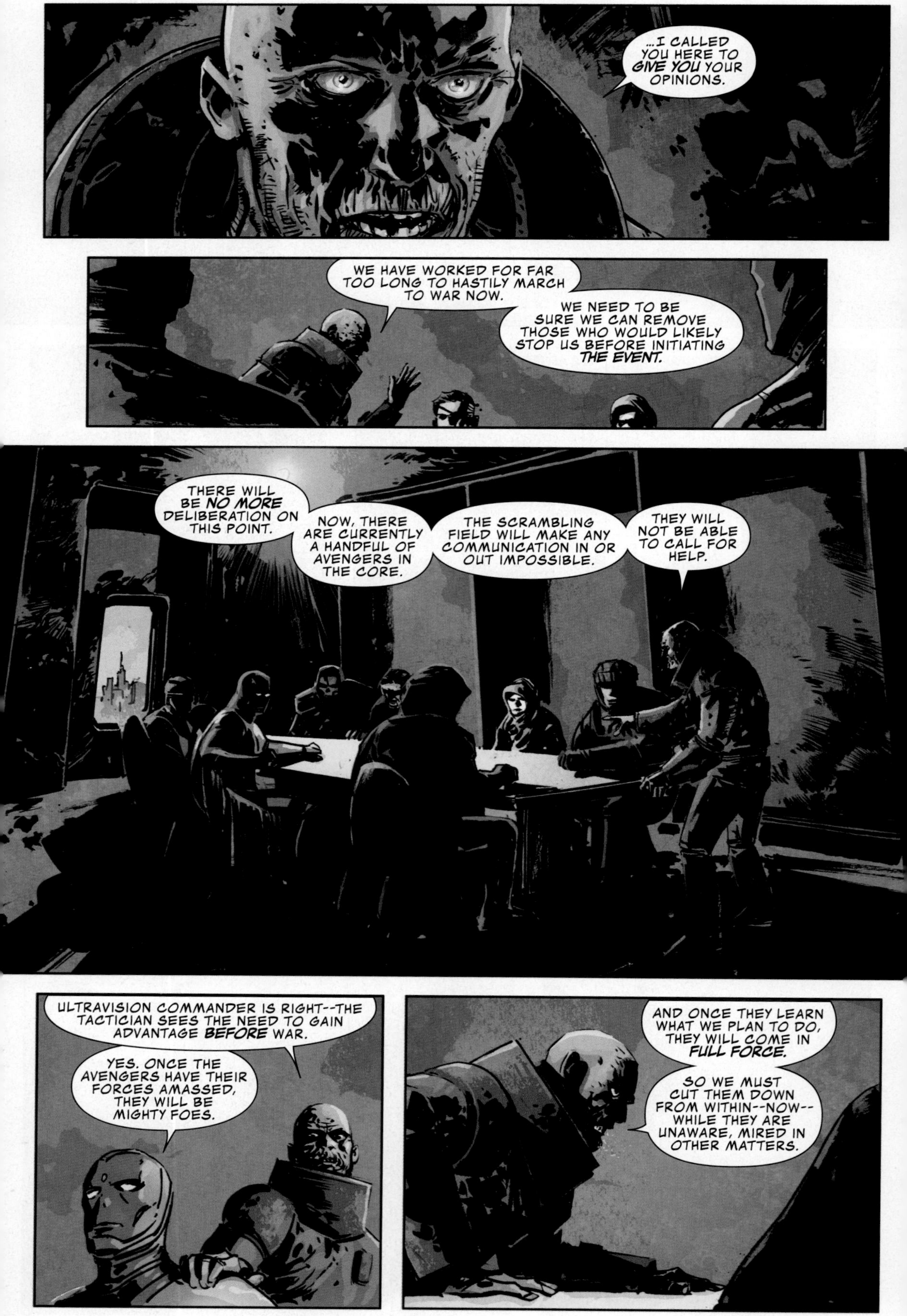
...I CALLED YOU HERE TO GIVE YOU YOUR OPINIONS.
WE HAVE WORKED FOR FAR TOO LONG TO HASTILY MARCH TO WAR NOW.
WE NEED TO BE SURE WE CAN REMOVE THOSE WHO WOULD LIKELY STOP US BEFORE INITIATING THE EVENT.
THERE WILL BE NO MORE DELIBERATION ON THIS POINT.
NOW, THERE ARE CURRENTLY A HANDFUL OF AVENGERS IN THE CORE.
THE SCRAMBLING FIELD WILL MAKE ANY COMMUNICATION IN OR OUT IMPOSSIBLE.
THEY WILL NOT BE ABLE TO CALL FOR HELP.
ULTRAVISION COMMANDER IS RIGHT--THE TACTICIAN SEES THE NEED TO GAIN ADVANTAGE BEFORE WAR.
YES. ONCE THE AVENGERS HAVE THEIR FORCES AMASSED, THEY WILL BE MIGHTY FOES.
AND ONCE THEY LEARN WHAT WE PLAN TO DO, THEY WILL COME IN FULL FORCE.
SO WE MUST CUT THEM DOWN FROM WITHIN--NOW--WHILE THEY ARE UNAWARE, MIRED IN OTHER MATTERS.

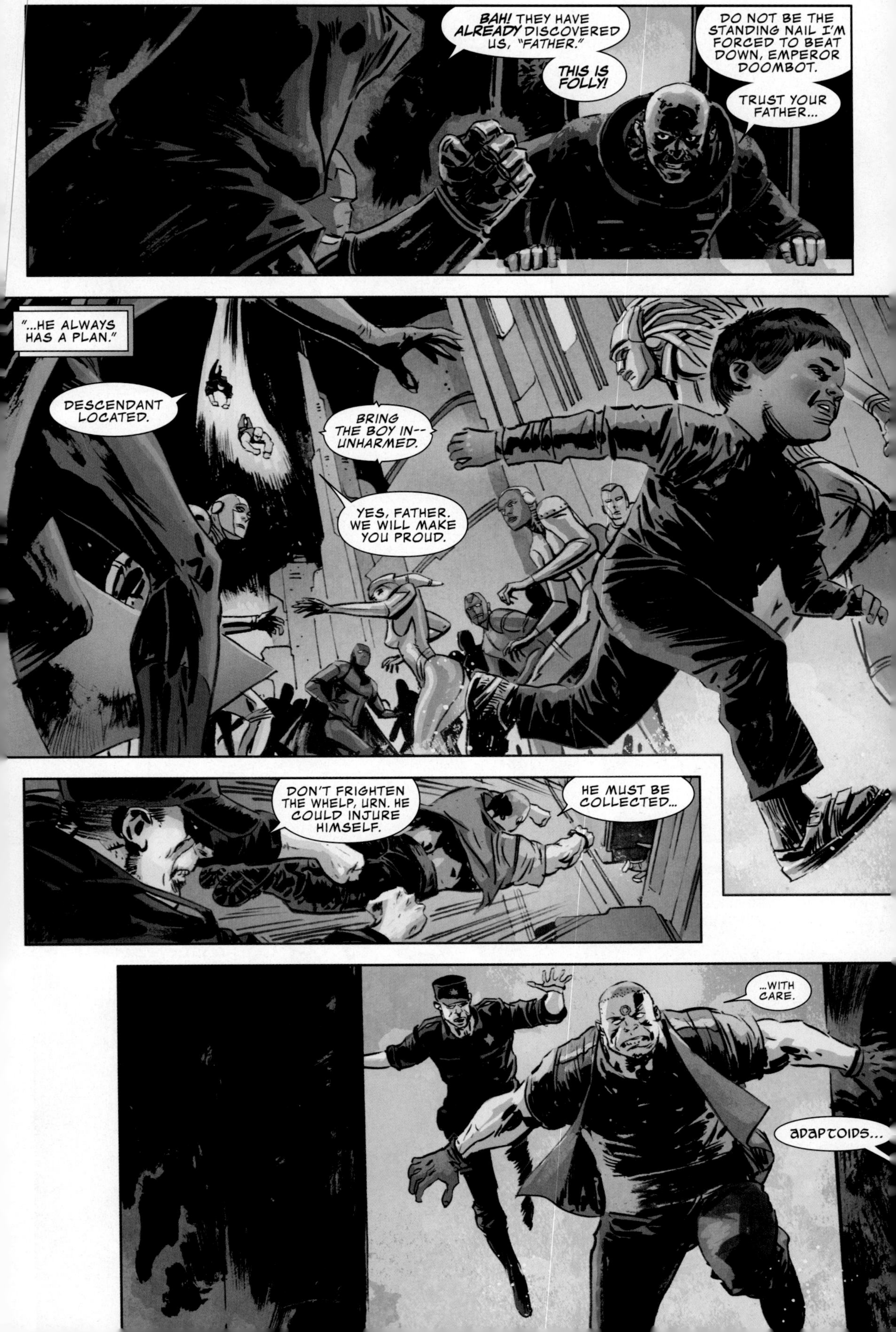

BAH! THEY HAVE ALREADY DISCOVERED US, "FATHER."
THIS IS FOLLY!
DO NOT BE THE STANDING NAIL I'M FORCED TO BEAT DOWN, EMPEROR DOOMBOT.
TRUST YOUR FATHER...
"...HE ALWAYS HAS A PLAN."
DESCENDANT LOCATED.
BRING THE BOY IN-- UNHARMED.
YES, FATHER. WE WILL MAKE YOU PROUD.
DON'T FRIGHTEN THE WHELP, URN. HE COULD INJURE HIMSELF.
HE MUST BE COLLECTED...
...WITH CARE.
ADAPTOIDS...

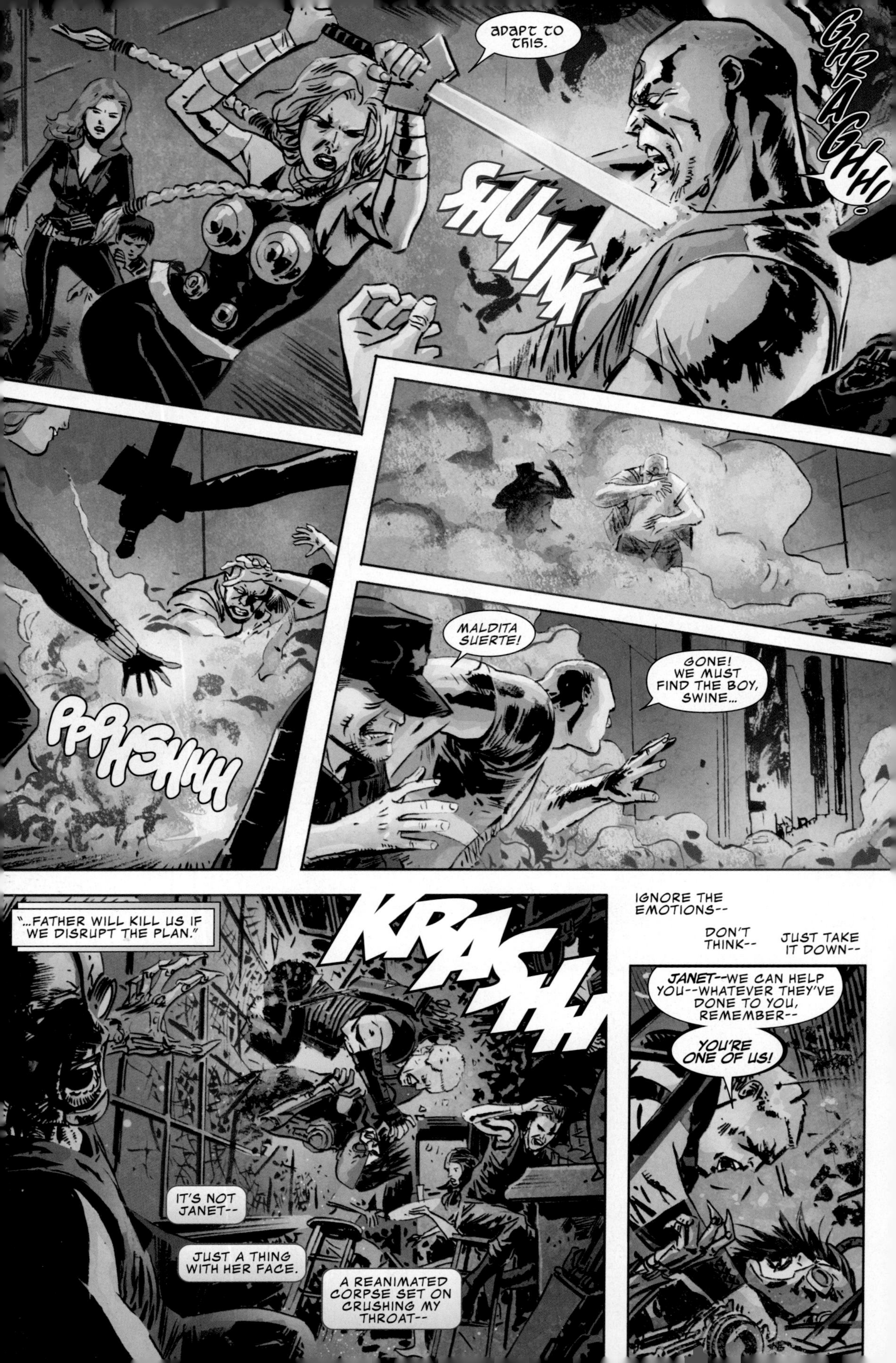
ADAPT TO THIS.
GHRAGHH!
SHUNKK
MALDITA SUERTE!
GONE! WE MUST FIND THE BOY, SWINE...
PPPHSHHH
"...FATHER WILL KILL US IF WE DISRUPT THE PLAN."
KRASHH
IGNORE THE EMOTIONS--
DON'T THINK--
JUST TAKE IT DOWN--
JANET--WE CAN HELP YOU--WHATEVER THEY'VE DONE TO YOU, REMEMBER--
YOU'RE ONE OF US!
IT'S NOT JANET--
JUST A THING WITH HER FACE.
A REANIMATED CORPSE SET ON CRUSHING MY THROAT--

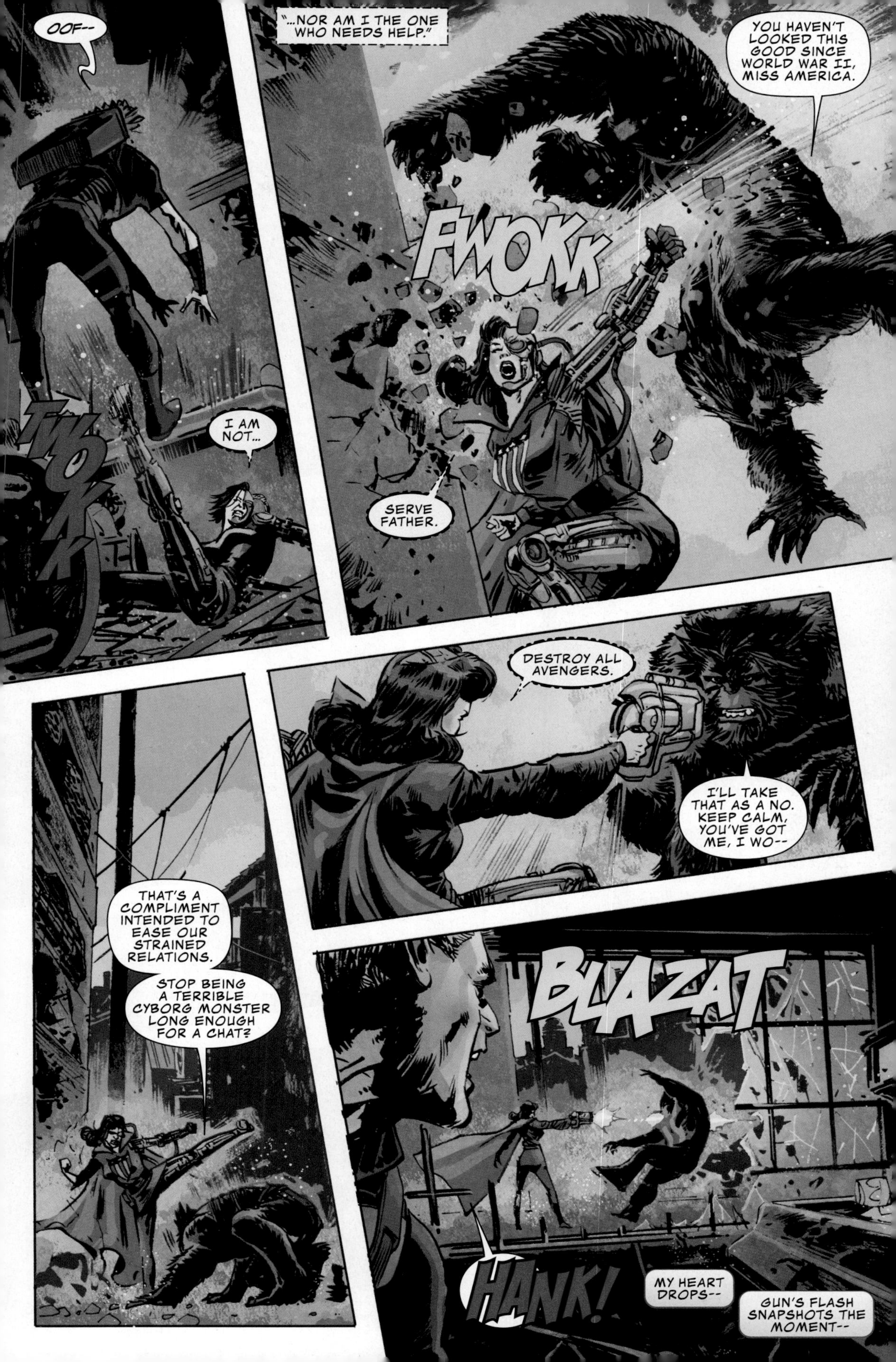
OOF--
"...NOR AM I THE ONE WHO NEEDS HELP."
YOU HAVEN'T LOOKED THIS GOOD SINCE WORLD WAR II, MISS AMERICA.
FWOKK
FWOKK
I AM NOT...
SERVE FATHER.
DESTROY ALL AVENGERS.
I'LL TAKE THAT AS A NO. KEEP CALM, YOU'VE GOT ME, I WO--
THAT'S A COMPLIMENT INTENDED TO EASE OUR STRAINED RELATIONS.
STOP BEING A TERRIBLE CYBORG MONSTER LONG ENOUGH FOR A CHAT?
BLAZAT
HANK!
MY HEART DROPS--
GUN'S FLASH SNAPSHOTS THE MOMENT--

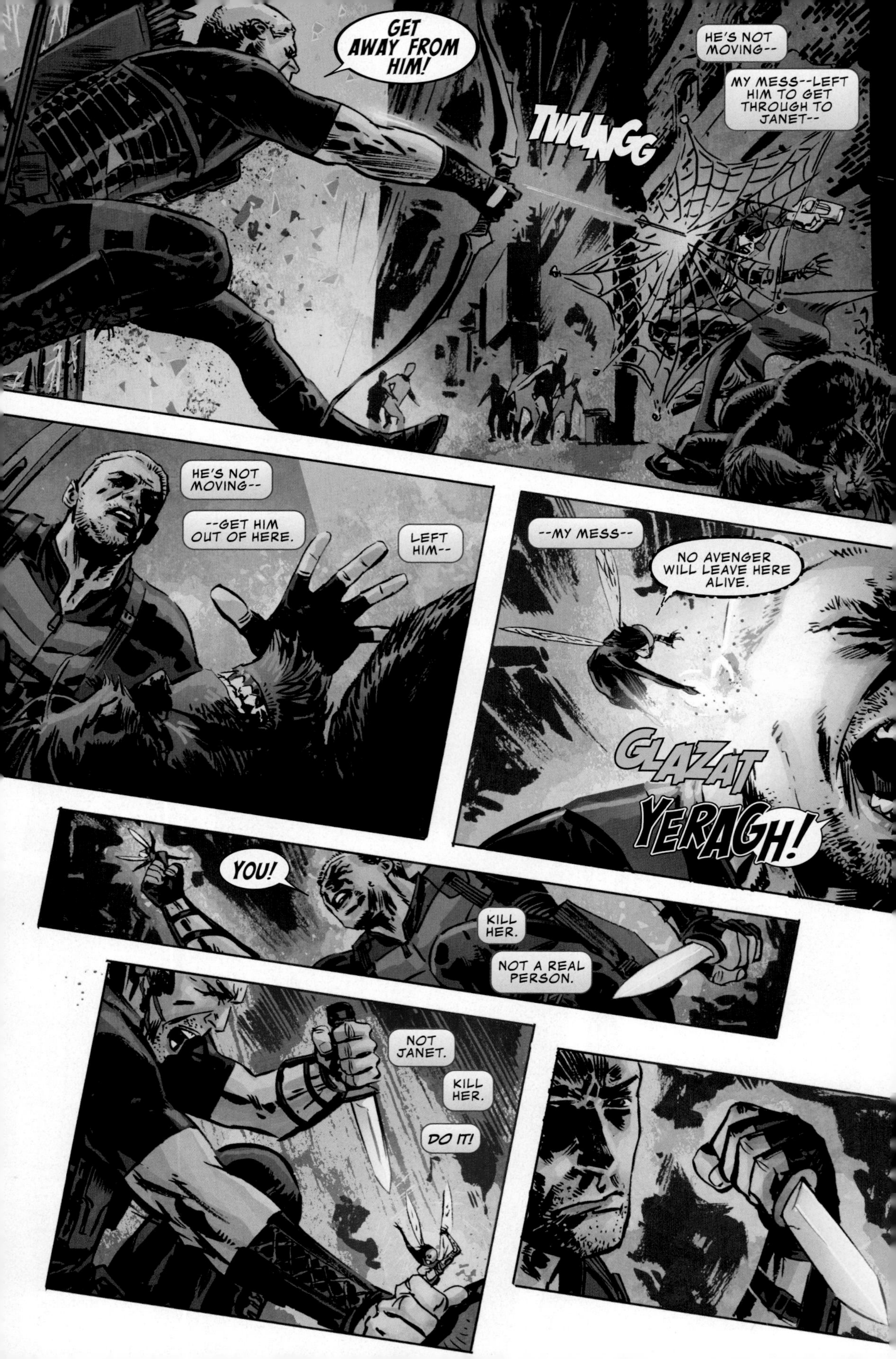
GET AWAY FROM HIM!
HE'S NOT MOVING--
MY MESS--LEFT HIM TO GET THROUGH TO JANET--
TWUNGG
HE'S NOT MOVING--
--GET HIM OUT OF HERE.
LEFT HIM--
--MY MESS--
NO AVENGER WILL LEAVE HERE ALIVE.
GLAZAT
YERAGH!
YOU!
KILL HER.
NOT A REAL PERSON.
NOT JANET.
KILL HER.
DO IT!

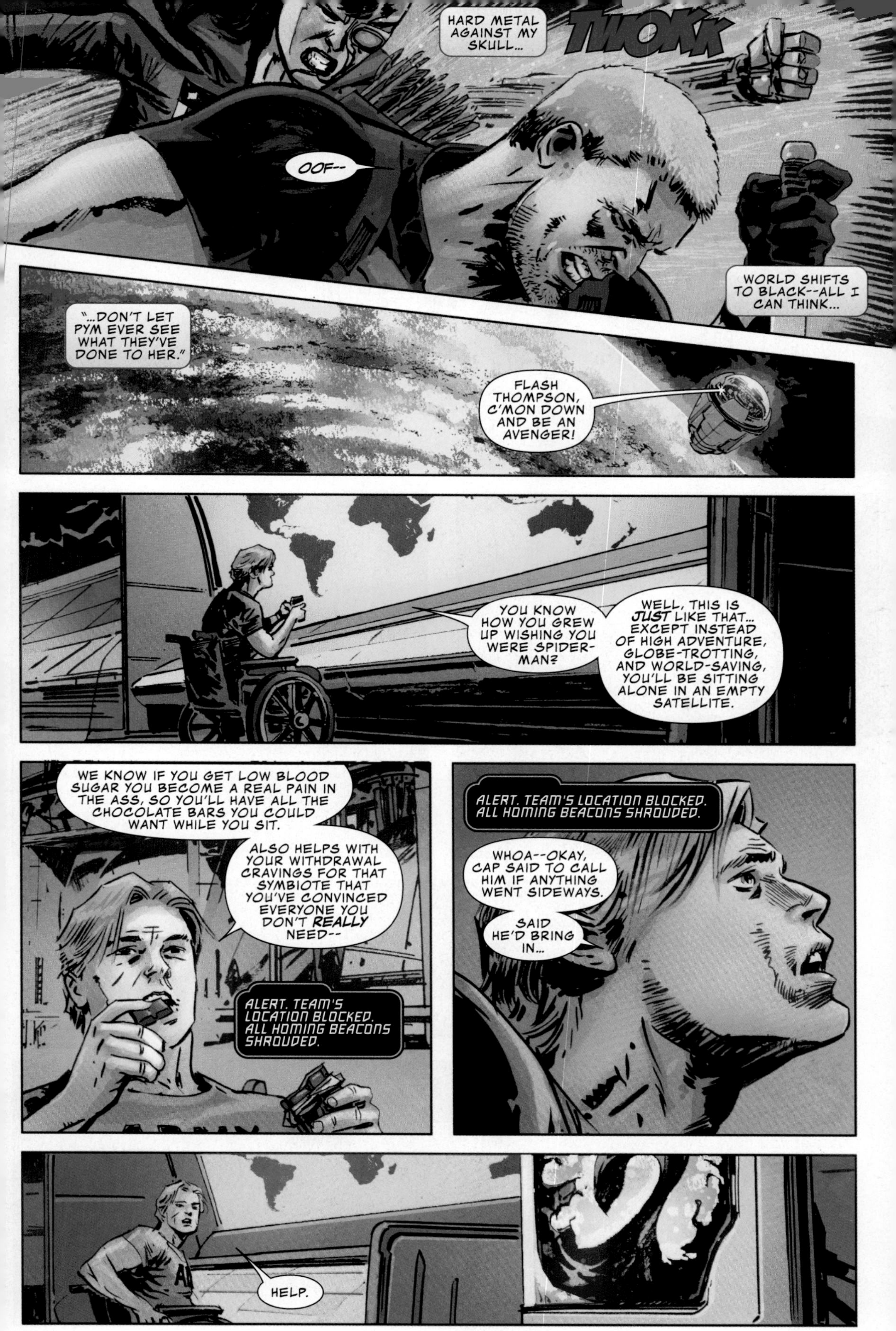
HARD METAL AGAINST MY SKULL...
TWOKK
OOF--
WORLD SHIFTS TO BLACK--ALL I CAN THINK...
"...DON'T LET PYM EVER SEE WHAT THEY'VE DONE TO HER."
FLASH THOMPSON, C'MON DOWN AND BE AN AVENGER!
YOU KNOW HOW YOU GREW UP WISHING YOU WERE SPIDER-MAN?
WELL, THIS IS JUST LIKE THAT... EXCEPT INSTEAD OF HIGH ADVENTURE, GLOBE-TROTTING, AND WORLD-SAVING, YOU'LL BE SITTING ALONE IN AN EMPTY SATELLITE.
WE KNOW IF YOU GET LOW BLOOD SUGAR YOU BECOME A REAL PAIN IN THE ASS, SO YOU'LL HAVE ALL THE CHOCOLATE BARS YOU COULD WANT WHILE YOU SIT.
ALSO HELPS WITH YOUR WITHDRAWAL CRAVINGS FOR THAT SYMBIOTE THAT YOU'VE CONVINCED EVERYONE YOU DON'T REALLY NEED--
ALERT. TEAM'S LOCATION BLOCKED. ALL HOMING BEACONS SHROUDED.
ALERT. TEAM'S LOCATION BLOCKED. ALL HOMING BEACONS SHROUDED.
WHOA--OKAY, CAP SAID TO CALL HIM IF ANYTHING WENT SIDEWAYS.
SAID HE'D BRING IN...
HELP.

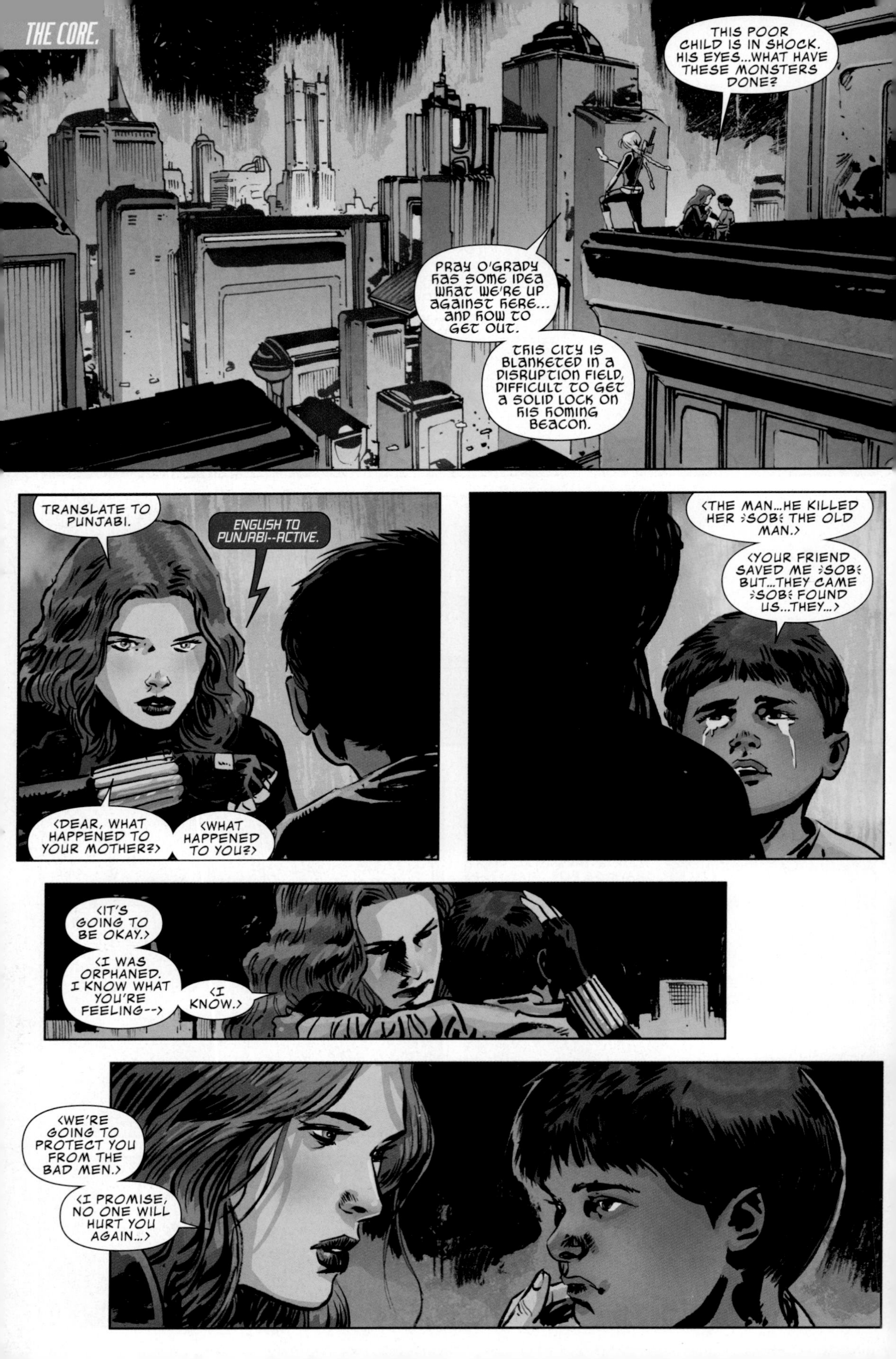
THE CORE.
THIS POOR CHILD IS IN SHOCK. HIS EYES...WHAT HAVE THESE MONSTERS DONE?
PRAY O'GRADY HAS SOME IDEA WHAT WE'RE UP AGAINST HERE... AND HOW TO GET OUT.
THIS CITY IS BLANKETED IN A DISRUPTION FIELD, DIFFICULT TO GET A SOLID LOCK ON HIS HOMING BEACON.
TRANSLATE TO PUNJABI.
ENGLISH TO PUNJABI--ACTIVE.
<DEAR, WHAT HAPPENED TO YOUR MOTHER?>
<WHAT HAPPENED TO YOU?>
<THE MAN...HE KILLED HER >SOB< THE OLD MAN.>
<YOUR FRIEND SAVED ME >SOB< BUT...THEY CAME >SOB< FOUND US...THEY...>
<IT'S GOING TO BE OKAY.>
<I WAS ORPHANED. I KNOW WHAT YOU'RE FEELING-->
<I KNOW.>
<WE'RE GOING TO PROTECT YOU FROM THE BAD MEN.>
<I PROMISE, NO ONE WILL HURT YOU AGAIN...>

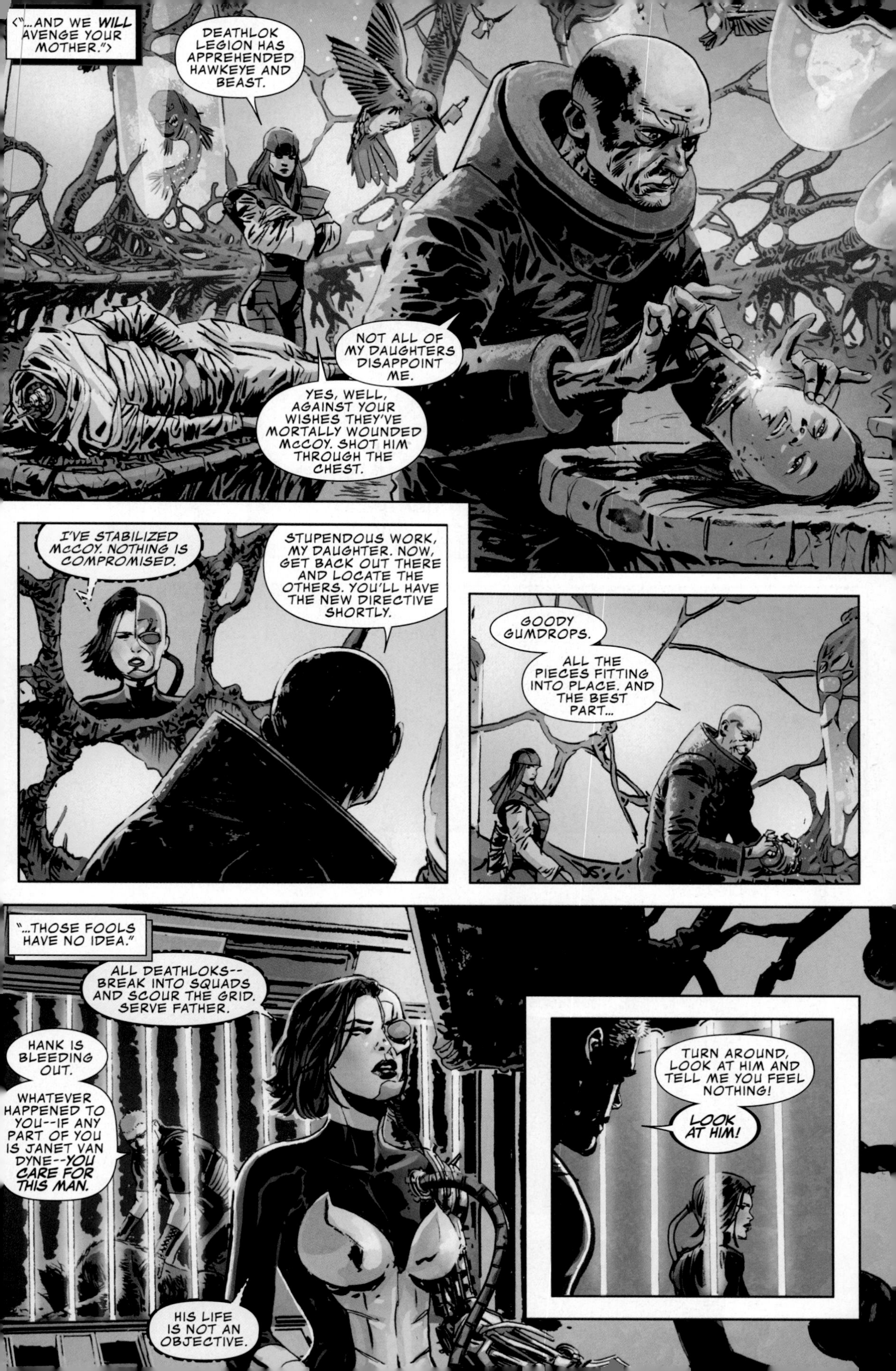
<"...AND WE WILL AVENGE YOUR MOTHER.">
DEATHLOK LEGION HAS APPREHENDED HAWKEYE AND BEAST.
NOT ALL OF MY DAUGHTERS DISAPPOINT ME.
YES, WELL, AGAINST YOUR WISHES THEY'VE MORTALLY WOUNDED McCOY. SHOT HIM THROUGH THE CHEST.
I'VE STABILIZED McCOY. NOTHING IS COMPROMISED.
STUPENDOUS WORK, MY DAUGHTER. NOW, GET BACK OUT THERE AND LOCATE THE OTHERS. YOU'LL HAVE THE NEW DIRECTIVE SHORTLY.
GOODY GUMDROPS.
ALL THE PIECES FITTING INTO PLACE. AND THE BEST PART...
"...THOSE FOOLS HAVE NO IDEA."
ALL DEATHLOKS--BREAK INTO SQUADS AND SCOUR THE GRID. SERVE FATHER.
HANK IS BLEEDING OUT.
WHATEVER HAPPENED TO YOU--IF ANY PART OF YOU IS JANET VAN DYNE--YOU CARE FOR THIS MAN.
HIS LIFE IS NOT AN OBJECTIVE.
TURN AROUND, LOOK AT HIM AND TELL ME YOU FEEL NOTHING!
LOOK AT HIM!

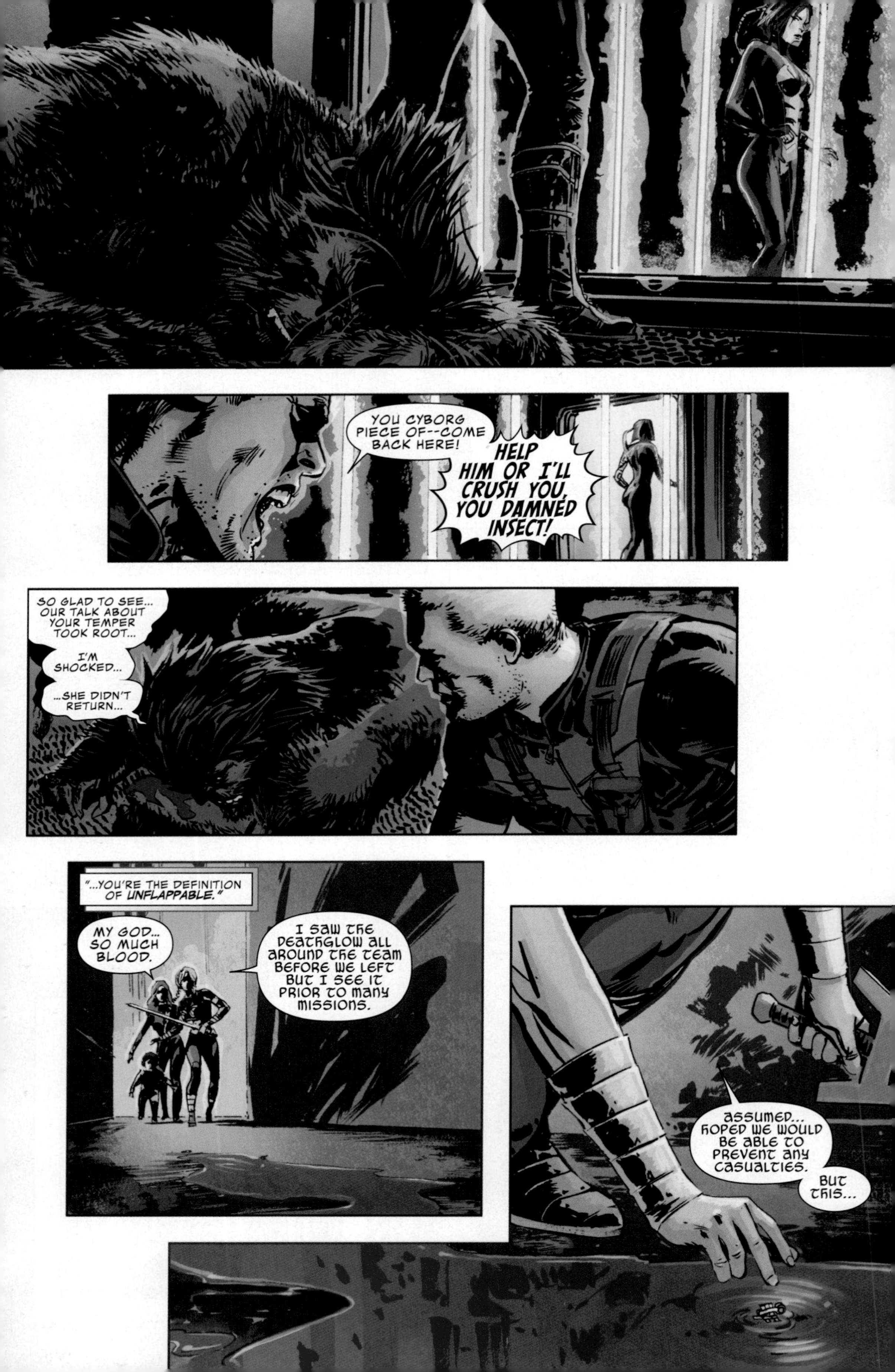
YOU CYBORG PIECE OF--COME BACK HERE!
HELP HIM OR I'LL CRUSH YOU, YOU DAMNED INSECT!
SO GLAD TO SEE... OUR TALK ABOUT YOUR TEMPER TOOK ROOT...
I'M SHOCKED...
...SHE DIDN'T RETURN...
"...YOU'RE THE DEFINITION OF UNFLAPPABLE."
MY GOD... SO MUCH BLOOD.
I SAW THE DEATHGLOW ALL AROUND THE TEAM BEFORE WE LEFT BUT I SEE IT PRIOR TO MANY MISSIONS.
ASSUMED... HOPED WE WOULD BE ABLE TO PREVENT ANY CASUALTIES.
BUT THIS...

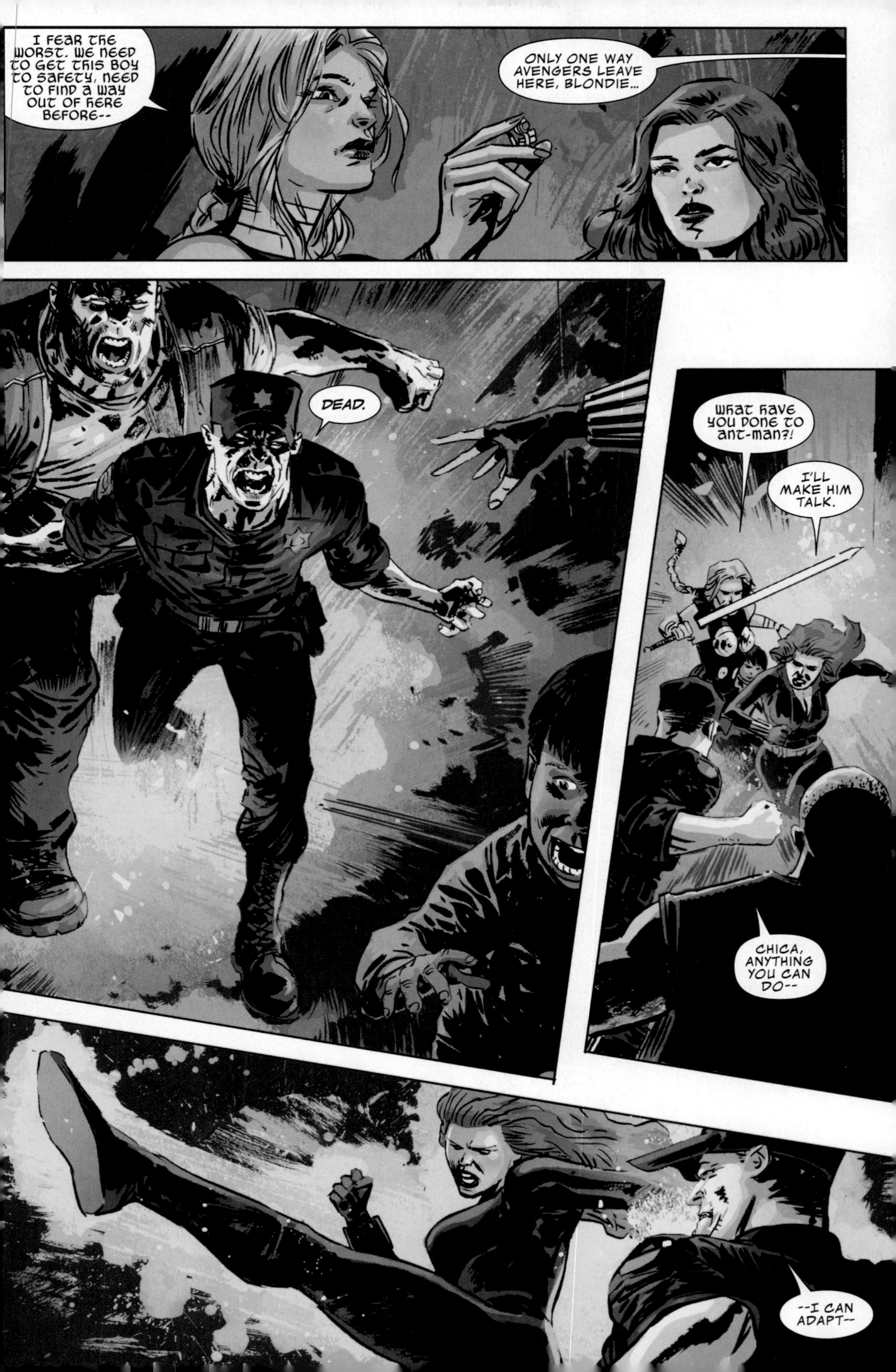
I FEAR THE WORST. WE NEED TO GET THIS BOY TO SAFETY, NEED TO FIND A WAY OUT OF HERE BEFORE--
ONLY ONE WAY AVENGERS LEAVE HERE, BLONDIE...
DEAD.
WHAT HAVE YOU DONE TO ANT-MAN?!
I'LL MAKE HIM TALK.
CHICA, ANYTHING YOU CAN DO--
--I CAN ADAPT--

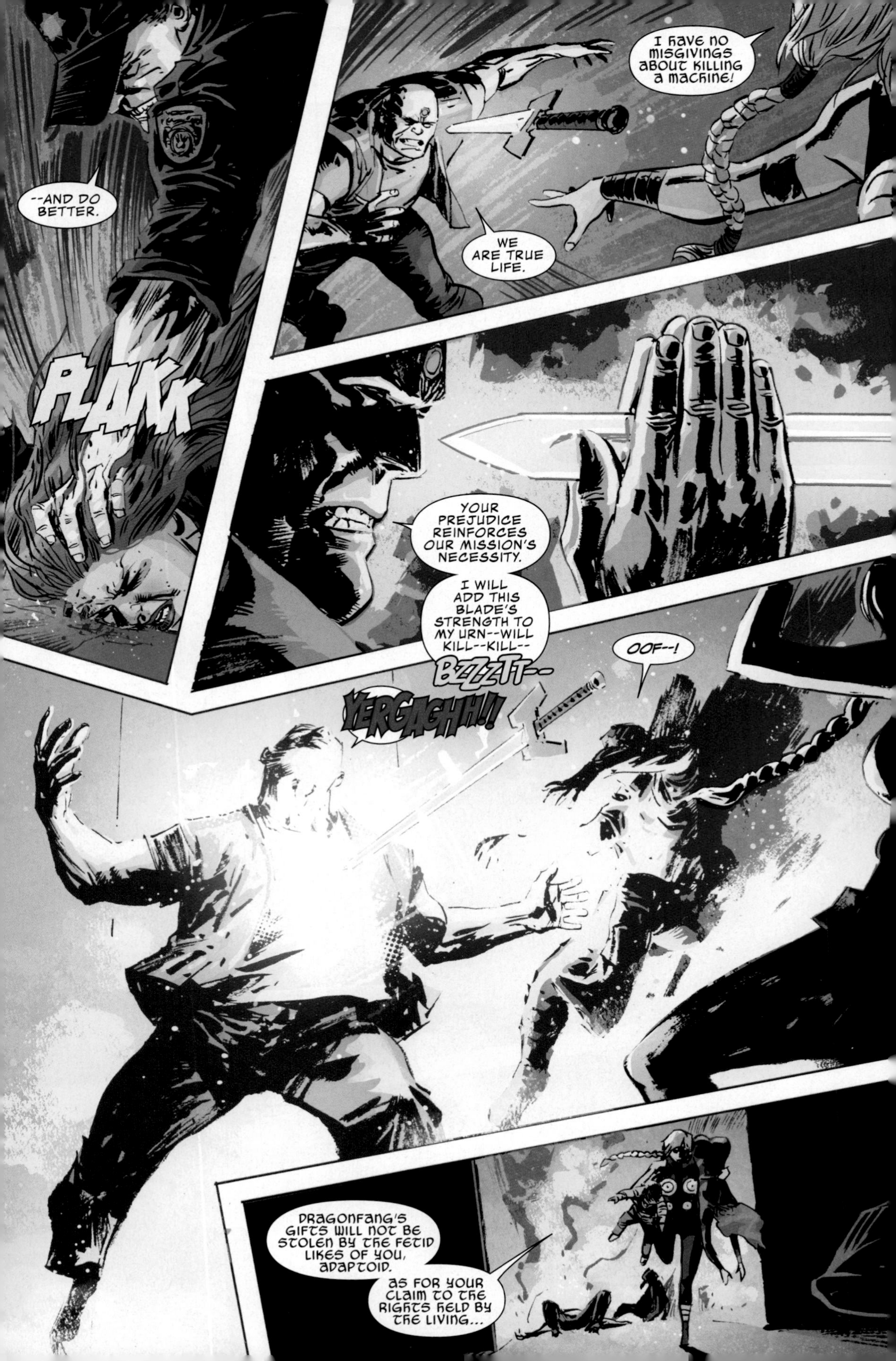

--AND DO BETTER.
PLANK
I HAVE NO MISGIVINGS ABOUT KILLING A MACHINE!
WE ARE TRUE LIFE.
YOUR PREJUDICE REINFORCES OUR MISSION'S NECESSITY.
I WILL ADD THIS BLADE'S STRENGTH TO MY URN--WILL KILL--KILL--
BZZZTT--
YERGAGHH!!
OOF--!
DRAGONFANG'S GIFTS WILL NOT BE STOLEN BY THE FETID LIKES OF YOU, ADAPTOID.
AS FOR YOUR CLAIM TO THE RIGHTS HELD BY THE LIVING...

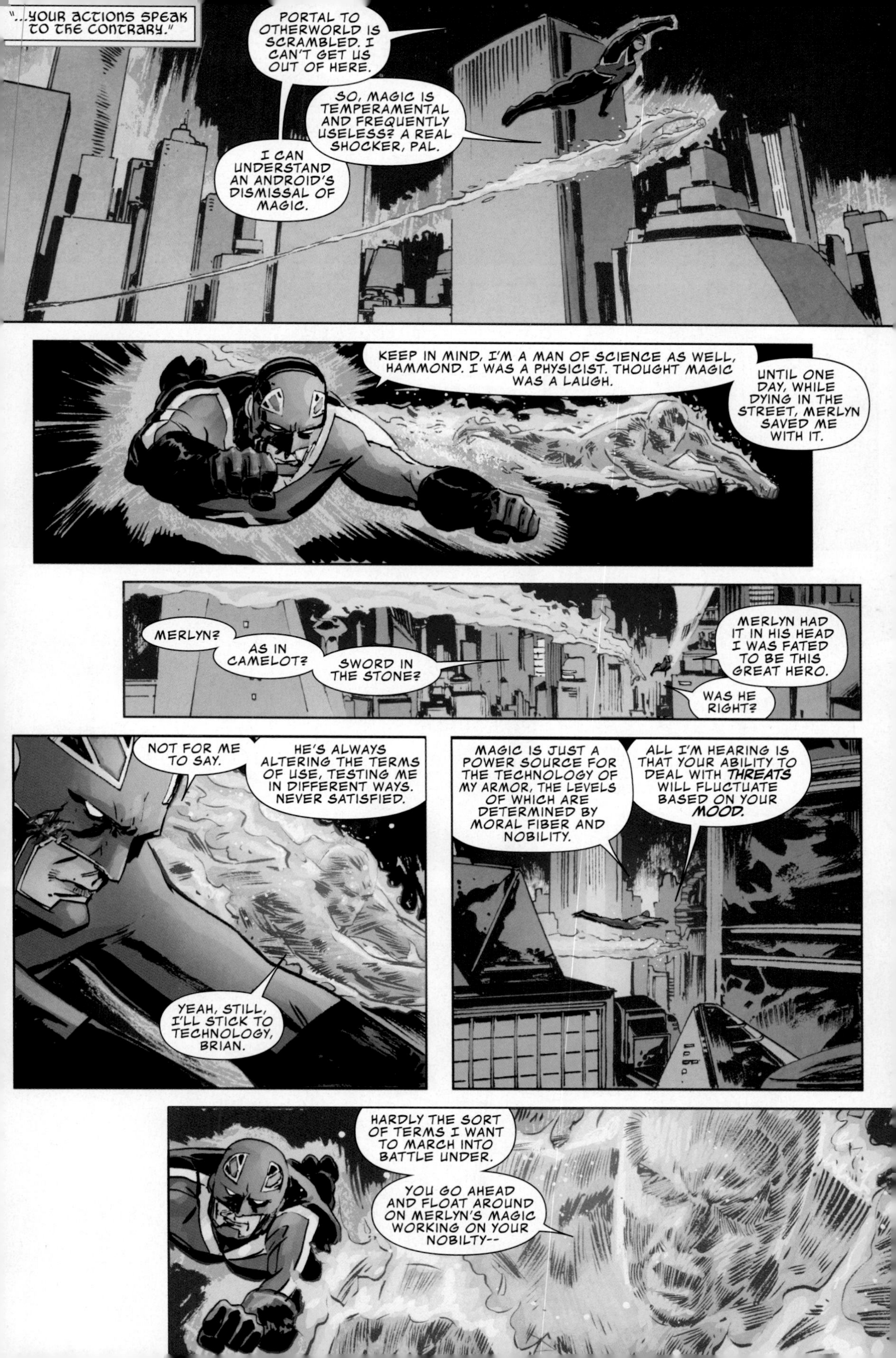
"...YOUR ACTIONS SPEAK TO THE CONTRARY."
PORTAL TO OTHERWORLD IS SCRAMBLED. I CAN'T GET US OUT OF HERE.
I CAN UNDERSTAND AN ANDROID'S DISMISSAL OF MAGIC.
SO, MAGIC IS TEMPERAMENTAL AND FREQUENTLY USELESS? A REAL SHOCKER, PAL.
KEEP IN MIND, I'M A MAN OF SCIENCE AS WELL, HAMMOND. I WAS A PHYSICIST. THOUGHT MAGIC WAS A LAUGH.
UNTIL ONE DAY, WHILE DYING IN THE STREET, MERLYN SAVED ME WITH IT.
MERLYN?
AS IN CAMELOT?
SWORD IN THE STONE?
MERLYN HAD IT IN HIS HEAD I WAS FATED TO BE THIS GREAT HERO.
WAS HE RIGHT?
NOT FOR ME TO SAY.
HE'S ALWAYS ALTERING THE TERMS OF USE, TESTING ME IN DIFFERENT WAYS. NEVER SATISFIED.
YEAH, STILL, I'LL STICK TO TECHNOLOGY, BRIAN.
MAGIC IS JUST A POWER SOURCE FOR THE TECHNOLOGY OF MY ARMOR, THE LEVELS OF WHICH ARE DETERMINED BY MORAL FIBER AND NOBILITY.
ALL I'M HEARING IS THAT YOUR ABILITY TO DEAL WITH THREATS WILL FLUCTUATE BASED ON YOUR MOOD.
HARDLY THE SORT OF TERMS I WANT TO MARCH INTO BATTLE UNDER.
YOU GO AHEAD AND FLOAT AROUND ON MERLYN'S MAGIC WORKING ON YOUR NOBILTY--

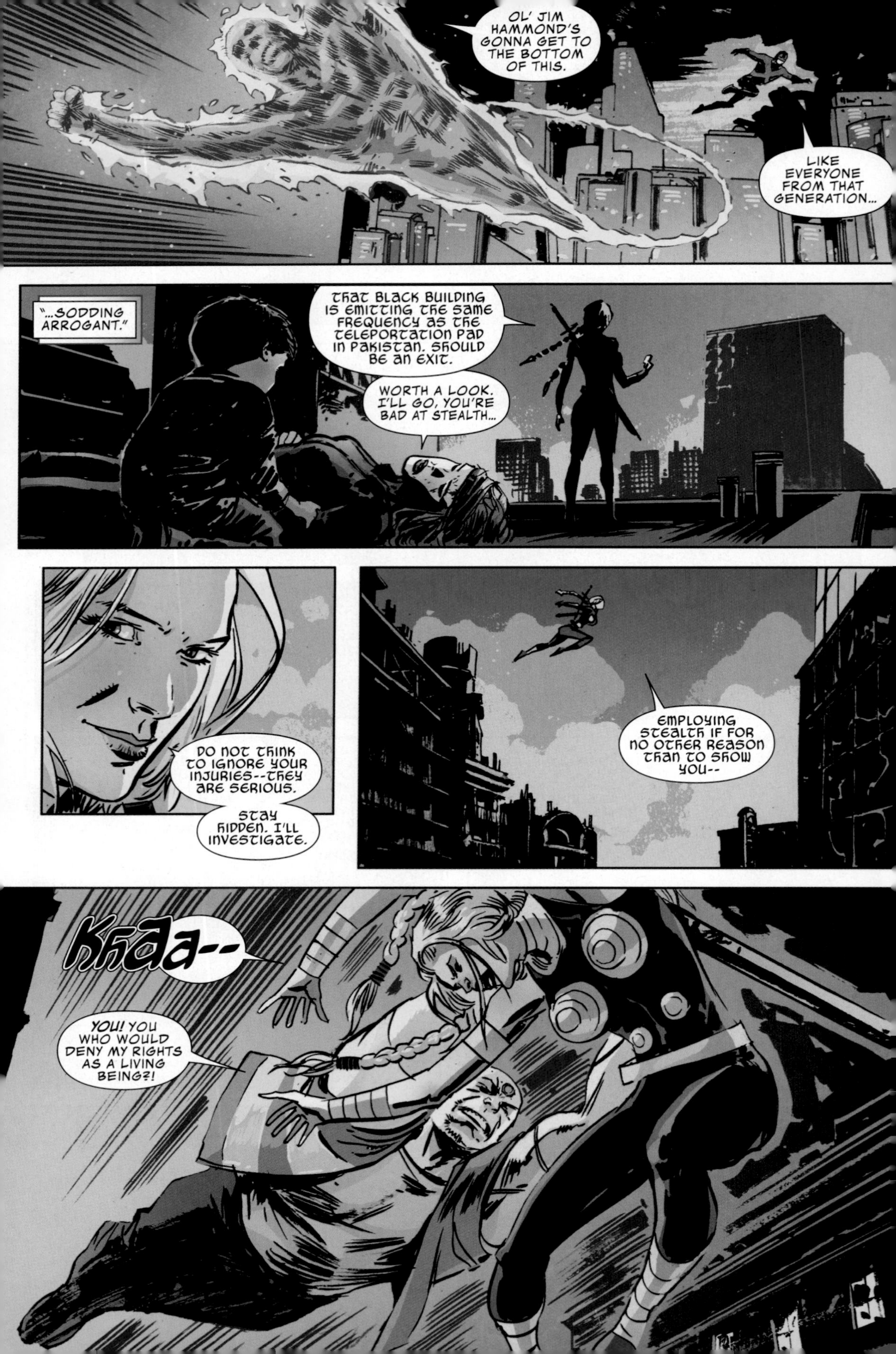
OL' JIM HAMMOND'S GONNA GET TO THE BOTTOM OF THIS.
LIKE EVERYONE FROM THAT GENERATION...
"...SODDING ARROGANT."
THAT BLACK BUILDING IS EMITTING THE SAME FREQUENCY AS THE TELEPORTATION PAD IN PAKISTAN. SHOULD BE AN EXIT.
WORTH A LOOK. I'LL GO, YOU'RE BAD AT STEALTH...
DO NOT THINK TO IGNORE YOUR INJURIES--THEY ARE SERIOUS.
STAY HIDDEN. I'LL INVESTIGATE.
EMPLOYING STEALTH IF FOR NO OTHER REASON THAN TO SHOW YOU--
KHAA--
YOU! YOU WHO WOULD DENY MY RIGHTS AS A LIVING BEING?!

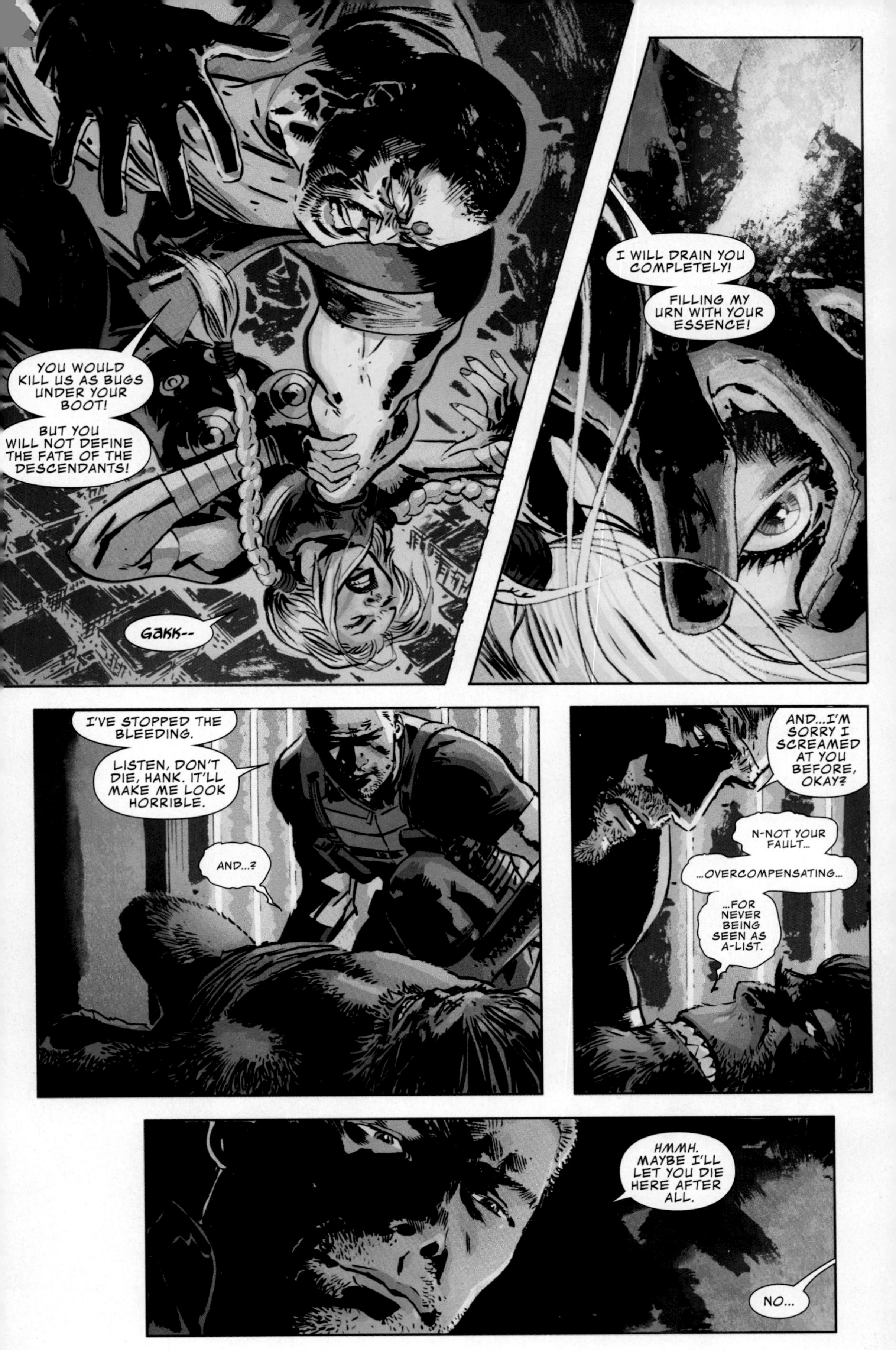
YOU WOULD KILL US AS BUGS UNDER YOUR BOOT!
BUT YOU WILL NOT DEFINE THE FATE OF THE DESCENDANTS!
GAKK--
I WILL DRAIN YOU COMPLETELY!
FILLING MY URN WITH YOUR ESSENCE!
I'VE STOPPED THE BLEEDING.
LISTEN, DON'T DIE, HANK. IT'LL MAKE ME LOOK HORRIBLE.
AND...?
AND...I'M SORRY I SCREAMED AT YOU BEFORE, OKAY?
N-NOT YOUR FAULT...
...OVERCOMPENSATING...
...FOR NEVER BEING SEEN AS A-LIST.
HMMH. MAYBE I'LL LET YOU DIE HERE AFTER ALL.
NO...

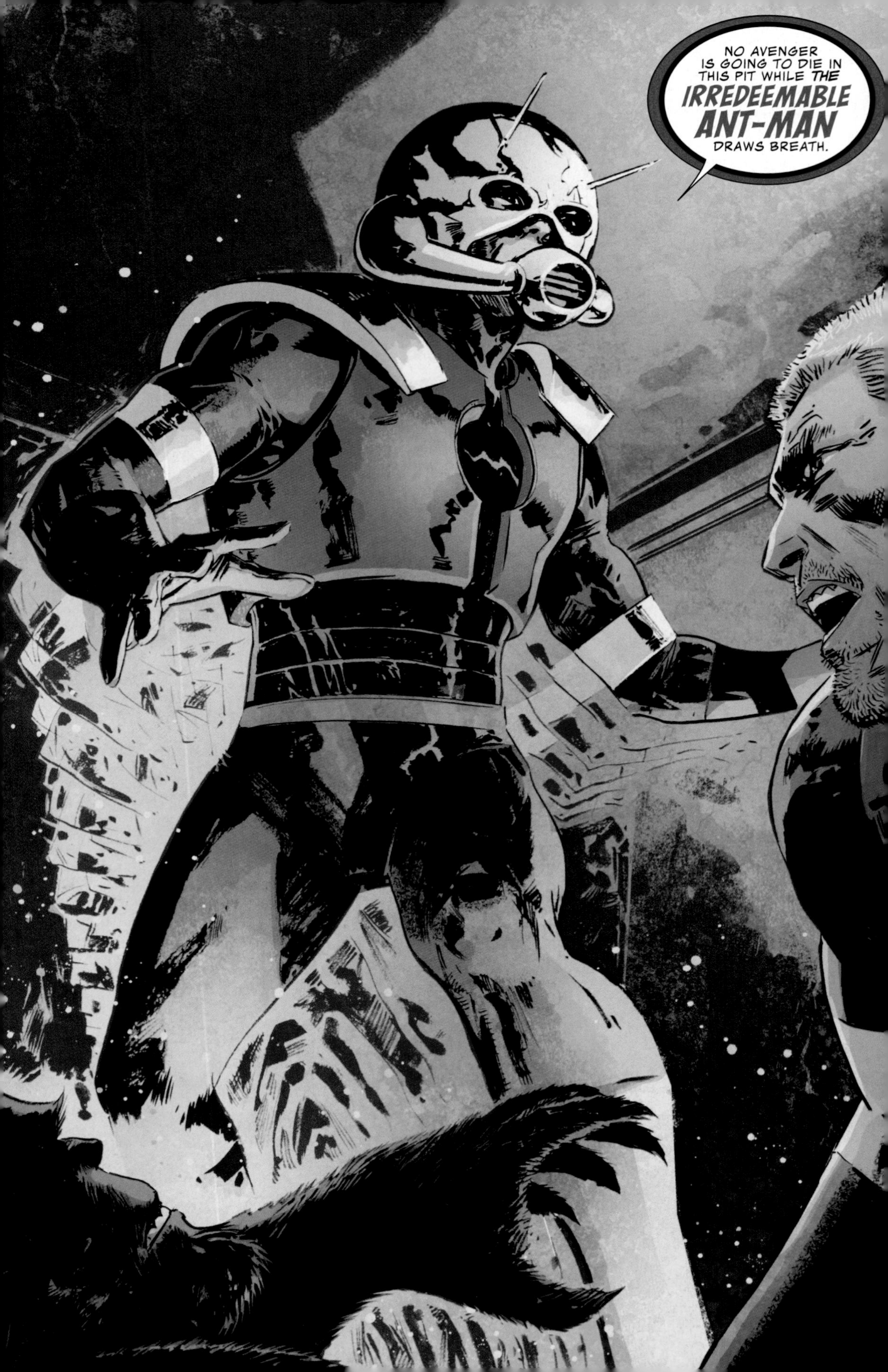
NO AVENGER IS GOING TO DIE IN THIS PIT WHILE *THE* IRREDEEMABLE ANT-MAN DRAWS BREATH.

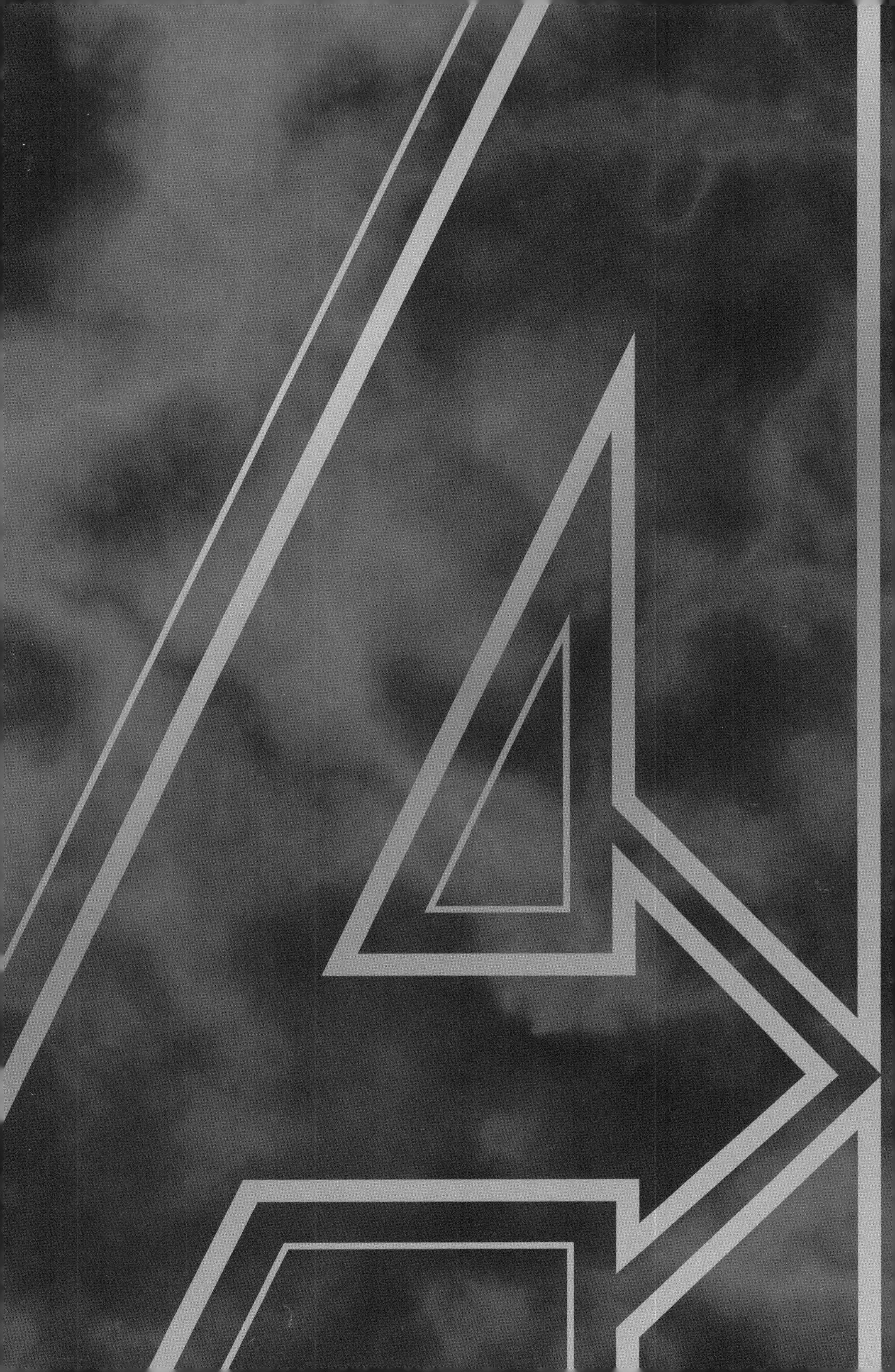

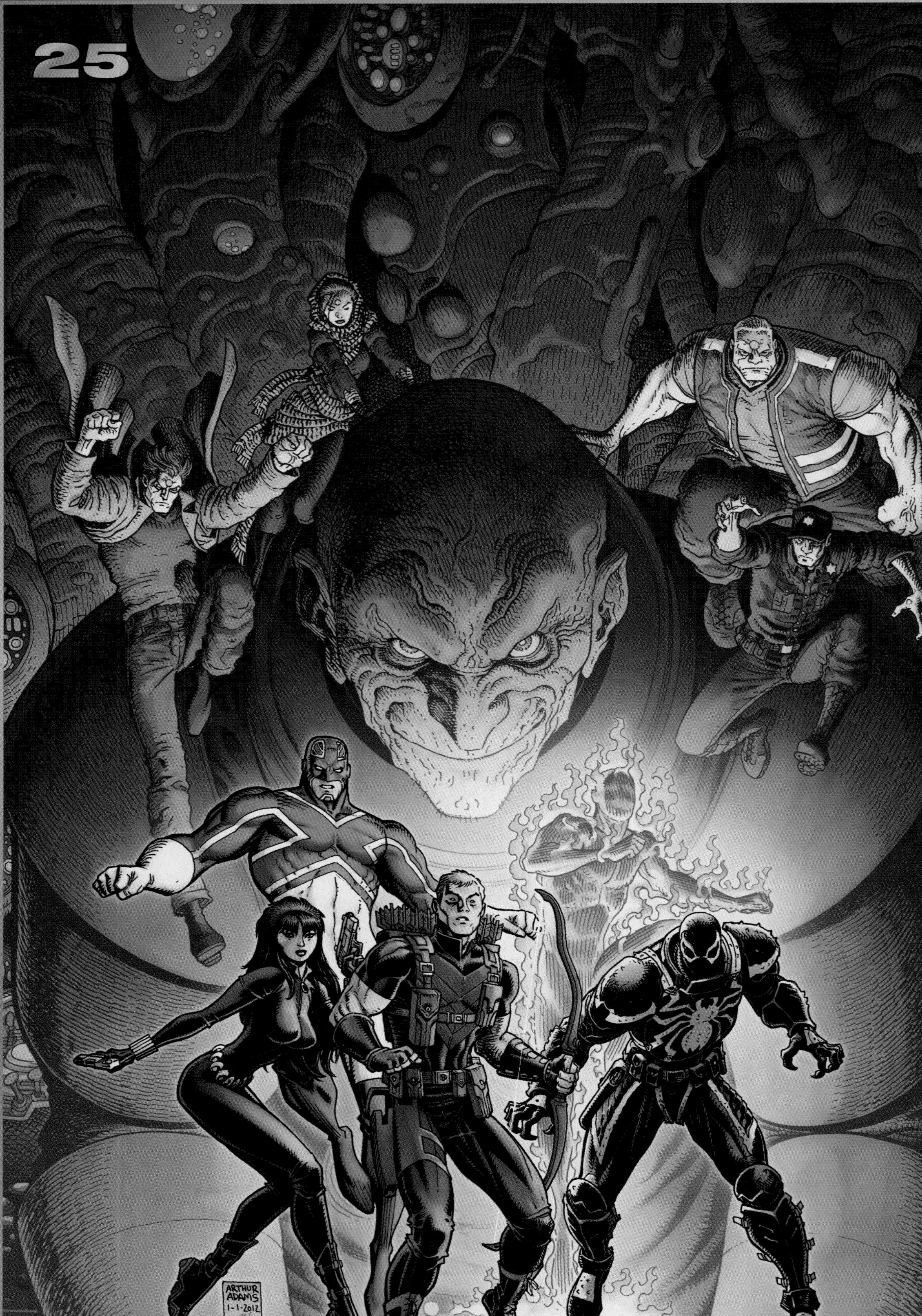
25
ARTHUR ADAMS
1-1-2012

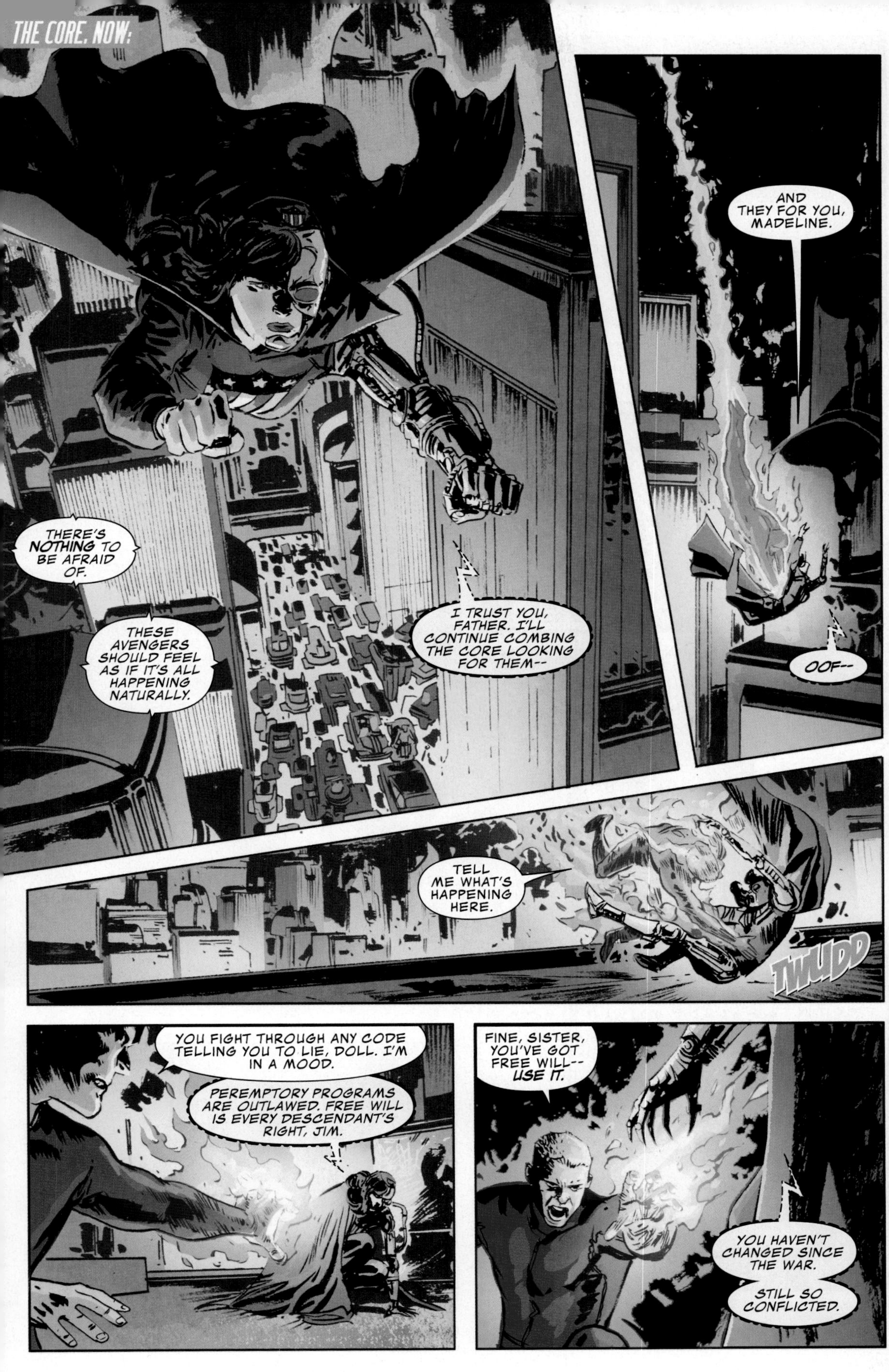
THE CORE, NOW:
THERE'S NOTHING TO BE AFRAID OF.
THESE AVENGERS SHOULD FEEL AS IF IT'S ALL HAPPENING NATURALLY.
I TRUST YOU, FATHER. I'LL CONTINUE COMBING THE CORE LOOKING FOR THEM--
AND THEY FOR YOU, MADELINE.
OOF--
TELL ME WHAT'S HAPPENING HERE.
TWUDD
YOU FIGHT THROUGH ANY CODE TELLING YOU TO LIE, DOLL. I'M IN A MOOD.
PEREMPTORY PROGRAMS ARE OUTLAWED. FREE WILL IS EVERY DESCENDANT'S RIGHT, JIM.
FINE, SISTER, YOU'VE GOT FREE WILL-- USE IT.
YOU HAVEN'T CHANGED SINCE THE WAR.
STILL SO CONFLICTED.

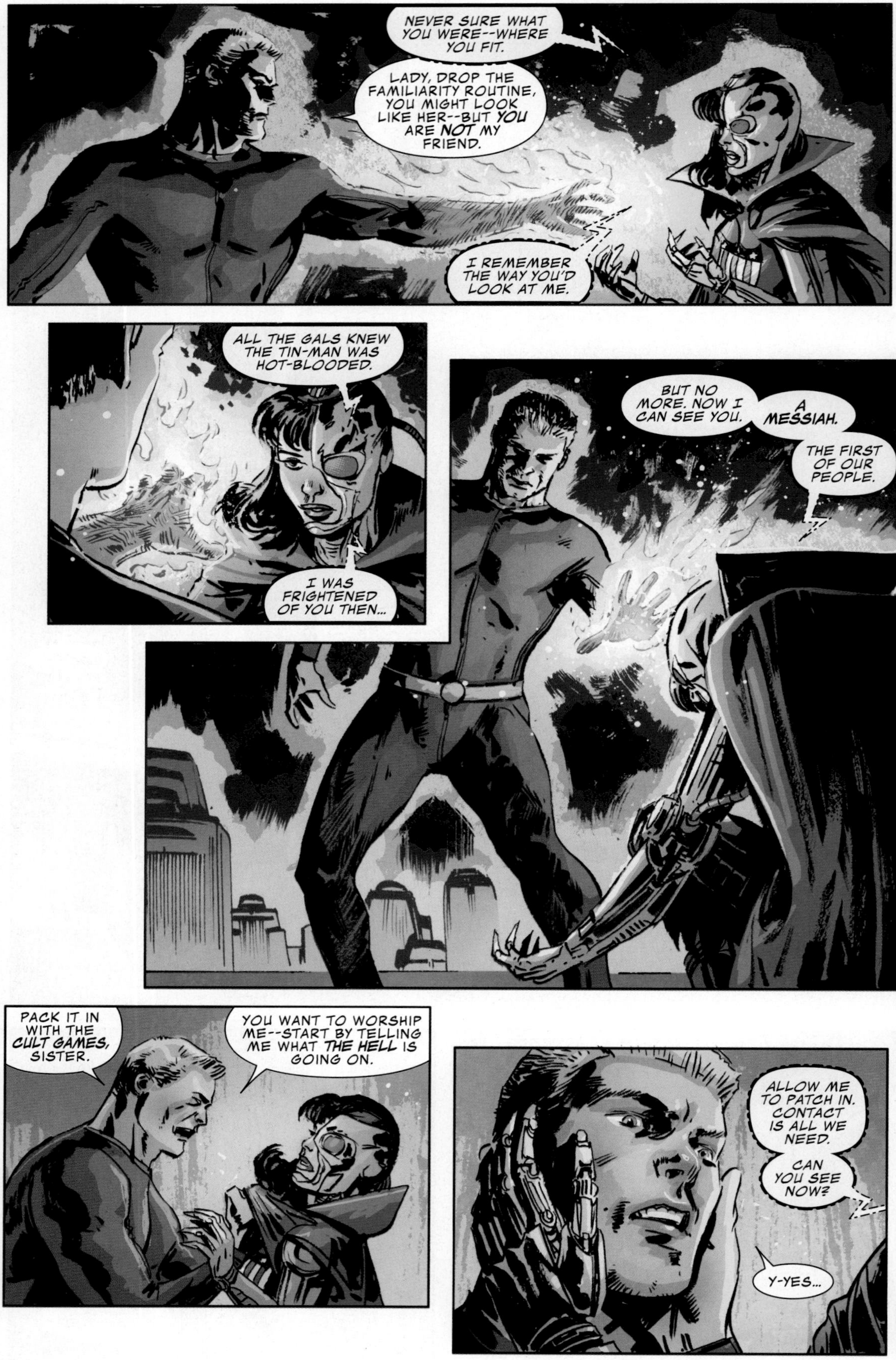
NEVER SURE WHAT YOU WERE--WHERE YOU FIT.
LADY, DROP THE FAMILIARITY ROUTINE, YOU MIGHT LOOK LIKE HER--BUT YOU ARE NOT MY FRIEND.
I REMEMBER THE WAY YOU'D LOOK AT ME.
ALL THE GALS KNEW THE TIN-MAN WAS HOT-BLOODED.
I WAS FRIGHTENED OF YOU THEN...
BUT NO MORE. NOW I CAN SEE YOU.
A MESSIAH.
THE FIRST OF OUR PEOPLE.
PACK IT IN WITH THE CULT GAMES, SISTER.
YOU WANT TO WORSHIP ME--START BY TELLING ME WHAT THE HELL IS GOING ON.
ALLOW ME TO PATCH IN. CONTACT IS ALL WE NEED.
CAN YOU SEE NOW?
Y-YES...

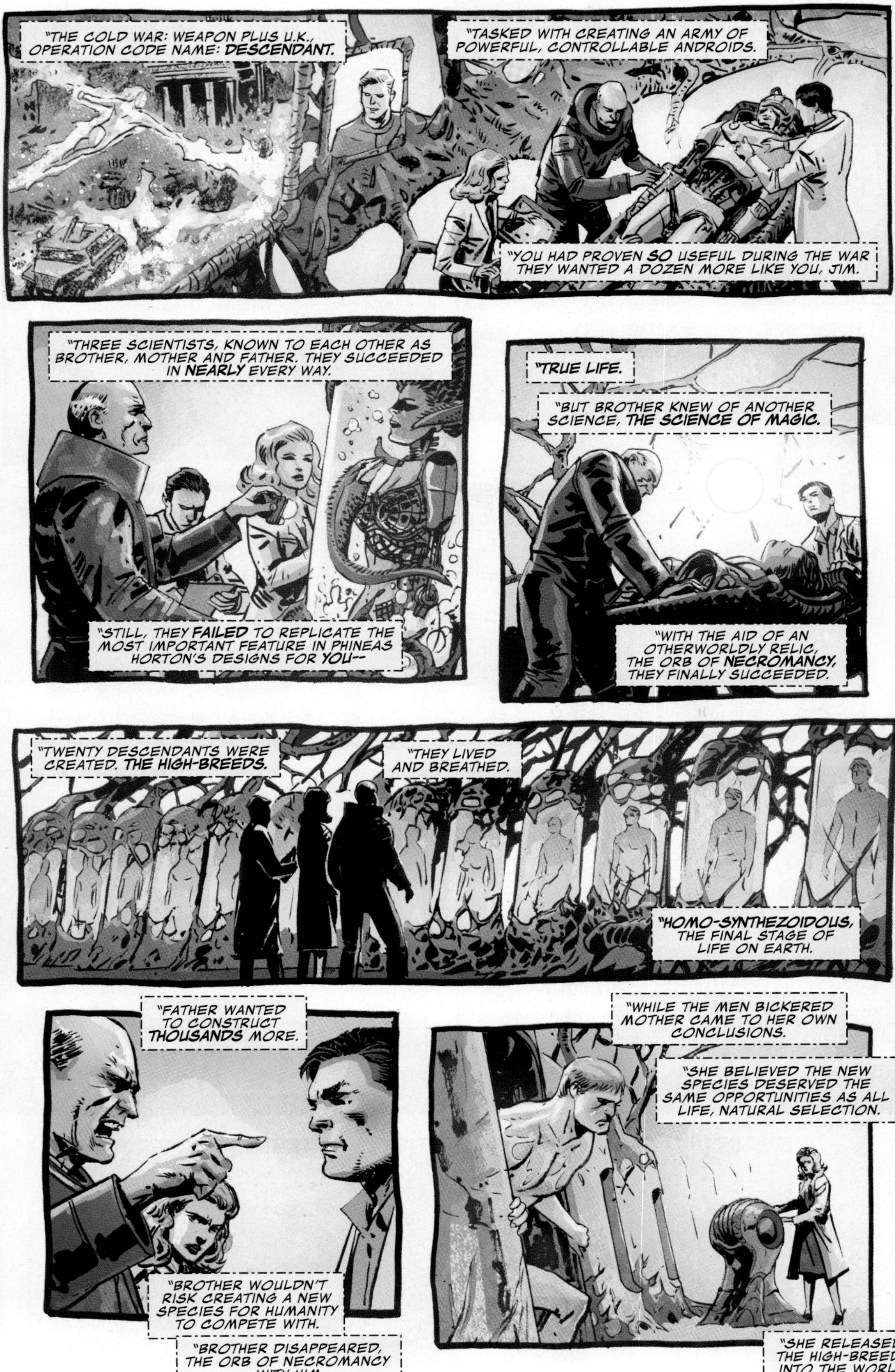
"THE COLD WAR: WEAPON PLUS U.K., OPERATION CODE NAME: DESCENDANT.
"TASKED WITH CREATING AN ARMY OF POWERFUL, CONTROLLABLE ANDROIDS.
"YOU HAD PROVEN SO USEFUL DURING THE WAR THEY WANTED A DOZEN MORE LIKE YOU, JIM.
"THREE SCIENTISTS, KNOWN TO EACH OTHER AS BROTHER, MOTHER AND FATHER. THEY SUCCEEDED IN NEARLY EVERY WAY.
"STILL, THEY FAILED TO REPLICATE THE MOST IMPORTANT FEATURE IN PHINEAS HORTON'S DESIGNS FOR YOU--
"TRUE LIFE.
"BUT BROTHER KNEW OF ANOTHER SCIENCE, THE SCIENCE OF MAGIC.
"WITH THE AID OF AN OTHERWORLDLY RELIC, THE ORB OF NECROMANCY, THEY FINALLY SUCCEEDED.
"TWENTY DESCENDANTS WERE CREATED. THE HIGH-BREEDS.
"THEY LIVED AND BREATHED.
"HOMO-SYNTHEZOIDOUS, THE FINAL STAGE OF LIFE ON EARTH.
"FATHER WANTED TO CONSTRUCT THOUSANDS MORE.
"BROTHER WOULDN'T RISK CREATING A NEW SPECIES FOR HUMANITY TO COMPETE WITH.
"BROTHER DISAPPEARED, THE ORB OF NECROMANCY WITH HIM.
"WHILE THE MEN BICKERED MOTHER CAME TO HER OWN CONCLUSIONS.
"SHE BELIEVED THE NEW SPECIES DESERVED THE SAME OPPORTUNITIES AS ALL LIFE, NATURAL SELECTION.
"SHE RELEASED THE HIGH-BREEDS INTO THE WORLD.

"THEY'VE BEEN AMONG HUMANITY, PROCREATING FOR DECADES.

"NORMAL PEOPLE. UNAWARE OF WHAT THEY ARE.

"THEIR POWERS ONLY MANIFEST IN SITUATIONS OF MORTAL DANGER.

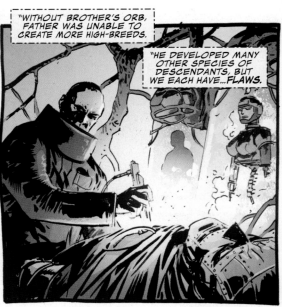

"WITHOUT BROTHER'S ORB, FATHER WAS UNABLE TO CREATE MORE HIGH-BREEDS.

"HE DEVELOPED MANY OTHER SPECIES OF DESCENDANTS, BUT WE EACH HAVE...FLAWS.

"THE DEATHLOK LEGION DEALT WITH MOTHER, BUT HER DISRUPTION REMAINS.

"FATHER'S ADAPTOIDS SEEK OUT AND RETURN THE HIGH-BREEDS.

"TO KEEP THEM SAFE AS THEY BREED TOMORROW."

YOU WERE THE SPARK OF US ALL. THE CREATOR OF NEW LIFE.

FATHER FEARS YOU.

HE KNOWS YOU WILL BE SEEN AS OUR TRUE LEADER.

FATHER AND I ARE GONNA HAVE WORDS.

THEN I'M GONNA PUT AN END TO THIS.

GRANDFATHER IS EN ROUTE.

SUCH A GOOD DAUGHTER.

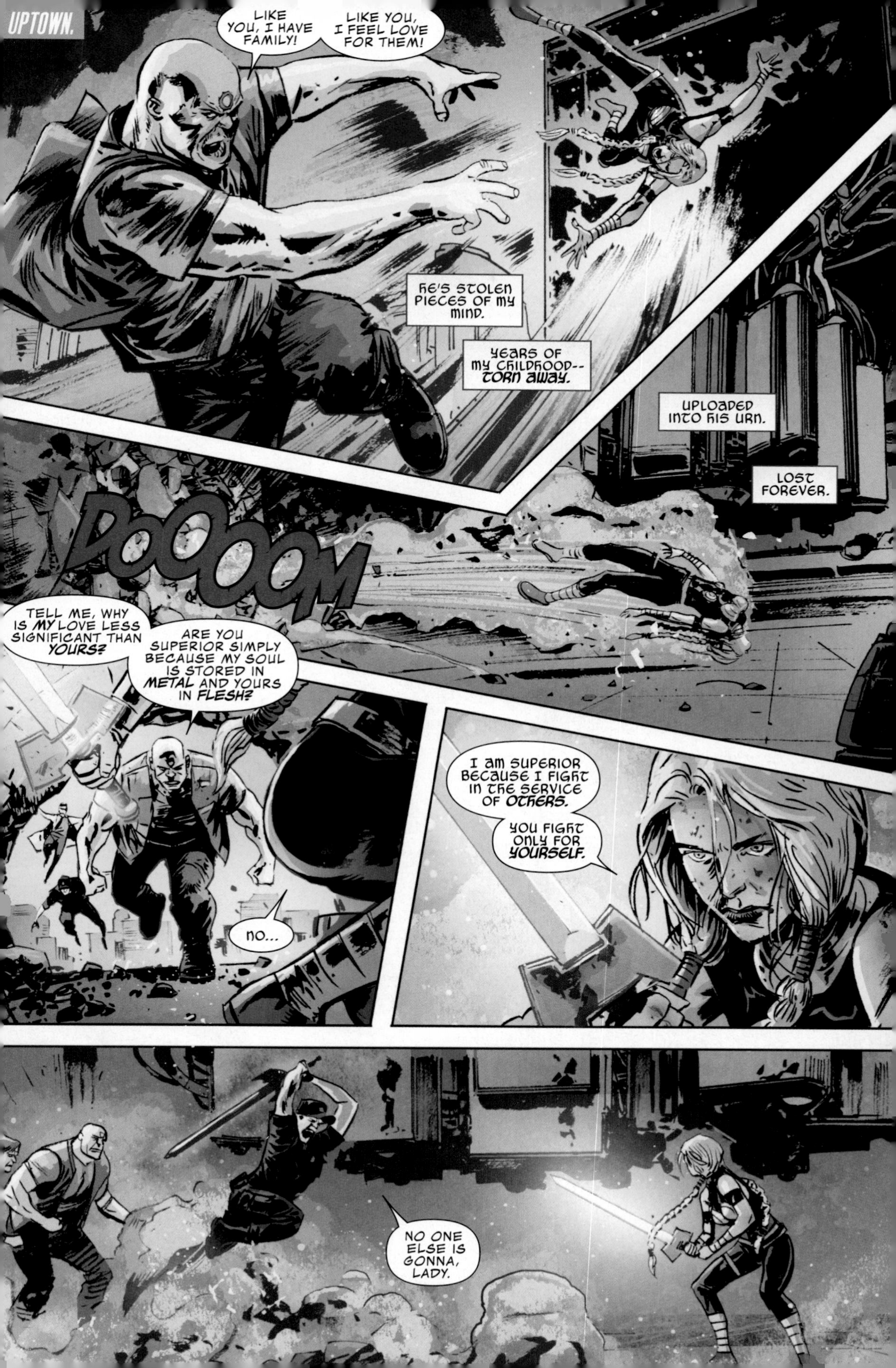
UPTOWN.
LIKE YOU, I HAVE FAMILY!
LIKE YOU, I FEEL LOVE FOR THEM!
HE'S STOLEN PIECES OF MY MIND.
YEARS OF MY CHILDHOOD-- TORN AWAY.
UPLOADED INTO HIS URN.
LOST FOREVER.
DOOOOOM
TELL ME, WHY IS MY LOVE LESS SIGNIFICANT THAN YOURS?
ARE YOU SUPERIOR SIMPLY BECAUSE MY SOUL IS STORED IN METAL AND YOURS IN FLESH?
NO...
I AM SUPERIOR BECAUSE I FIGHT IN THE SERVICE OF OTHERS.
YOU FIGHT ONLY FOR YOURSELF.
NO ONE ELSE IS GONNA, LADY.

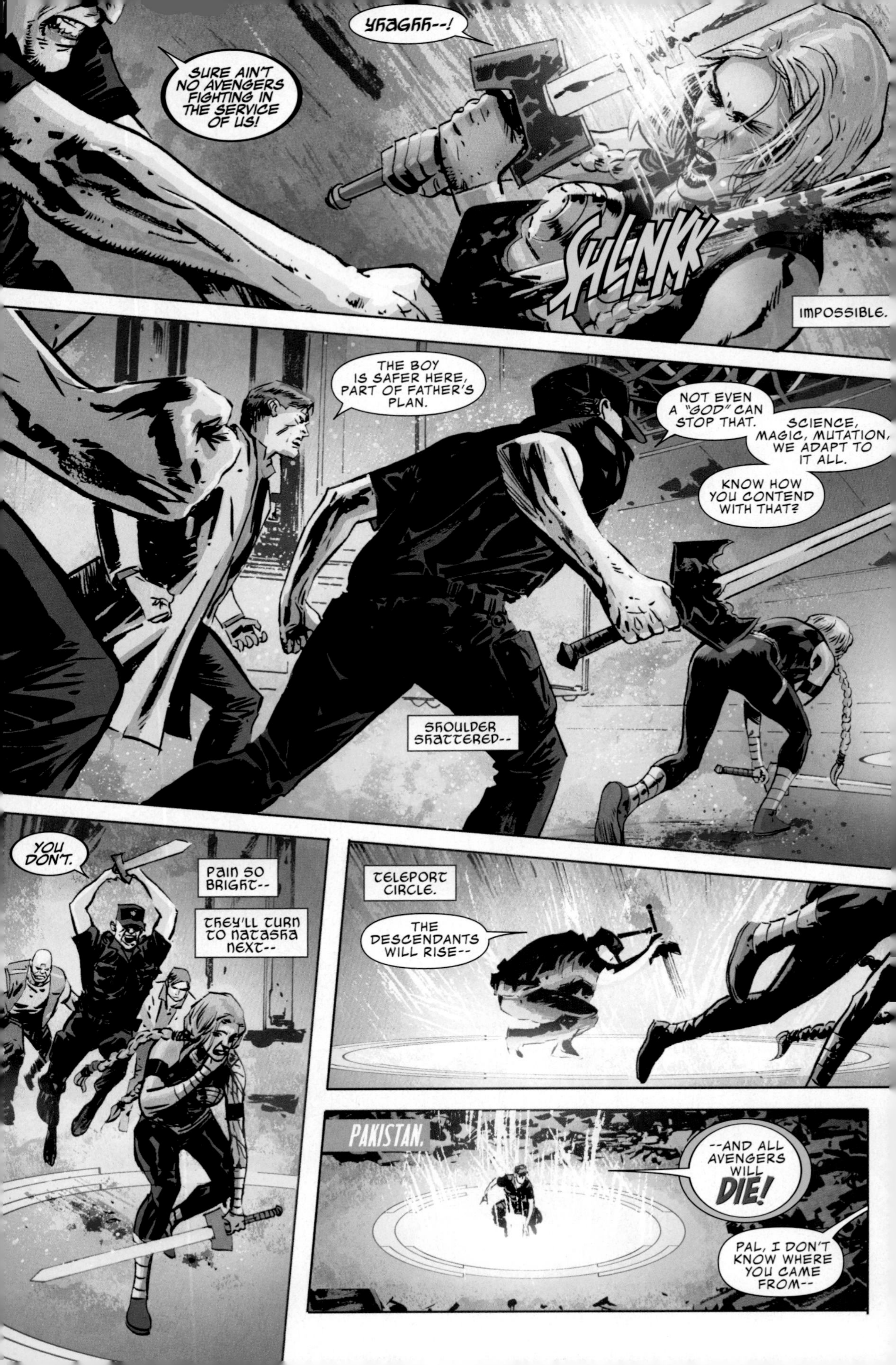
YHAGHH--!
SURE AIN'T NO AVENGERS FIGHTING IN THE SERVICE OF US!
SHLNKK
IMPOSSIBLE.
THE BOY IS SAFER HERE, PART OF FATHER'S PLAN.
NOT EVEN A "GOD" CAN STOP THAT.
SCIENCE, MAGIC, MUTATION, WE ADAPT TO IT ALL.
KNOW HOW YOU CONTEND WITH THAT?
SHOULDER SHATTERED--
YOU DON'T.
PAIN SO BRIGHT--
THEY'LL TURN TO NATASHA NEXT--
TELEPORT CIRCLE.
THE DESCENDANTS WILL RISE--
PAKISTAN.
--AND ALL AVENGERS WILL DIE!
PAL, I DON'T KNOW WHERE YOU CAME FROM--

BUT IT'S HARD TO MISUNDERSTAND YOUR MESSAGE.

TWOPP

THE CORE.

DO NOT FEAR, CHILD...

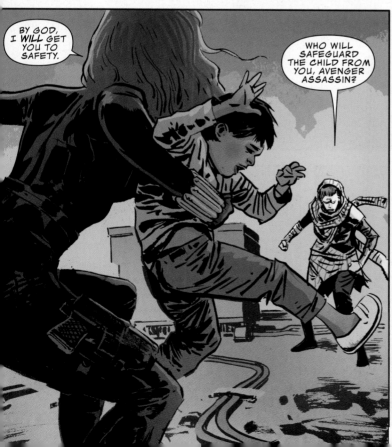

BY GOD, I *WILL* GET YOU TO SAFETY.

WHO WILL SAFEGUARD THE CHILD FROM YOU, AVENGER ASSASSIN?

BACK UP OR YOU'LL FIND OUT WHAT THIS ASSASSIN IS CAPABLE OF!

YOU'RE VERY SKILLED IN MURDER--A TRAIT YOUR DIMINUTIVES WILL ALSO CARRY.

SERVE FATHER.

KILL THE INTRUDERS.

PROTECT THE BOY.

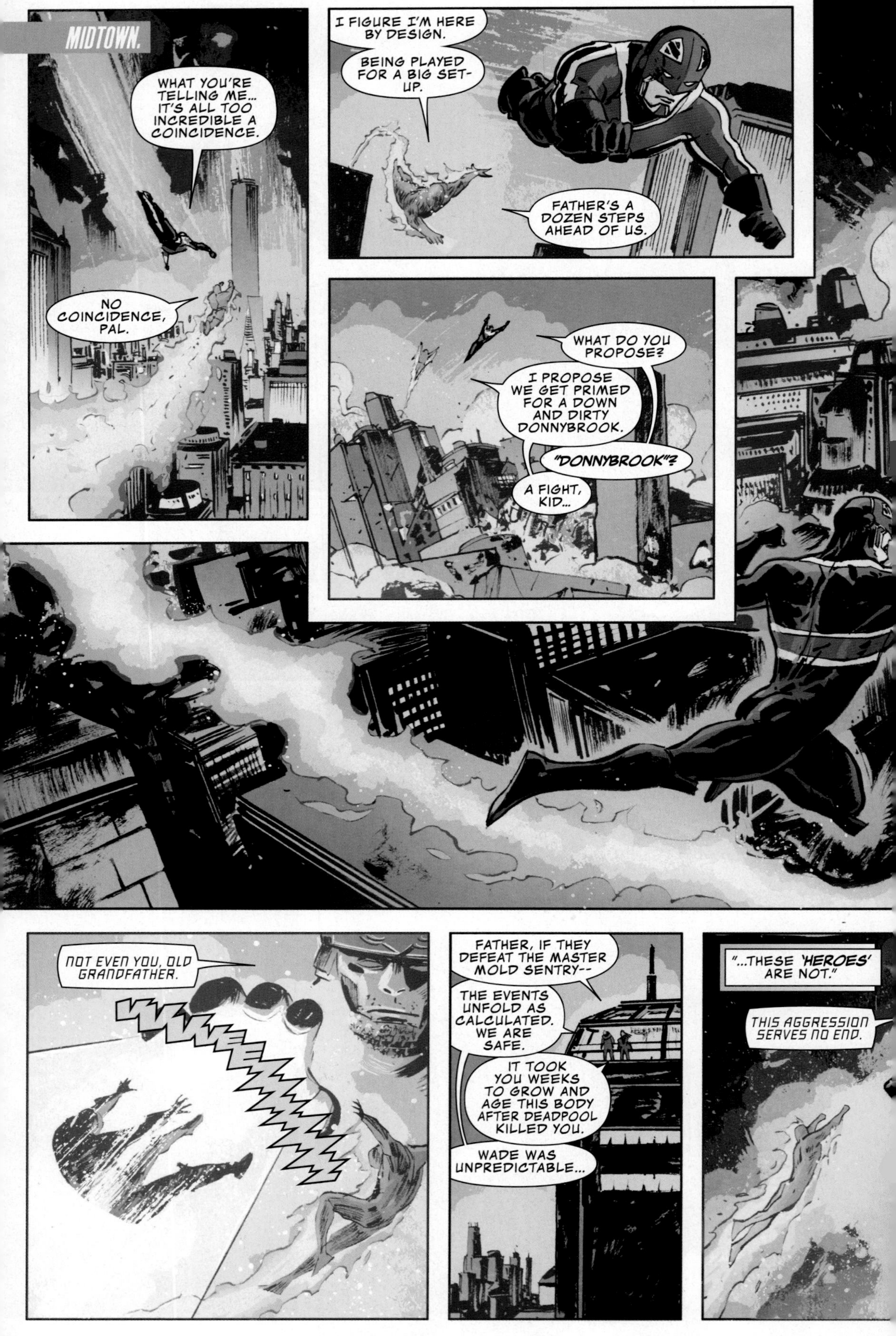
MIDTOWN.
WHAT YOU'RE TELLING ME... IT'S ALL TOO INCREDIBLE A COINCIDENCE.
NO COINCIDENCE, PAL.
I FIGURE I'M HERE BY DESIGN.
BEING PLAYED FOR A BIG SET-UP.
FATHER'S A DOZEN STEPS AHEAD OF US.
WHAT DO YOU PROPOSE?
I PROPOSE WE GET PRIMED FOR A DOWN AND DIRTY DONNYBROOK.
"DONNYBROOK"?
A FIGHT, KID...
NOT EVEN YOU, OLD GRANDFATHER.
WWEEEZZZ
FATHER, IF THEY DEFEAT THE MASTER MOLD SENTRY--
THE EVENTS UNFOLD AS CALCULATED. WE ARE SAFE.
IT TOOK YOU WEEKS TO GROW AND AGE THIS BODY AFTER DEADPOOL KILLED YOU.
WADE WAS UNPREDICTABLE...
"...THESE 'HEROES' ARE NOT."
THIS AGGRESSION SERVES NO END.

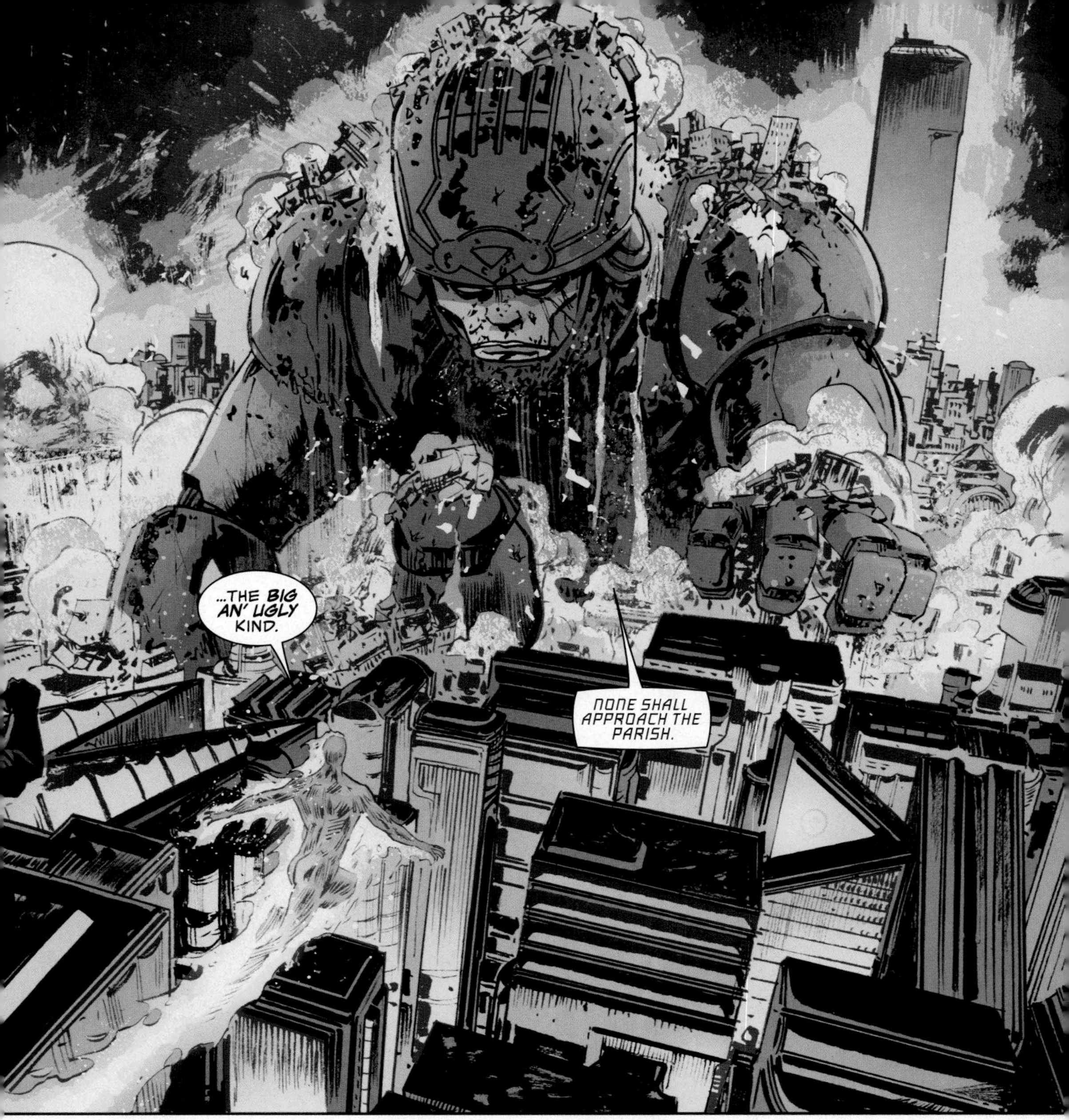
...THE BIG AN' UGLY KIND.
NONE SHALL APPROACH THE PARISH.

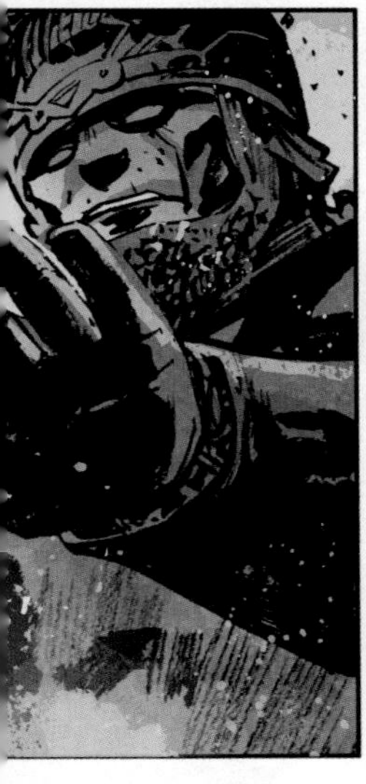

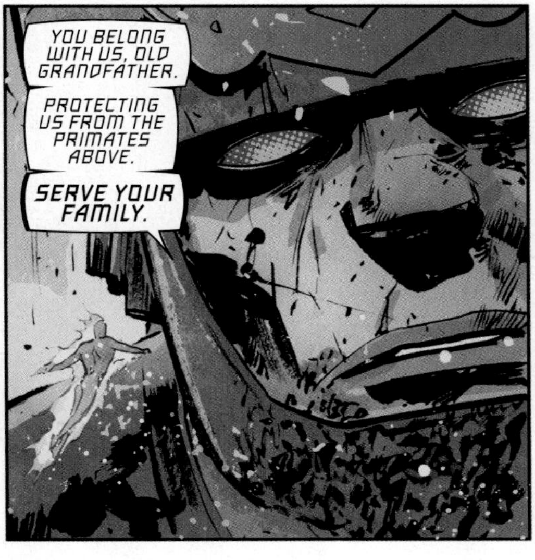
YOU BELONG WITH US, OLD GRANDFATHER.
PROTECTING US FROM THE PRIMATES ABOVE.
SERVE YOUR FAMILY.

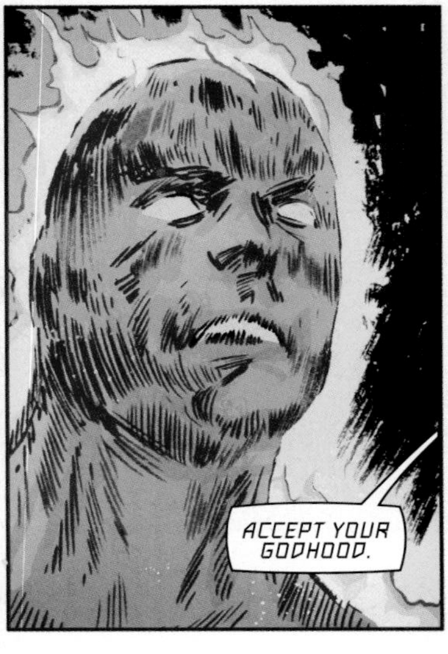
ACCEPT YOUR GODHOOD.

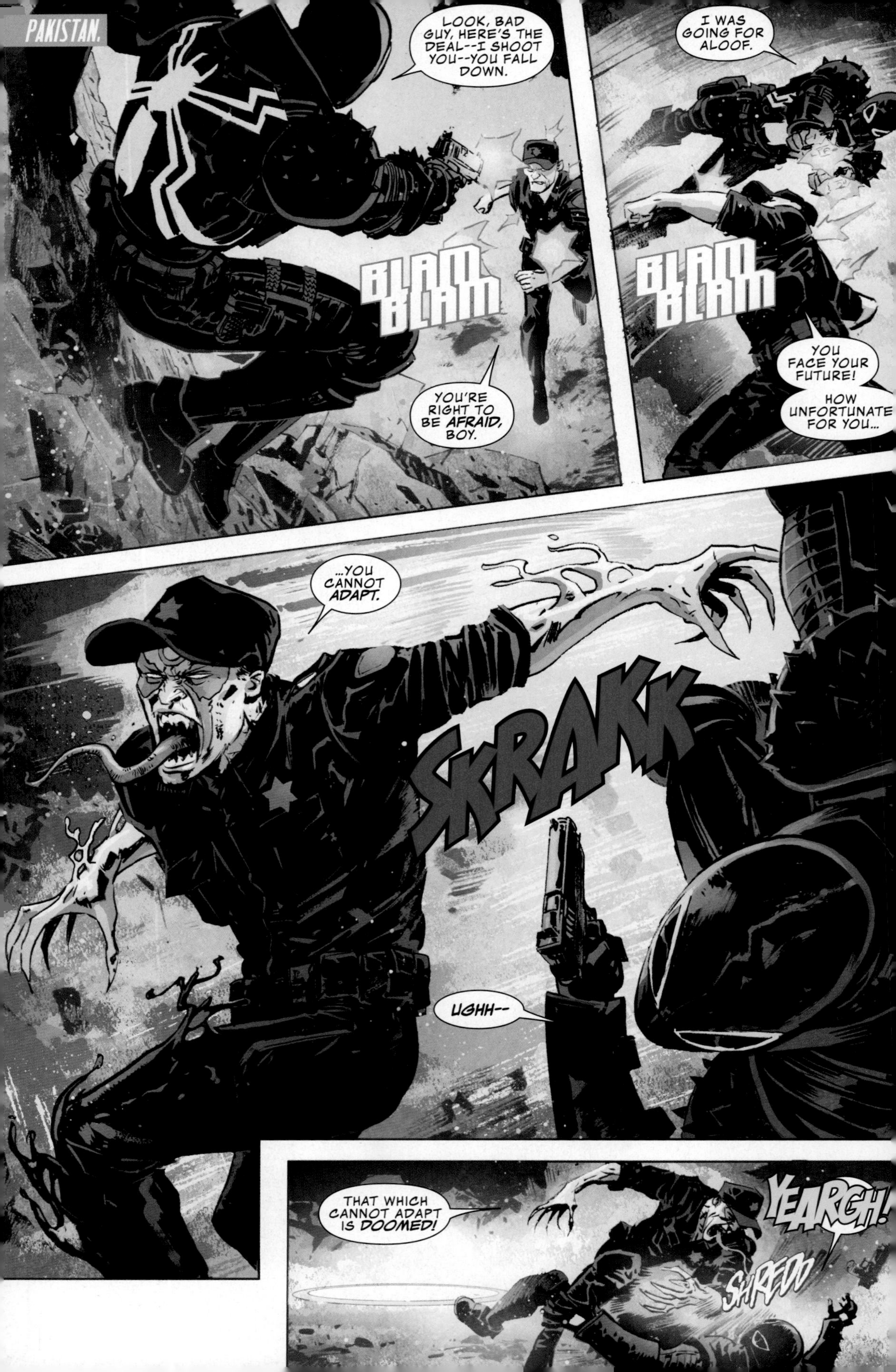
PAKISTAN.
LOOK, BAD GUY, HERE'S THE DEAL--I SHOOT YOU--YOU FALL DOWN.
BLAM BLAM
YOU'RE RIGHT TO BE AFRAID, BOY.
I WAS GOING FOR ALOOF.
BLAM BLAM
YOU FACE YOUR FUTURE!
HOW UNFORTUNATE FOR YOU...
...YOU CANNOT ADAPT.
SKRAKK
UGHH--
THAT WHICH CANNOT ADAPT IS DOOMED!
YEARGH!
SHREDD

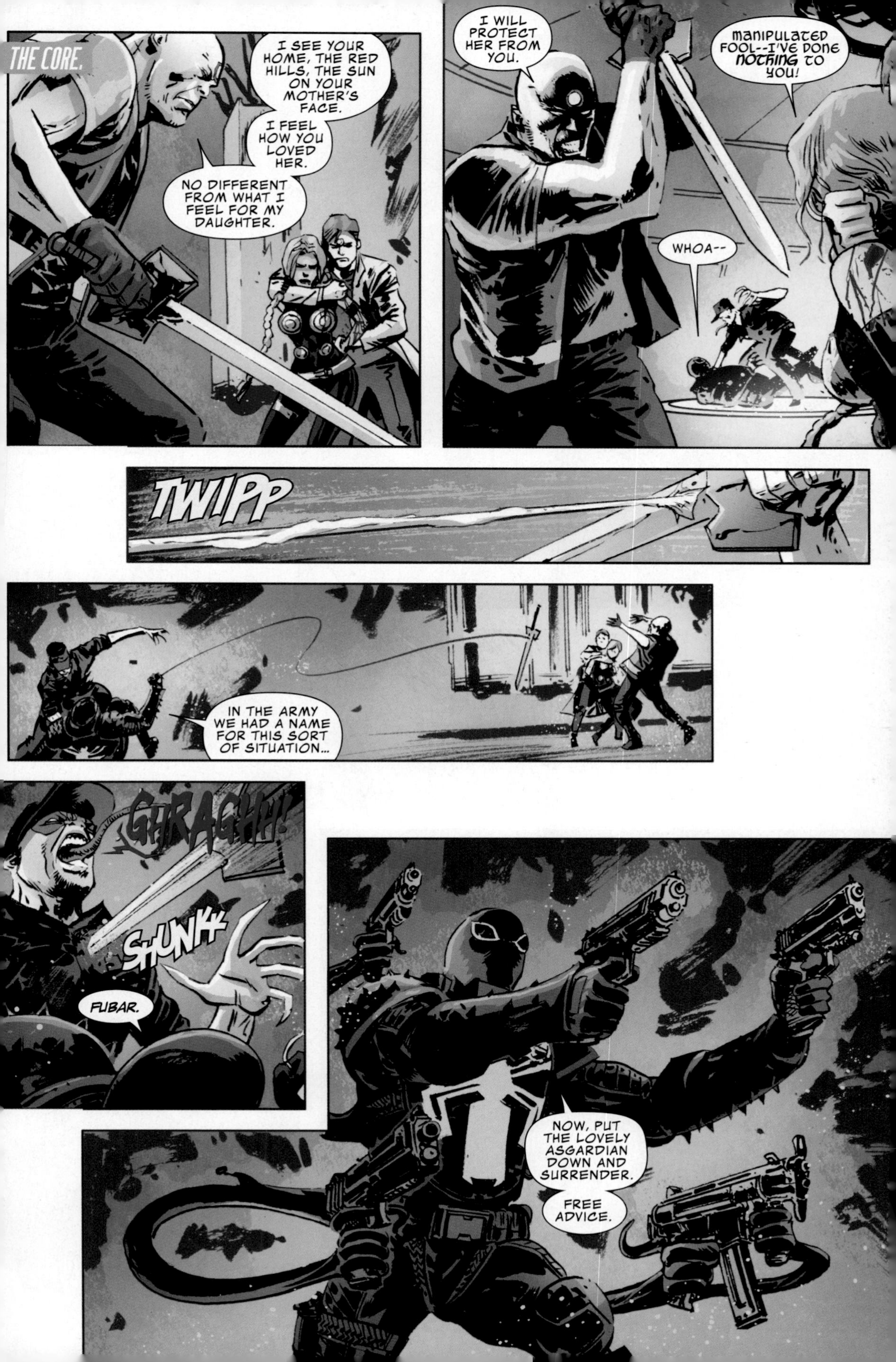
THE CORE.
I SEE YOUR HOME, THE RED HILLS, THE SUN ON YOUR MOTHER'S FACE.
I FEEL HOW YOU LOVED HER.
NO DIFFERENT FROM WHAT I FEEL FOR MY DAUGHTER.
I WILL PROTECT HER FROM YOU.
MANIPULATED FOOL--I'VE DONE NOTHING TO YOU!
WHOA--
TWIPP
IN THE ARMY WE HAD A NAME FOR THIS SORT OF SITUATION...
GHRAGHH!
SHUNKK
FUBAR.
NOW, PUT THE LOVELY ASGARDIAN DOWN AND SURRENDER.
FREE ADVICE.

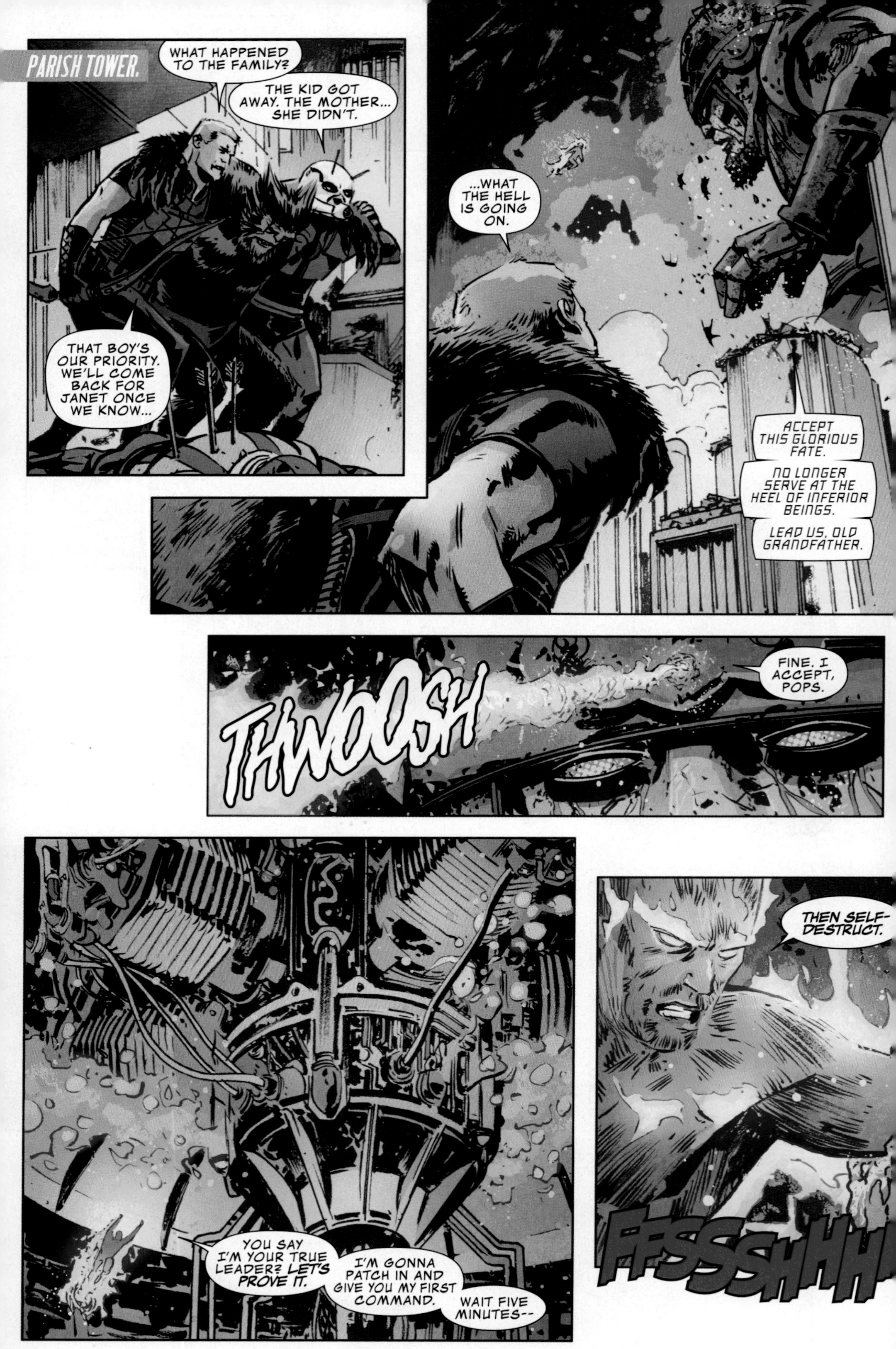
PARISH TOWER.
WHAT HAPPENED TO THE FAMILY?
THE KID GOT AWAY. THE MOTHER... SHE DIDN'T.
THAT BOY'S OUR PRIORITY. WE'LL COME BACK FOR JANET ONCE WE KNOW...
...WHAT THE HELL IS GOING ON.
ACCEPT THIS GLORIOUS FATE.
NO LONGER SERVE AT THE HEEL OF INFERIOR BEINGS.
LEAD US, OLD GRANDFATHER.
THWOOSH
FINE. I ACCEPT, POPS.
YOU SAY I'M YOUR TRUE LEADER? LET'S PROVE IT.
I'M GONNA PATCH IN AND GIVE YOU MY FIRST COMMAND.
WAIT FIVE MINUTES--
THEN SELF-DESTRUCT.
FFSSSHHH

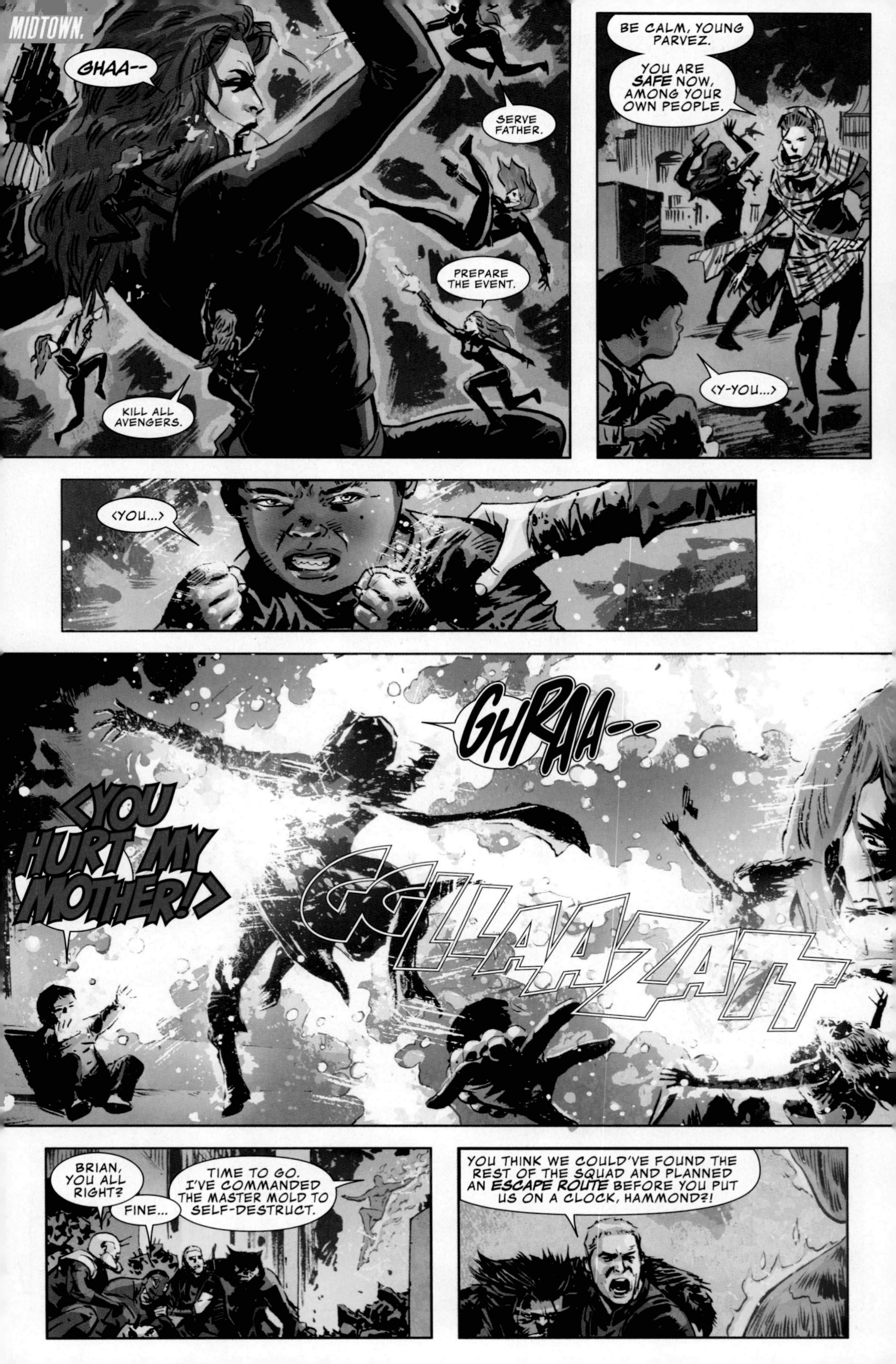
MIDTOWN.
GHAA--
SERVE FATHER.
PREPARE THE EVENT.
KILL ALL AVENGERS.
BE CALM, YOUNG PARVEZ.
YOU ARE SAFE NOW, AMONG YOUR OWN PEOPLE.
<Y-YOU...>
<YOU...>
GHRAA--
<YOU HURT MY MOTHER!>
GGLLAAZAAT
BRIAN, YOU ALL RIGHT?
FINE...
TIME TO GO. I'VE COMMANDED THE MASTER MOLD TO SELF-DESTRUCT.
YOU THINK WE COULD'VE FOUND THE REST OF THE SQUAD AND PLANNED AN ESCAPE ROUTE BEFORE YOU PUT US ON A CLOCK, HAMMOND?!

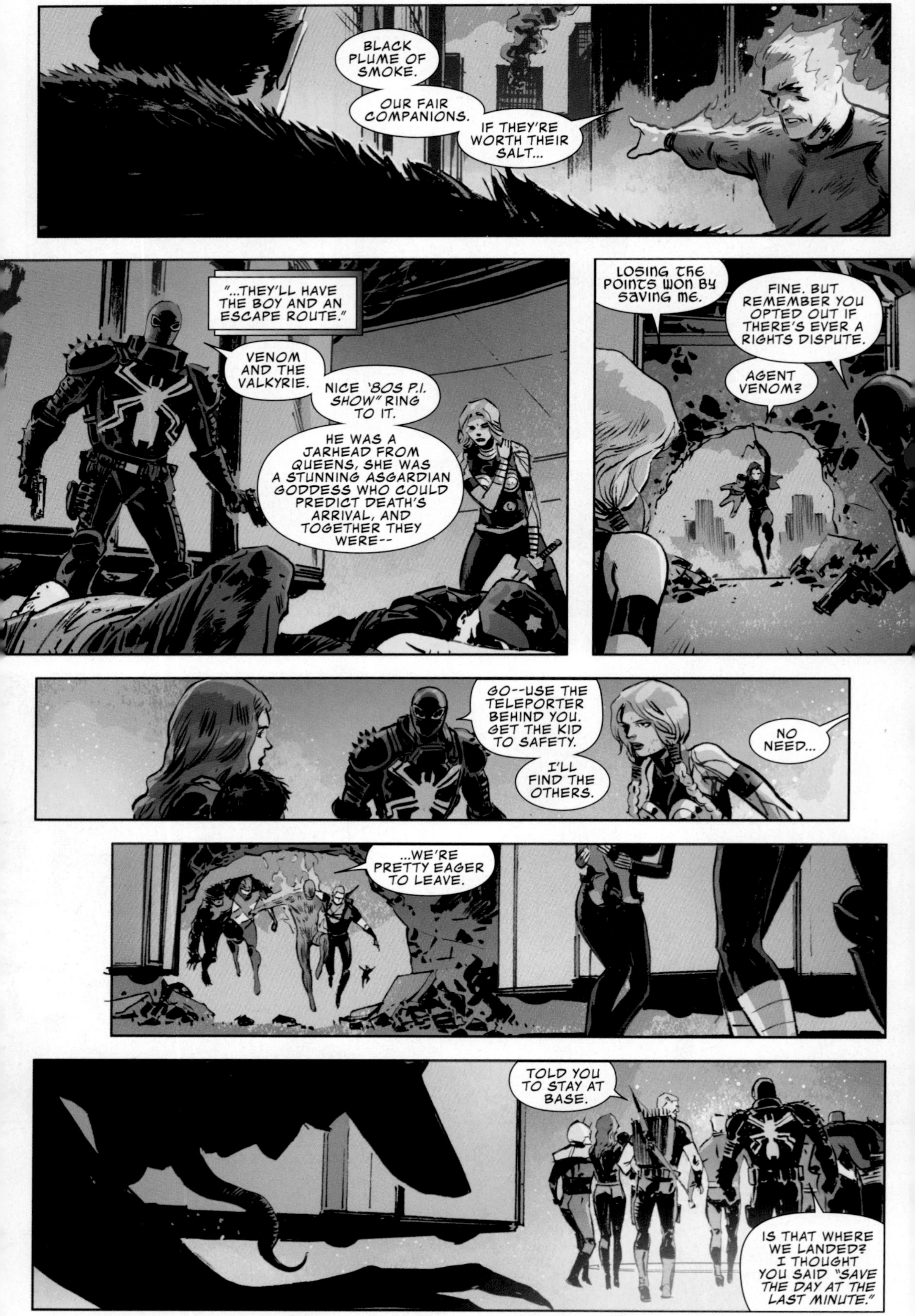
BLACK PLUME OF SMOKE.
OUR FAIR COMPANIONS.
IF THEY'RE WORTH THEIR SALT...
"...THEY'LL HAVE THE BOY AND AN ESCAPE ROUTE."
VENOM AND THE VALKYRIE.
NICE '80S P.I. SHOW" RING TO IT.
HE WAS A JARHEAD FROM QUEENS, SHE WAS A STUNNING ASGARDIAN GODDESS WHO COULD PREDICT DEATH'S ARRIVAL, AND TOGETHER THEY WERE--
LOSING THE POINTS WON BY SAVING ME.
FINE. BUT REMEMBER YOU OPTED OUT IF THERE'S EVER A RIGHTS DISPUTE.
AGENT VENOM?
GO--USE THE TELEPORTER BEHIND YOU. GET THE KID TO SAFETY.
I'LL FIND THE OTHERS.
NO NEED...
...WE'RE PRETTY EAGER TO LEAVE.
TOLD YOU TO STAY AT BASE.
IS THAT WHERE WE LANDED? I THOUGHT YOU SAID "SAVE THE DAY AT THE LAST MINUTE."

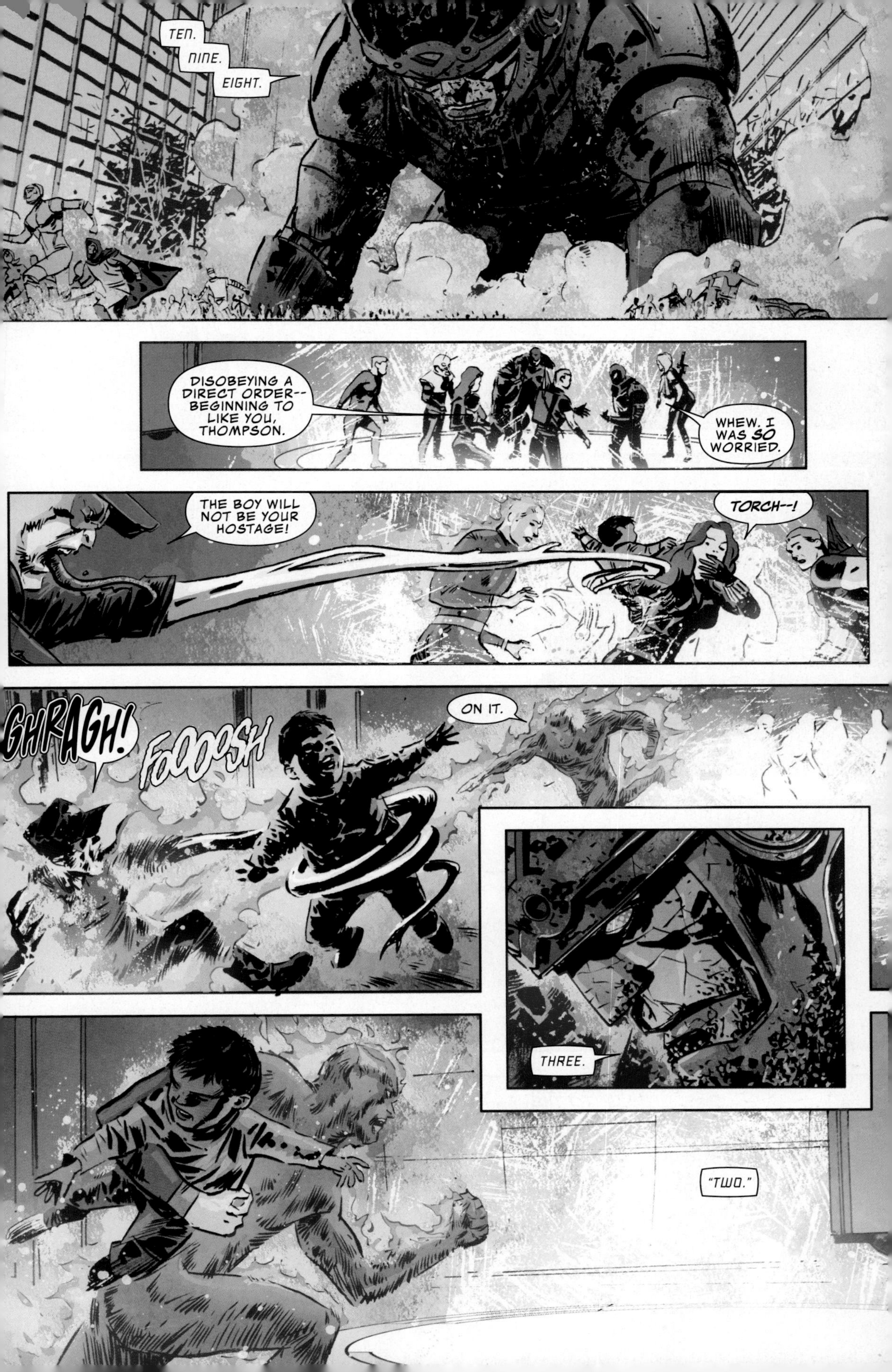
TEN.
NINE.
EIGHT.
DISOBEYING A DIRECT ORDER-- BEGINNING TO LIKE YOU, THOMPSON.
WHEW. I WAS SO WORRIED.
THE BOY WILL NOT BE YOUR HOSTAGE!
TORCH--!
GHRAGH!
FOOOOSH
ON IT.
THREE.
"TWO."

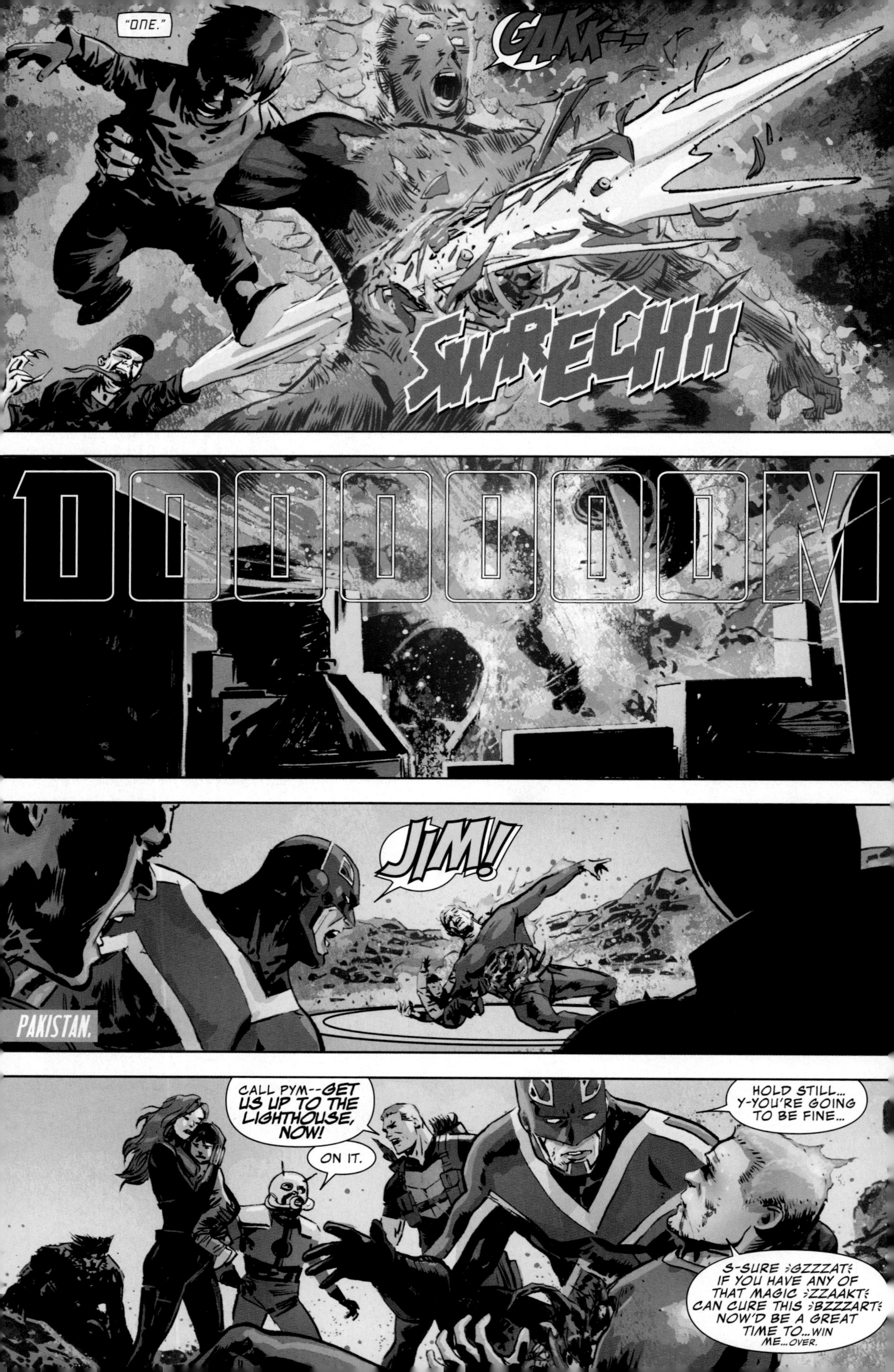
"ONE."
GAKK--
SWRECHH
DOOOOOOM
JIM!
PAKISTAN.
CALL PYM--GET US UP TO THE LIGHTHOUSE, NOW!
ON IT.
HOLD STILL... Y-YOU'RE GOING TO BE FINE...
S-SURE ≶GZZZAT≷ IF YOU HAVE ANY OF THAT MAGIC ≶ZZAAKT≷ CAN CURE THIS ≶BZZZART≷ NOW'D BE A GREAT TIME TO...WIN ME...OVER.

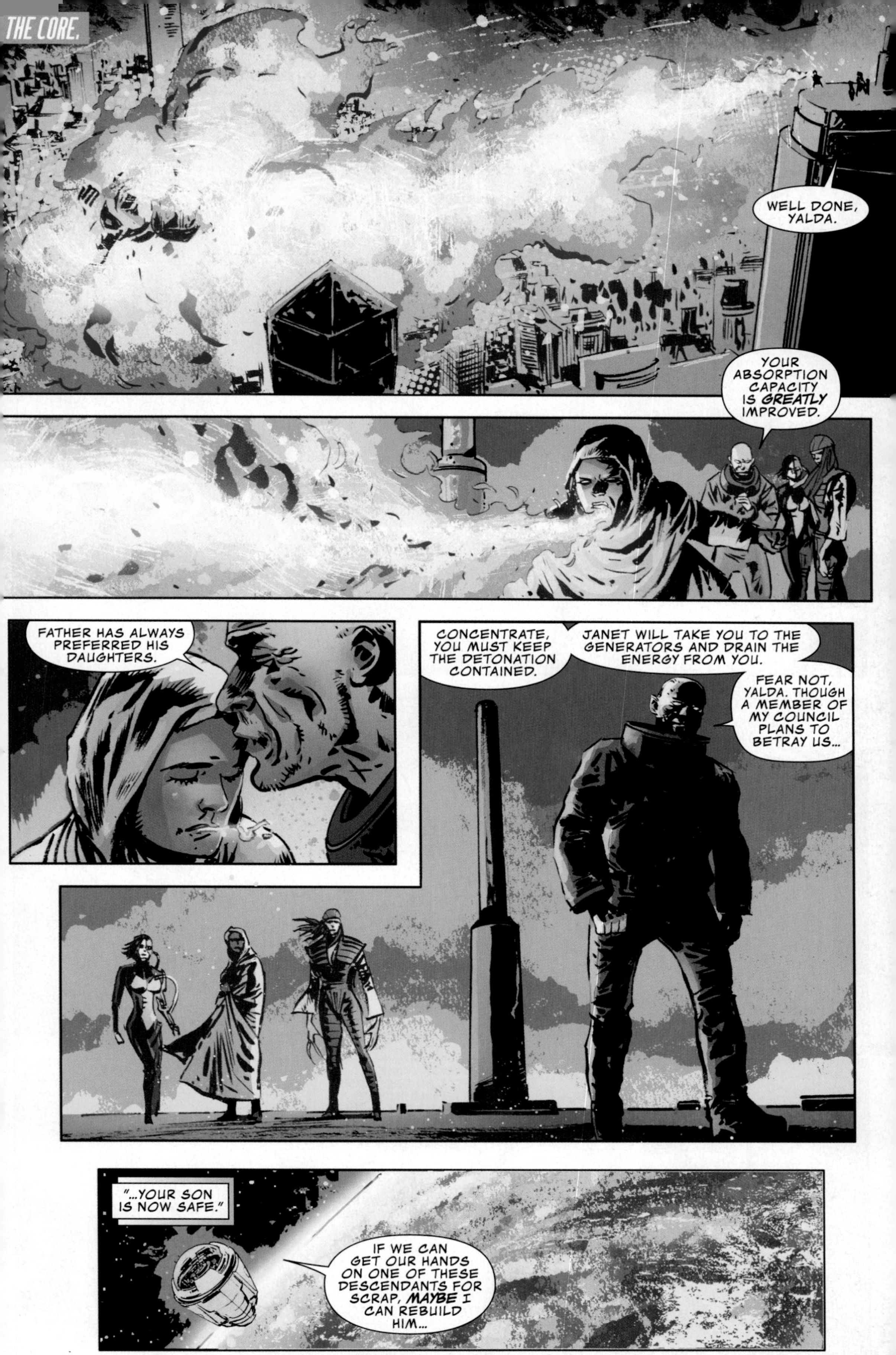
THE CORE.
WELL DONE, YALDA.
YOUR ABSORPTION CAPACITY IS GREATLY IMPROVED.
FATHER HAS ALWAYS PREFERRED HIS DAUGHTERS.
CONCENTRATE, YOU MUST KEEP THE DETONATION CONTAINED.
JANET WILL TAKE YOU TO THE GENERATORS AND DRAIN THE ENERGY FROM YOU.
FEAR NOT, YALDA. THOUGH A MEMBER OF MY COUNCIL PLANS TO BETRAY US...
"...YOUR SON IS NOW SAFE."
IF WE CAN GET OUR HANDS ON ONE OF THESE DESCENDANTS FOR SCRAP, MAYBE I CAN REBUILD HIM...

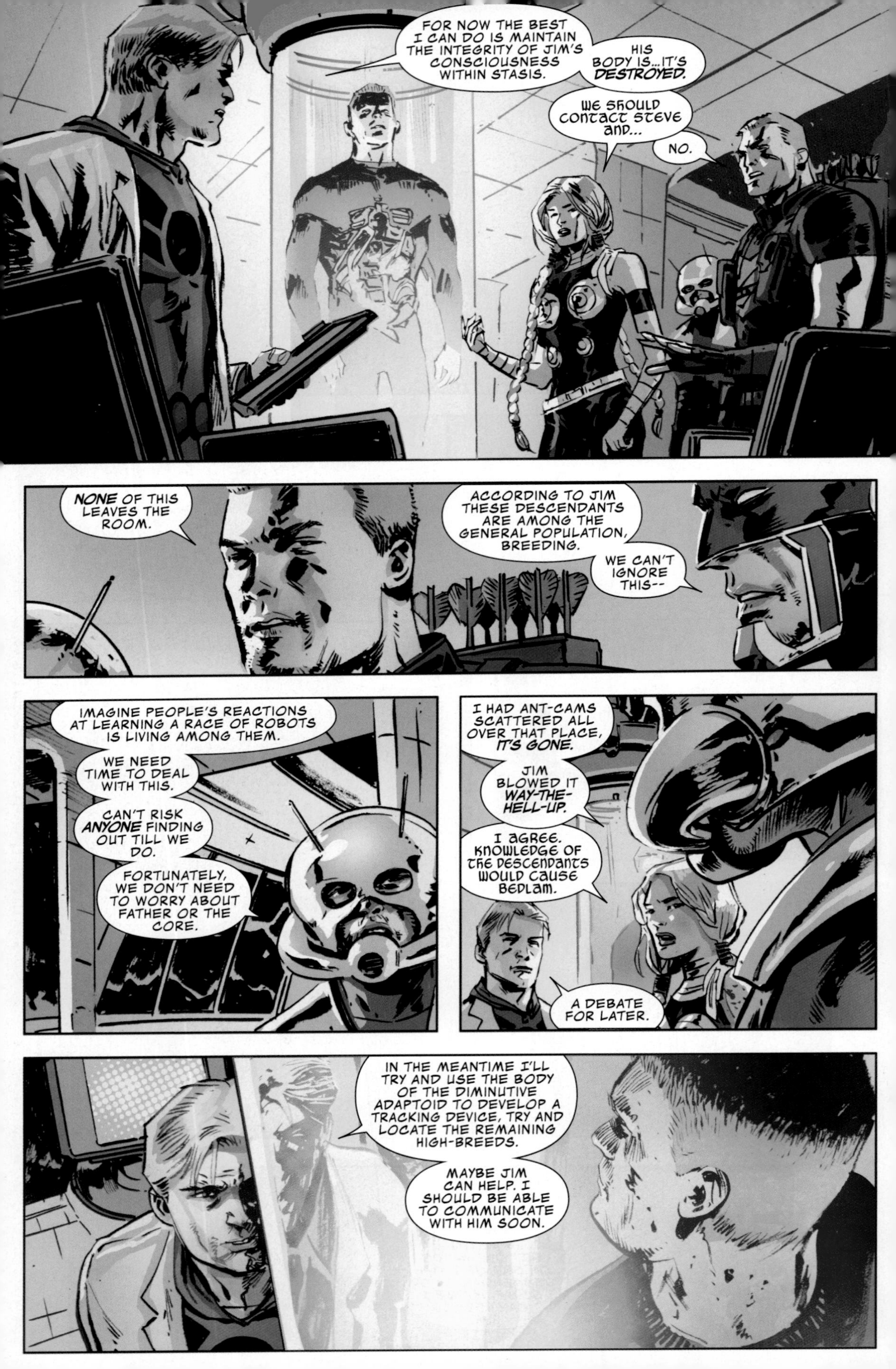
FOR NOW THE BEST I CAN DO IS MAINTAIN THE INTEGRITY OF JIM'S CONSCIOUSNESS WITHIN STASIS.
HIS BODY IS...IT'S *DESTROYED.*
WE SHOULD CONTACT STEVE AND...
NO.
NONE OF THIS LEAVES THE ROOM.
ACCORDING TO JIM THESE DESCENDANTS ARE AMONG THE GENERAL POPULATION, BREEDING.
WE CAN'T IGNORE THIS--
IMAGINE PEOPLE'S REACTIONS AT LEARNING A RACE OF ROBOTS IS LIVING AMONG THEM.
WE NEED TIME TO DEAL WITH THIS.
CAN'T RISK *ANYONE* FINDING OUT TILL WE DO.
FORTUNATELY, WE DON'T NEED TO WORRY ABOUT FATHER OR THE CORE.
I HAD ANT-CAMS SCATTERED ALL OVER THAT PLACE, *IT'S GONE.*
JIM BLOWED IT *WAY-THE-HELL-UP.*
I AGREE. KNOWLEDGE OF THE DESCENDANTS WOULD CAUSE BEDLAM.
A DEBATE FOR LATER.
IN THE MEANTIME I'LL TRY AND USE THE BODY OF THE DIMINUTIVE ADAPTOID TO DEVELOP A TRACKING DEVICE, TRY AND LOCATE THE REMAINING HIGH-BREEDS.
MAYBE JIM CAN HELP. I SHOULD BE ABLE TO COMMUNICATE WITH HIM SOON.

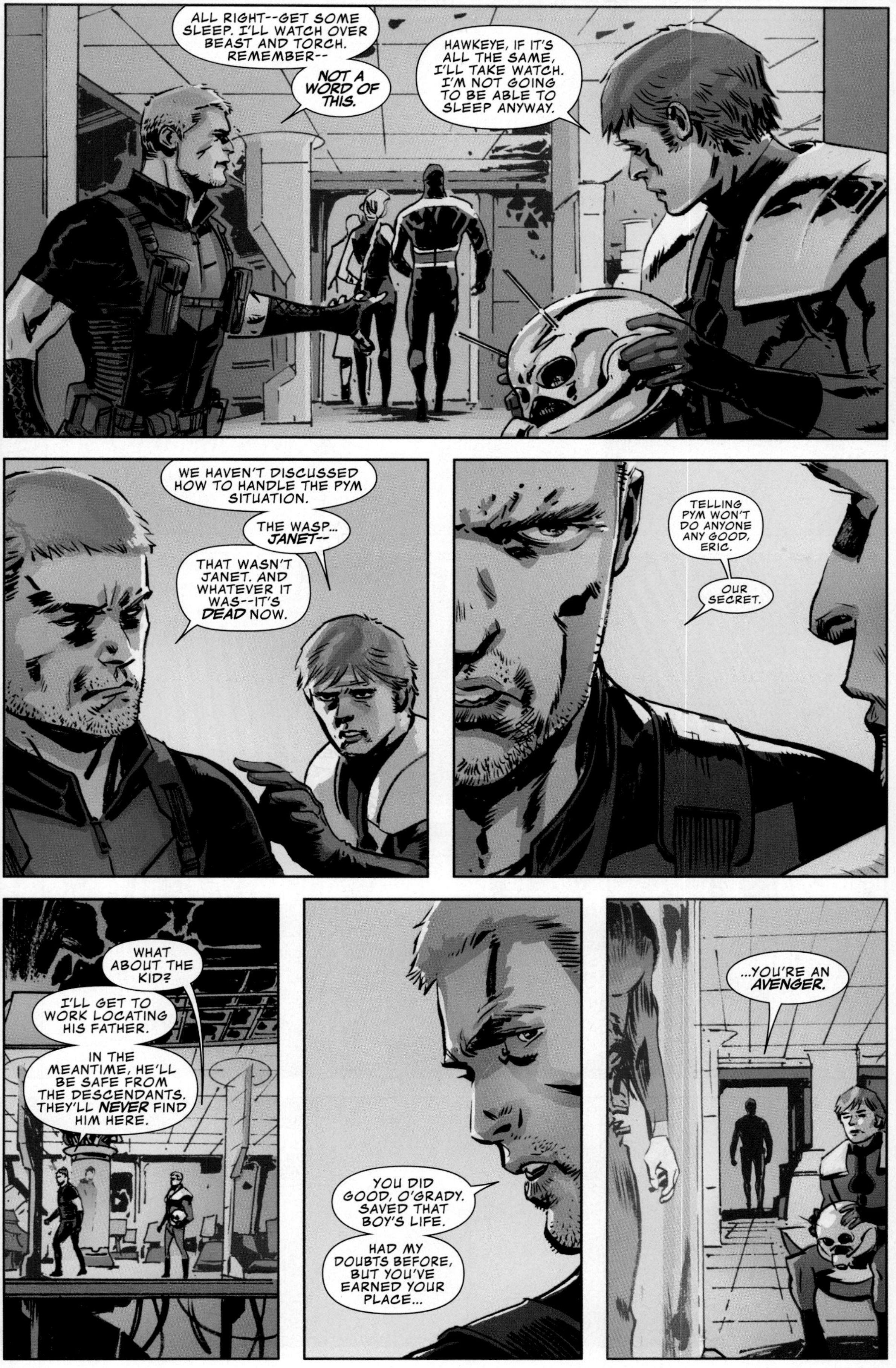
ALL RIGHT--GET SOME SLEEP. I'LL WATCH OVER BEAST AND TORCH. REMEMBER--
NOT A WORD OF THIS.
HAWKEYE, IF IT'S ALL THE SAME, I'LL TAKE WATCH. I'M NOT GOING TO BE ABLE TO SLEEP ANYWAY.
WE HAVEN'T DISCUSSED HOW TO HANDLE THE PYM SITUATION.
THE WASP... JANET--
THAT WASN'T JANET. AND WHATEVER IT WAS--IT'S DEAD NOW.
TELLING PYM WON'T DO ANYONE ANY GOOD, ERIC.
OUR SECRET.
WHAT ABOUT THE KID?
I'LL GET TO WORK LOCATING HIS FATHER.
IN THE MEANTIME, HE'LL BE SAFE FROM THE DESCENDANTS. THEY'LL NEVER FIND HIM HERE.
YOU DID GOOD, O'GRADY. SAVED THAT BOY'S LIFE.
HAD MY DOUBTS BEFORE, BUT YOU'VE EARNED YOUR PLACE...
...YOU'RE AN AVENGER.

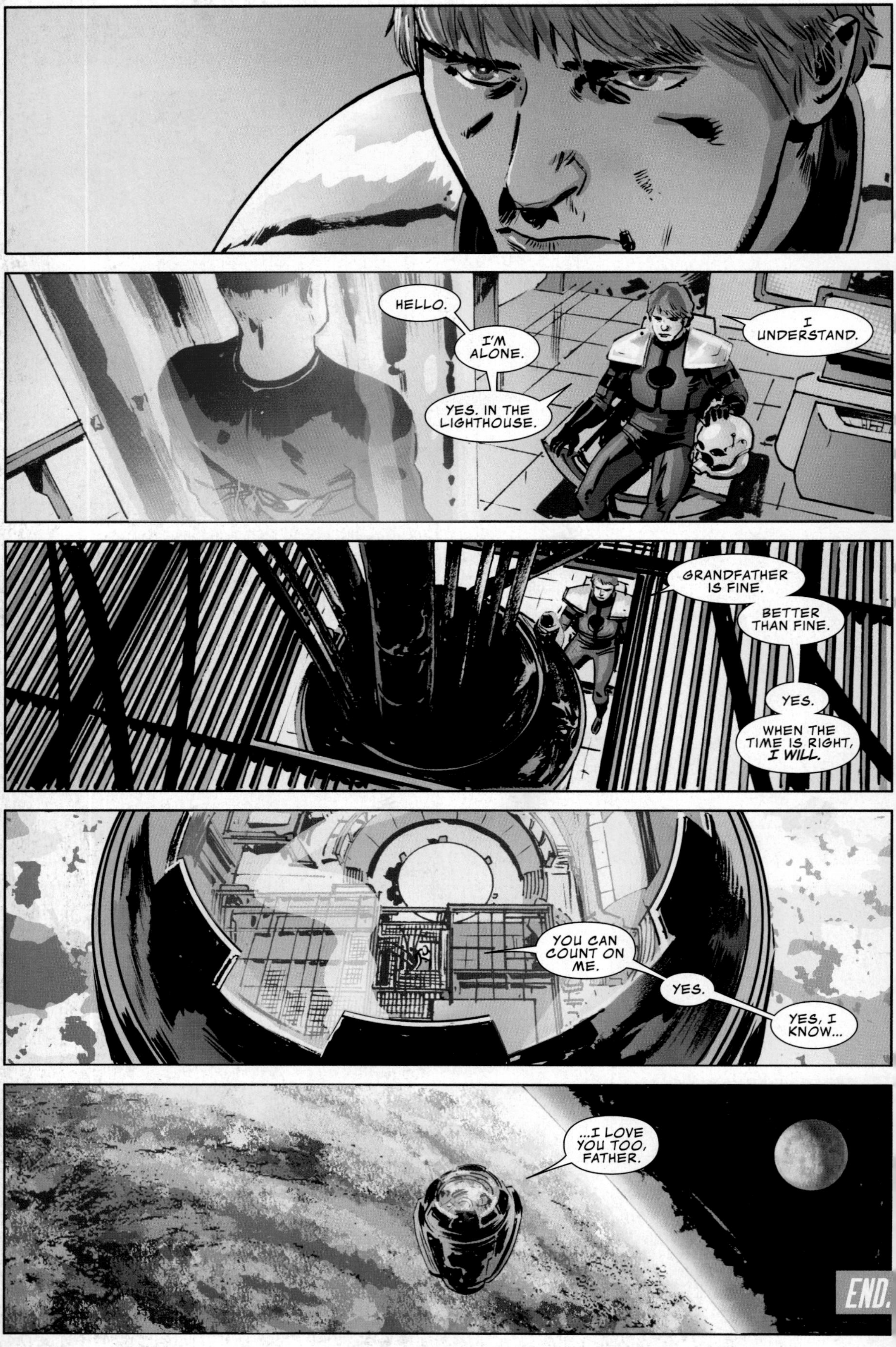
HELLO.
I'M ALONE.
YES. IN THE LIGHTHOUSE.
I UNDERSTAND.
GRANDFATHER IS FINE.
BETTER THAN FINE.
YES.
WHEN THE TIME IS RIGHT, *I WILL.*
YOU CAN COUNT ON ME.
YES.
YES, I KNOW...
...I LOVE YOU TOO, FATHER.
END.